Observer: The Ronnie Lee and Jackie Bancroft
Spencer Morgan Story, a tale of people, greed,
envy, manipulation---even crime

by

Glen Aaron

Books of The Prison Trilogy

by Glen Aaron

"Such is the remorseless progression of human society, shedding lives and souls as it goes on its way. It is an ocean into which men sink who have been cast out by the law and consigned, with help most cruelly withheld, to moral death. The sea is the pitiless social darkness into which the penal system casts those it has condemned, an unfathomable waste of misery. The human soul, lost in those depths, may become a corpse. Who shall revive it?" --- Victor Hugo

~~~

All three books of The Prison Trilogy are available at Amazon.com, and by request through your favorite bookstore:

> ➤ ***Observer: The Ronnie Lee and Jackie Bancroft Spencer Morgan Story, a tale of people, greed, envy, manipulation – even crime!***

> ➤ *Observer: The George Trofimoff Story, the tale of America's highest-ranking military officer convicted of spying*

> ➤ *Observer: The Prison People; The Prison Experience*

We like giving you gifts!

- Please visit us at www.glenaaron.com, where one **free copy** of Glen Aaron's *Revived In Rio* will be given away each Friday in 2015.

We like connecting with you!

- Please visit www.glenaaron.com for information about the author.
- Follow Glen on Facebook, www.facebook.com/AuthorGlenAaron.
- And on Twitter: twitter.com/OBSERVERauthor.

Table of Contents

Chapter

Introduction

INTRODUCTION

"I find the conduct of the upper class so exactly like that of the lower classes that I am thankful I was born in the middle."
(Mary Priestley, wife of Joseph Priestley, made this statement when she and Joseph had been moved to the estate of Lord Shelburne, where Joseph could continue his research on the elements of air and electricity.)

Ron Morgan always knew what he wanted --- to be rich and beautiful, to live in the places you see in *Architectural Digest*.

He knew certain things about the rich: that they were different, that they liked beautiful things, power, and influence, that, if they saw that another had something more beautiful or impressive, they had to have it, too. He also knew that every rich person would take advantage of him if given the chance. So he devised ways to reverse this probability. While making it appear that they were getting a good deal, a special deal, he always made money.

Ron had developed his expertise in interior decorating over the course of many years. It took him even longer to perfect a personality that attracted and pleased wealthy clients. His involvement as an interior decorator for the wealthy, his intuitive knowledge of how to deal with them, was also an evolution of fits and starts.

Although it didn't hurt that Ron was gay, in his early life he had had difficulty figuring that out. He tried a heterosexual marriage. It didn't work.

Then, in his fiftieth year, in the New Mexico mountain village of Ruidoso, Ron met Jackie Bancroft Spencer ("Jackie"), a wealthy *Wall Street Journal* heiress possessed of a unique personality. Jackie was building a stunning theater for the performing arts in Ruidoso for which she would pay $23 million cash. At the same time, she was caring for her terminally-ill second husband, Dr. A.N. ("A.N.") Spencer. Ron Morgan came to know Jackie by creating interior decor for her home, making suggestions regarding the theater, and, in the end, assisting with A.N.'s care during his final illness.

I was Ron Morgan's lawyer for many years. On numerous occasions, I defended lawsuits and negotiated a way out of touchy problems. Ultimately, I placed Ron in bankruptcy protection in El Paso, Texas. Not long after, he introduced me to Jackie. Through numerous golf games and dinners, I became fascinated with this lady, her history and that of the Bancrofts and their ownership of The *Wall Street Journal*.

Two years later, Ron, a 52-year old gay man, and Jackie, a 75-year old heterosexual heiress, decided to marry. At the time she met Ron, Jackie was married to Dr. A.N. Spencer; it was her second marriage. She wanted to travel the world after A.N.'s death, and she wanted Ron to travel with her. For his part, Ron had his own designs on what this should cost Jackie. Whether pressing for marriage was a manifestation of Ron's ulterior financial desires, or whether it was at Jackie's urging is unknown. What is known is that Jackie accepted, indeed relished, the arrangement.

While the relationship was filled with intrigue, greed and Machiavellian manipulation from within and without, the ultimate mystery for me was the nature of Jackie's illness---the illness that led to her death---while she and Ron were on a world cruise. It was my task to get her off the ship in the middle of the Atlantic and arrange for medical care in Albuquerque, New Mexico. That would be my last service on her behalf.

I have always been an observer of people: what motivates them to do what they do, how they view their quality of life, why and how this plays out in relationships. This book has a dual purpose: to share my observations of Jackie and Ron's unusual relationship, and to share my experiences as Jackie's sometime-confidante and as Ron's lawyer until Jackie's death. Ultimately, these experiences with my last client would change my life.

1

In 2003, May Day took on a new meaning for me. At about 2:30 a.m., I received a frantic call at my home in Midland, Texas, from my client, Ron Morgan. It was what we used to call 'ship-to-shore telephonic.' I supposed this call was via satellite but it still had that hollow sound.

Ron was in a state of panic. He and his wife, Jackie Bancroft Spencer Morgan, were on one of their extended cruises on the plush Radisson Seven Seas ship. The cruise was for five months, making numerous ports-of-call around the world, and cost about a hundred-thousand dollars a month. This was the cost of the cruise only and did not include the several-hundred-thousand-dollar purchases at the ports-of-call. Ron and Jackie lived in separate staterooms, a fact that would later haunt Ron.

I had kept up with the cruise itinerary pretty well because Ron and Jackie shipped their purchases from a port-of-call to my law office in Midland, Texas, for storage. There were many purchases for antiques and art, just as there had been on their previous Radisson Seven Seas' adventure about a year-and-a-half earlier.

"I have waited a lifetime for this. I'm having so much fun," Jackie had said to me before that last cruise.

At first, I thought this wee-hour call from Ron was to check whether a certain purchase had arrived at my office. As an interior decorator, he was experienced at keeping up with inventory.

This night, however, and the nights to follow, would be quite different. Jackie, typically robust and always wanting to be on the go at 77 years of age, was ill, seriously ill. Now, on a ship in the middle of an ocean somewhere in the world, this turn in her health was a concern.

"Glen, something is really wrong with Jackie. I don't know what to do!" Ron screamed into the ship's phone.

"Okay, settle down. Let me get up-to-speed here. What is the nature of her illness?"

"I don't know. One of her legs is horribly swollen."

"Did she fall?" I asked.

"No, no, it's something worse. Something internal. Here, talk to the nurse."

Basically, the nurse told me that she didn't know what was wrong with Jackie. She had been ill several days, and had become progressively worse. The best the nurse could do was to keep her as comfortable as possible.

I asked to speak to the doctor, and the nurse told me she was the sole source of medical care; the ship did not have a doctor onboard. The thought struck me that, for a hundred grand a month, you would think they would have a doctor, but I didn't take the time to raise hell about it. The sense of urgency was clearly there, and some decisions had to be made.

I asked the nurse to let me speak to Ron again.

"Ron, where are you? Where is the ship located at this time?"

"I don't know. We're somewhere in the Atlantic, I think."

"Is the Captain there? Let me speak to the Captain," I said.

"He isn't here right now. He isn't available. Stay by the phone. I'll have him call you back."

I agreed. I was glad for the break. It gave me the chance to think the situation through. Apparently, Jackie was in an almost critical state. When I asked the nurse if Jackie was cogent, did she respond to questions, I was told that she was almost comatose. She was sedated because of pain, and barely responsive. When I asked, "Would she be able to speak with me," the nurse said Jackie just wasn't capable.

We had a real problem on our hands. My first thought was, we'll just have a medical evac fly in, snatch her off the ship, and bring her back. How naïve. She was thousands of miles out in the Atlantic, in the middle of nowhere. Neither helicopter nor any other evac conveyance that could land on a ship is capable of flying that far.

After about thirty minutes, the phone rang. It was the captain of the Radisson Seven Seas. He was professional, acknowledged that Jackie was in need of medical assistance greater than what the ship could provide, but offered no solution. I asked for the current location of the ship, which turned out to be in the Atlantic, far off the West Coast of Africa. I sat in my easy chair at home trying to determine the next logical move.

The phone rang. It was Ron. He was quite frantic. Something had to be done, and quick. I told him I would be proposing a plan to the captain within thirty minutes. Try to stay calm.

Truth of the matter was, I had no plan. I kept wondering why Ron had let Jackie reach this advanced state without calling me. For the last five years of my professional relationship with him, Ron would hardly spit on the street without calling me first, or so it seemed. Had he waited because he wanted Jackie to die? I knew Ron's devious side, and I knew that he often counted the days until she was gone. There were many conversations between Jackie, Ron and me as to how he should be compensated after her death. She was amazingly forthright on the subject to both of us.

Was this concern just an act on Ron's part? He was pretty good at putting on an act. Surely, Ron hadn't become overly anxious about his post-Jackie life, and when she became ill on the ship, delayed, delayed. On the other hand, I knew how Ron was, that at times he had difficulty making a decision. Maybe that's how this thing had gotten out of hand. Then, too, I knew how Jackie was. "Demanding" would be an understatement.

Ron and Jackie had leased a Lear jet based out of Midland for their U.S. travels. The plane was owned, and often piloted, by my good friend, Dallas Smith. Not only was he an expert at navigation; he had a company that manufactured oil field equipment in China and imported it to the West Texas oil fields. I had been representing local oil firms and families in foreign countries for years. He was the man I needed in this crisis. Between the two of us, we should be able to figure out the logistics for this thing. Beyond that, I needed to mobilize my office team, particularly Teresa, my legal assistant, and Cuatro, my son, who was the office manager. They were expert at putting plans into action.

Within thirty minutes, at 4:00 a.m., Dallas, Teresa, and Cuatro were sitting in my conference room. We were speaking with the Captain of the ship, reviewing Jackie's condition as best the Captain could ascertain it, and identifying the exact longitude of the Radisson Seven Seas. Within reachable distance of this location was an island, Ascension. It was the closest location that could provide medical services. The decision was made to change course and head for the island.

Ascension is very small and owned by the British. Essentially, it is a military base and was an important fueling stop in Britain's Falkland Islands' war with Argentina.

The decision having been made to get medical help for Jackie at Ascension, we felt some relief and could return to the day's work. I wasn't too pleased that it would take the Radisson Seven Seas ten hours to reach Ascension, but that was the nearest medical help, and the best we could do. The Captain was instructed to notify me immediately upon the ship's arrival.

About the time we thought we had put the emergency to rest, the captain called again. There were several problems. When he had first called the medical facility at Ascension, the British commandant he spoke with was cooperative and said they would accept Jackie on an emergency basis. The Radisson Seven Seas had no sooner changed course for Ascension than the commandant of the island called and said that they could not receive the Radisson Seven Seas without approval from the Royal Air Force (RAF) Commander for British-owned Atlantic islands, who was stationed in England. Beyond that, the Ascension base medical facility did have a doctor. However, after the ship's nurse described Jackie's symptoms and condition, they had no idea whether they had facilities sufficient to treat her.

Back to the drawing board! I called the ship's captain and instructed him to maintain course for Ascension. I would get the necessary approval for docking of the Radisson Seven Seas at Ascension, and acceptance at the medical facility for Jackie. I was speaking through my ass. I had no idea how I was going to get this done.

What I did know was that Dallas was pretty good at breaking through bureaucratic barriers. Aside from manufacturing and importing from China, he knew 'pilot-speak' and had been the sheriff of Midland County.

Somehow, he got hold of the British RAF commander in England and acquired the necessary permission for the Radisson Seven Seas to be received at Ascension and for Jackie to be admitted for emergency care. We did have to fax a few documents, such as a waiver of liability, to the commander, but it looked like we were set.

Cuatro had been rearranging schedules, canceling appointments, and checking on how we might airlift Jackie and Ron from Ascension once Jackie was stabilized. Teresa had been multitasking, helping Dallas locate the commander of Ascension, and then break through secretarial barriers to speak with him.

By this time, it was mid-day. We sighed in relief and tried to get on with our other obligations of the day. We thought that was the end of it, and hoped for the best for Jackie.

But about 8:00 p.m., as I had just sat down with a glass of wine and was seriously thinking about bed, the phone rang. It was the Radisson Seven Seas' first-mate asking me to hold for the captain. When he came on, the captain stated that they were at Ascension, but in rough seas. It was impossible to dock. What did I suggest now?

I was dumbstruck. The thought entered my mind that surely this captain had more leadership skills than I was feeling at the moment. Surely, he must be highly trained and making a huge salary floating a boat around the world for only the rich. Why was I the one making all the decisions? I hardly knew where the Atlantic was. I lived in the desert.

Again, I suppressed my reaction and told the captain I would call him back in thirty minutes. Again, I summoned my team. Again, we were at the law office within thirty minutes.

Dallas had brought flight maps for the area around Ascension. A straight line to the East would take a ship to port cities in either Angola or the Congo. This didn't seem like a good alternative. A straight line to the West would bring the ship to port cities in Brazil. This seemed like the best bet, but what then? These ports didn't have modern medical facilities. What would be the next step?

The captain, in another call, suggested calling the Brazilian port of Fortaleza. The Radisson Seven Seas could make for Fortaleza and dock there, but, once docked, what was to be done with Jackie? The captain estimated their time of arrival (ETA) at forty-eight hours hence, and we had better have a plan of how to get medical help for Jackie at docking.

Sitting in my conference room, we studied maps and tried to determine routes to major cities where, hopefully, there would be adequate medical care. I knew from talking to the ship's nurse that we needed good diagnostics. I was told that it could be a bowel blockage requiring surgery, or it could be the onset of kidney failure, or perhaps there was a cancer implication. Basically, the nurse didn't know what was wrong with Jackie. She was doing her best to keep Jackie as comfortable as possible.

The logistics of this situation were terrible, and they just kept getting worse. We studied the maps. We could have a private jet waiting at the port of Fortaleza and then fly Jackie either south to Rio, or north to Caracas. In either case, we had to make a decision quickly. You don't just go entering sovereign countries and say I want medical help. There are hoops to jump through and red tape to master. Beyond that, either of these destinations required a long flight from the port. Could Jackie even survive the flight?

I called the ship and discussed the options with Ron. He, of course, didn't know the right answer. None of us did. He said he would talk it over with Jackie, and call me back. That told me she must be hanging in there, that she vacillated between being semi-comatose and cogent. I suspected this was in part due to sedation. Although the nurse did not know the source of Jackie's sickness, she seemed dedicated to managing her pain.

When Ron called back, he said Jackie was insistent that she wasn't going to have a bunch of South Americans treating her, and most certainly not operating on her. I was glad to hear it, not because it solved any problems but because it sounded like the old Jackie. No one ever told Jackie what to do; she told *you*. She told Ron to tell me to get her to Albuquerque to the hospital. That was it---no ifs, ands, or buts about it.

While the Radisson Seven Seas made for the Brazilian Port of Fortaleza, Dallas, Teresa and Cuatro tried to locate a jet on which we could place a doctor, nurse, and medical equipment, a jet that could make it to Fortaleza as quickly as possible, refuel, and return to Albuquerque, New Mexico. Within itself, this was no easy task. You don't just go retro-fitting leased jets for medical evacuation in less than twenty-four hours.

We located a private evac-service in Miami that had just what we needed: Gulf-Stream II, and a contractual relation with a doctor and a nurse to be placed onboard. They could head for Fortaleza within four hours. It was quite an expensive operation, but, fortunately, in this case, money was not a concern.

However, the Miami company advised that the plane would have to land at Houston upon its return; there was no way to clear customs at Albuquerque. We knew intuitively that time was running out for Jackie. Another delay, trying to clear customs, an intermediate stop on the way to the hospital, just wasn't going to work.

In a crisis, it helps to be rich and to have contributed substantial sums to the party in power. Jackie, like all Bancrofts, had always been a staunch Republican. This was one time it paid off.

Simultaneously, Teresa contacted the Immigration Service while I contacted the State Department. We were fortunate to get both agencies talking to each other, and, within four hours, we had emergency clearance for the Gulf-Stream II to fly directly into Albuquerque.

It had been a long two days and nights, and my team and I were gassed. As we each struggled back to our daily routine, we learned that Jackie had made it to the hospital in Albuquerque.

We checked on her daily through hospital information. With what she had been through, and the delay in receiving adequate medical attention, I didn't want to bother her.

She lived for about seven days, then passed.

Now, for the rest of the story.

2

I met Ronnie Lee Morgan in the late 1980s after rehabbing from a car wreck. The physical therapy clinic where I received treatment had a small gym and a weight trainer. The number of people allowed to use the facility for weight training was restricted since the main purpose was physical rehabilitation.

Counting our trainer, there were six of us. All were professional people --- engineers, geologists, myself, a lawyer, and Ron, who, at the time, owned an upscale antique store called "Jackson-Morgan."

As time went on, when any one of our little group needed legal advice or service, they would call me. I had a small boutique law firm that covered various aspects of law practice, some known, some not so well-known, but very private and confidential.

Ron called me one morning and asked if I could drop by his store. He had a legal matter he would like me to review. I would be glad to, I told him, and suggested the following morning. He said that would be a good time but seemed quite anxious.

The following morning, I drove out to the chic shopping area where Jackson-Morgan was located. The building that housed Jackson-Morgan was a large, tall building with an atrium, like an arboretum, in the middle, and a fountain shooting water twenty feet in the air. As it fell, the water landed on staggered slate rocks into a gentle waterfall that flowed into varied creeks running through vegetation. Goldfish swam in the creeks and numerous species of colored ducks frequented various parts of the arboretum. The whole thing was enclosed. While the center of the building was open to the top, you felt as if you were somewhere in the Northeast, in the middle of nature. A wealthy oilman had built the structure. His oil company was headquartered there, along with a bank, numerous offices in the upper floors, and commercial and retail outlets on the ground floor, all opening into the nature scene with the unending sound of gentle falling water.

"Ron, how are you this morning? I have never been to your store. It is quite impressive," I said as I entered Jackson-Morgan.

"Thank you. We have armoires from France, beds from Italy and Spain. There are a number of unique items. Some of it is on consignment. Some, I have imported," Ron explained.

As I looked around, I wondered who bought these things; they were quite pricey. But, having grown up in Midland, Texas, I knew there was no end to what people would build or pay for. The herd mentality --- if one had something nice or unusual, a neighbor, friend, or competitor must "one-up"--- had been the norm in Midland for quite some time. His billboard, located just before the Country Club's entrance, came to mind. It seemed to say it all: "If you have to ask, you can't afford it," it said. Ron and his shop intrigued me.

Ron led me to a small cramped office in the back. A desk was stacked with disheveled papers. We sat down:

"My partner has been stealing from me. I want us to break up. He needs to go back to California."

"I'm sorry to hear that," I responded, trying to sound empathetic. Over the years, I had handled many cases of partner fallout. Sometimes, it can arise from employment, or just a different view that can't be reconciled of how the business should be run.

"How long have you been together?" I asked.

"About three years," Ron responded.

I was learning that if I wanted information from Ron, I would have to drag it out of him. This would be the seminal beginning of that phenomenon that would become the habit and practice for years to come.

"How do you know that Mr. Jackson (Jackson-Morgan) has been stealing from you?" I asked.

"Mr. Jackson? Who is he?"

"Why, isn't Mr. Jackson of Jackson-Morgan who you are talking about?" I asked.

"No. There is no Jackson. That's just a name I liked, so I put it up there. I thought it sounded sophisticated. I'm talking about my partner I live with. He's been stealing from me. I know he has. I want him out of my house."

It took me a moment to re-center. I had no idea my workout partner was gay. Not that it made any difference. I have never been homophobic, and people's sexual preferences are of little concern to me. It was just that I had no idea. In the back of my mind, as I tried to restart the conversation, I wondered if our other workout partners knew.

Ron could never give me an intelligible explanation of how he knew his partner was stealing from him. The story always seemed to have an ethereal fog, so I let it drop. It seemed more an excuse than a crime, but when people split up, pegging to a contrived event is often the case.

I met Ron's significant other; his name was Tim. He was probably ten to fifteen years younger than Ron, and looked like what you would expect a typical California beach boy to look like --- tall, trim, blonde, and tan. He had been in town about three years. He was a stylist and worked at an upscale boutique. I had called in advance so as not to conflict with an appointment.

We met for coffee at the little shop next door, split a muffin, and he explained the situation of an impending breakup and the problem of the house being in both their names. Tim was a friendly, spontaneous, outgoing fellow, but a little guarded, as one might expect.

He pretty well knew that it was time to separate. He seemed to want out of the relationship as much as Ron. After my initial explanation, Tim said:

"You know Ron can be brutal."

"How do you mean?" I asked.

"He is very controlling, and there is something deep inside that is dark."

"Dark?"

"I don't know what it is. It doesn't start out that way, but you come to know it."

The revelation made me feel uncomfortable, as if I were prying into the life of a friend, knowing something that wasn't supposed to be revealed. I passed Tim's statement with a non-sequitur and moved on to the business at hand.

It turned out that Tim had been thinking about returning to California, anyway, and he had little interest in the house. So, Ron's problem was solved.

That was the beginning of my attorney/client relationship with Ronnie Lee Morgan. It was a quaint, humble beginning. Over the course of the following year, Ron would have a little problem here and there and call upon me to handle it. Occasionally, I would be at the same social function and we would greet each other. But, mainly, we showed up at the gym three times a week and lifted weights with our other partners until we were blue in the face.

I began to notice that Ron had a way with women, wealthy women.

This occurred to me because, it turned out, we represented some of the same ladies. I would be handling legal matters, and, for some reason, we --- the client, Ron, and I --- would suddenly realize we all knew each other. With several clients, it so happened that we had lunch together, the three of us. On other occasions, we traveled together: I would be handling a legal matter while Ron would be re-designing a home for the same lady.

In those early years, it was a frequent hobby with wealthy women to buy homes in such varied places as New Orleans, Baton Rouge, Dallas, Manzanilla, Mexico, and, of course, Midland. Our mutual clients refurbished and re-designed houses and condos with emphasis on interior design, and then resold them. As long as I represented heiresses and wealthy widows who participated in this hobby, it had been a mystery to me; I never knew of a profit being made. Perhaps that was not the purpose, but one thing was for sure: It provided a good income for Ron.

My role was to handle disputes with contractors, or, in most cases, "subs," or to negotiate purchases and sales. There were often legal issues outside what Ron and his client were doing. I represented a young Midland heiress in federal court in Louisiana, and state court in Texas. She was fighting for her financial life against the FDIC. She had become involved in building a hotel in Odessa, Texas. It went way over budget and went broke, as did the bank that financed it. This client only had about twenty million left of her inheritance, and the FDIC was suing her over the failed hotel construction debt. They were after her cash and the houses she and Ron had remodeled. I was defending against the takeover. By strange coincidence, she was a newspaper heiress like Jackie, whom I had not yet met, but by no means as wealthy.

On another occasion and for a different client, my client owned a home on "the point" overlooking Manzanilla and the bay below and sold it on contract to an evangelist from Oklahoma City. He had stopped paying the monthly installments, but he and his entourage would not vacate the premises. I was dispatched from Midland to handle the problem. Once accomplished, Ron was sent to remodel the place.

In these days, I began to observe Ron's dual personality. Perhaps it was dual, perhaps it was more than that. The ladies loved to go to "Market" with Ron and naturally got quite excited as they dreamed up designs. Interestingly, though they spent a lot of money, they were always money-conscious. They liked going to market in Dallas because Ron had them believing that, because he had a license to get into the Market, he could make purchases "at cost" and he would give them this good deal. They would just pay him for his interior design work.

The Dallas Market lends itself to buying. It is well-established and known worldwide. It is a twelve-story building with huge square footage and easy access to hundreds of shops filled with glitzy furniture and unique lighting, including chandeliers and sconces. Just as the ambiance of a Vegas casino drives one's energy to gamble, the bright lighting and endless array of high-end goods at the Market excites one to buy. After a full day of shopping with Ron, his client and he would settle in at a nearby quaint exclusive hotel for a night's rest but not before having a nice, long dinner to discuss what they had seen that day, what was interesting, and what else should be purchased. It was not unusual for one of these shopping tours to cost fifty- to a hundred-thousand dollars.

Ron always showed the ladies respect and knew just what to say and when to say it. He had unending patience with his clients but also knew exactly when to take the lead and bring an issue to a decision. There were times, of course, when he would become frustrated; he might even threaten to return home. In time, the ladies might fear his rejection. I never knew whether this was because of Ron, himself, or what they saw as a social stigma of going to Market with an interior decorator and returning either because they couldn't make a decision or they couldn't afford it. Ego has its complexities.

It was a mystery to me how women felt so at ease with Ron. Their conversations were totally different from their conversations with me. Even when Ron was "snippy" or condescending to them, it was well-accepted. His acceptance with women, especially wealthy women, didn't seem to exist in the heterosexual world. I began to observe this conundrum early on in my association with Ron, and had numerous opportunities to further observe it as the years passed.

In the styling studios of the world, I knew that many gay stylists entertained, joked, and had fun with their female clientele. I've known many ladies whose best friend or roommate was a gay man. This was different. Ron was not effeminate, but he enjoyed female acceptance as if he were. Of greater interest to me was how he'd taken that odd acceptance women have of gay men --- where they let down their defensive shield --- and learned how to separate them from their money, using the pseudo-art of interior decorating.

Had I been blind all these years? Was this common practice and I just hadn't noticed? Without letting on or saying anything, I determined within myself to make Ron my private study. Human nature, socialization, and psychological interplay had always been a hobby of mine through my varied law practice, representing a potpourri of people and class, and a practice that, on occasion, took me to various parts of the world, studying people and what makes them tick. I decided that Ron would be a most interesting study.

Evening talks with my wife, Jane, enhanced this hobby, this predilection for studying human traits. She chaired the sociology department at our community college and often helped me design open-ended questions for *voir dire* when I was preparing to select a jury for a trial. Oddly, as I now reflect, I had never shared my observations regarding Ron until the final days of my representing him. In the days to come, Jane and I would be mutually shocked as events unfolded.

In those early years that I knew him, Ron had three sources of income. There was Jackson-Morgan, the high-end retail shop, and interior decorating; but there was also the scheme --- perhaps it should be called a "profession" --- of selling and trading jewelry. He had learned the trade working for a man in Lubbock when he first attended college there. Periodically, Ron gravitated to selling a piece of jewelry as an aside to his interior decorating. The two professions run hand-in-hand, if you know how to pull it off. Women who collect sparkly things as a passion are known in the industry as "crows." A good crow has an addictive nature towards collecting, and as Ron gained their trust and confidence --- that he knew what he was doing when it came to jewelry --- the crow was an easy mark for a sale of a piece Ron could acquire or take on consignment. The wealthiest crows are called "whales."

As far as I know, Ron never dealt with a "hip-pocketer," unless it was his Midland jeweler connection. A hip-pocketer is a savvy middle person, a jewelry freelancer who buys from pawnshops and jewelers in distress, or works out a deal with big players like Blue Nile, Cash America Pawn, or Neiman-Marcus—then resells the jewelry or puts it on "memo." Memo simply means consignment: you only pay for it if and when you sell it, otherwise, you return it. Often, a hip-pocketer is his own enforcer, and it is probably not wise to stiff him. With Ron's propensity to get behind in invoices, or not pay them at all, it was a good thing he didn't deal with known hip-pocketers.

He did, however, have his loyal Lubbock source where he once worked and learned the trade. On occasion, he took on some of the same trade nuances as if dealing with a hip-pocketer. Later, when he met Jackie, he also met and got to know a lady in Midland who played this role.

It all came together then, a wealthy lady who liked to buy, and a hip-pocketer of sorts who kept close the industry trade secrets while working with Ron. A standard markup in the jewelry business is a "keystone." If Ron could buy it for a thousand, he would sell it for two thousand, or, if he had it on consignment from an individual, he would shoot for a triple key: buy it for a hundred to sell for three hundred, then discount from there. Typically, as in the early years, if Ron was using his Lubbock source or his Midland source, he'd do a split-profit deal with the source. Of course, the buyer always thought he or she was getting a special, unusual deal. "What is a fine lie?" asked Oscar Wilde (himself a great jewelry aficionado), and answered, "Simply that which is its own evidence." A diamond's rarity or worth is an illusion, the supply being cannily managed by DeBeers. The fact that people buy jewelry specifically to display their wealth can make the salesman feel that his customers somehow deserve to be ripped off. If it were any other business, the techniques used in trading and selling jewelry would be illegal.

Greed hustles even the hustlers, and so it was with Ron. The jeweler's trade is in Veblen (named for Thorstein Veblen, the Norwegian-American economist who coined the term "conspicuous consumption") goods: goods that controvert the basic economic formula that, as prices decrease, demands increase. Veblen goods increase their appeal as they increase in price. The principle has its application in the jewelry industry as well as the profession of interior design. Your importance is gauged only by whether you can afford it, and whatever the item is, a yellow diamond, a stainless steel Daytona Cosmograph, or a ten-carat Kashmir sapphire ring, you obsessively want it. You want it even more if it is, or it's about to be, on someone else. Envy is one of the great emotions, whether you sell jewelry or remodel a house for the rich. Envy is effortless. It's another woman's bigger engagement ring, bigger house, better breasts, or latest bracelet from David Yurman.

Envy and greed is where Ron Morgan lived. It was his life's blood and the currency of those he served. To be successful in that service, you must be both cause and effect. You must be capable of tapping into the driving source of consumption, as well as providing the supply for the unquenchable desire. Selling baubles to the impressionably rich with décor of *arriviste flauntis* is a talent within itself, and Ron had that talent. The day would come, however, when sale and purchase would be indistinguishable, and it would not be the mere appearance of wealth but wealth, itself.

This was Ron Morgan's arena, his stage, his world, and I was his lawyer. A few years later, he would meet Jackie Bancroft Spencer, and it would finally all come together for him. Not only would he be the salesman, he would become the consumer.

3

In some ways, Midland, Texas, is just like any other small American city with this exception: there is extreme wealth at the top thirty-plus percent, and the wealthy very much want you to know they are wealthy. In every case, it comes from striking oil. It is Western wealth, not East Coast blueblood money. Bostonian elitism, from which Jackie's first husband, Hugh Bancroft, Jr., and her wealth came, has its own rules for acceptance and participation, though the Northeastern establishment has now been absorbed by a broader national and international elite. In the East, there is a certain social etiquette mimicking British aristocracy. Not so in the West, in Midland, Texas. There, it is in your face.

The key to the uppercrust in Midland is made of one thing --- money. Not sumptuary codes, special drinks, or summer colonies, other than the mountain village of Ruidoso, New Mexico, within driving distance, where Midlanders escape the brutal heat of summer or ski in the winter. Gentility is neither expected nor required. Nor is there a requirement of attending a certain school or college, using a certain bank or law firm; or when or how you acquired your money. Nor must you have an estate in the Eastern sense. At minimum, you do have to live in a McMansion and, within that competitive spirit, one larger than your neighbor's. You are more noted if you shop in Dallas or New York, and though you might own a thoroughbred or quarter horse champion, or play polo, it is not required for admittance. Within Midland's elite, there is a pipeline, efficient in its communication. It is a pipeline that whispers who got what, and where they got it. The only requirement to be elite is to have money, or at the very least *appear* to have it, lots of it, and to be of conservative attitude and religious mind.

If one were to pull up the Chamber of Commerce site of Midland, it would show the formulaic presentation of a town having an outstanding community performing arts theatre, five golf courses, including three or four country clubs, state-of-the-art medical services, many banks, and so on. Oh yes, and many, many churches. Midland is very religious, of the Pentecostal nature. Even the mainstream denominations have a Pentecostal flair. Almost everyone has a fish on their car, and a Republican sticker either denouncing the other party or reaffirming that Midland is the hometown of George W. and Laura Bush.

Behind it all, there is a subliminal jealousy of others and an underlying hypocrisy that comes with instant wealth, the kind that, because the hole you stuck in the ground was lucky enough to hit black gold, makes you smarter and better than the next guy. The working class takes on the aura of their masters, and, indeed, blindly follows along in the same principles, beliefs and opinions. It is important for an oilman's wife to be coiffed and styled at just the right couturier by just the right stylist and seamstress, belong to the Republican Women's Club, serve on the acceptable eleemosynary committees and boards, and play golf or tennis with the girls at the club. She may have the Texas twang accent, or not, but she is dressed to the "nines" and ornamented with gold and diamonds when she leaves the house.

I have watched the Midland woman, young and old, as she conforms herself into a knowing codification of the tribe's tastes, proclivities, and accoutrements, her canned political and religious attitude and desired acceptance in the clubs that provide the social ladder. In Midland, wealth holds the appearance of knowledge, of worthiness, and importance. It just so happens that, aside from driving a sporty Mercedes or the like, a Midland lady must have her house done by an interior decorator who is most admired. One who can make the house look like it stepped out of *Architectural Digest*, or perhaps mimic some castle in Europe. On occasion, Midlanders have brought interior designers from as far away as Italy. The size of the house, the size of the car, the size of the pickup truck, the speed of the car, the speed of the horse, or the size and speed of the private plane, these are all of importance to the Midland elite.

Gravitas is not as evident as is competitiveness in the people who run the town. Oddly, the proletariat seek only to be like the elite. As for the men, they are controlled, top-down, by canned conservative liturgy in both politics and religion. A young man growing up in Midland or coming to live there quickly learns that this is "Bush country" and differences of opinion are not acceptable. You can either follow the ideology of the majority, or quietly be invited to leave. It makes no difference whether one is speaking to the CEO of an oil company, a banker, a priest or preacher, or a field hand. The mantra is the same.

The demographics of population were slowly beginning to change in the '80s, however. Gradually, in the decades to come, the ethnicity mix would change. The Black and Hispanic population, particularly in the latter, would increase. To the disgust of true Midlanders, Midland was "browning." The upper third remained white, nevertheless, and, when one oilman passed on, his trust babies would continue the social process. The oil bust of the '80s was a humbling experience to Midland. Even the major bank, First National Bank of Midland, proud as it was, failed. The social elite continued, and, for the most part, weathered the economic downturn.

This was the atmosphere in which Ronnie Lee Morgan struggled for acceptance at age forty. He had grown up in a small town east of Abilene, worked in a family-owned furniture store, and, as a young man, struggled with his own sexuality. He attended Texas Tech in Lubbock, and developed a unique style of salesmanship working in a jewelry store. He had an eye for all things beautiful, and an entrepreneurial drive. But in Midland, he found it easier to associate with the younger *nouveau riche* or the plentiful trust babies than with the older elite. The key to developing that clientele required a certain breakthrough, a break coddled by the older money, that is, money made in the last half of the 20th Century. It also meant having the unique opportunity of making over a house belonging to one of the wealthiest families. If that break should come, all the rest would follow. It never did. That didn't mean he didn't have the opportunity to remodel or decorate this room or that for the socially acceptable. He did. However, the grand jobs, the million-dollar jobs, never materialized.

Aside from socializing and advertising, Ron's *entre* was his high-end antique and import shop. The problem was, it was also high rent, and, as far as I could tell, required turning the inventory at least four times a year. The Midland economy is based entirely on the price of oil, and, interestingly, when the price of oil is down, as it was in the late '80s and early '90s, even the wealthy are not wont to spend money.

My representation of Ron in that period was, for the most part, fighting off Jackson-Morgan creditors. For years, he had ordered inventory, sold it but never paid the invoices. "Subs" who weren't paid for their work filed liens on houses of the younger set where Ron had done makeovers. Even though Ron had made very good money on occasion taking ladies to Market and contracting makeovers, the lawsuits mounted and the liability exposure was more than he could handle By 1993, Ron had not gotten his big break into Midland's top, wealthiest echelons, and his reputation had taken such a beating at the store, the burden was just too great. It became necessary to close Jackson-Morgan. I placed him in Chapter 7 bankruptcy and he left town, heading back to Lubbock, the home of his original entrepreneurial schemes. At the time, I actually thought I would not see Ron again. Ours had been an interesting enough lawyer/client relationship.

My mind during the early '90s was distracted; I was buried in litigation. Downturns in the price of oil meant that every service provider, drilling company, or oil operator started suing each other, not to mention litigation by the banks. The problem was that no one had the money to pay his debts because the price of oil had dropped. The syndrome even filtered down to lawyers handling the litigation. Unpaid account receivables just kept rising.

At one point, I had heard that Ron moved from Lubbock to El Paso and was getting restarted there. Little did I know that a saga was about to begin involving Jackie Bancroft Spencer, a *Wall Street Journal* heiress, and one of the richest ladies in America, a name I wouldn't have recognized if someone had mentioned it. Since I had never read tea leaves, I couldn't have known that forces were combining to provide assisted professional suicide.

Neither could I have guessed that my early acquaintance with Ron Morgan would test my hobby of observing human nature to its limits.

4

Several years had passed since I heard from Ron after he left Midland. He had contacted my staff on a few occasions, seeking minor services.

One day, he walked into my office for a visit, and we caught up on what he was doing and what was going on in his life. Finally, we got to the real purpose of his visit.

Ron had tried his hand at starting a small sandwich shop in Lubbock. It went broke, and, again, the creditors were after him. He had moved to El Paso and started over working in a furniture store. The start had been slow, but things were picking up. His name was gradually coming to the attention of some of the up-and-comers. He had also organized cheap Mexican labor to make artificial plants and trees, which provided a high profit margin. So, part of his visit was to have me counter his creditors in Lubbock, but there was more.

Some months before, a wealthy gay rancher by the name of Sam Vest contracted Ron to restyle and redecorate his ranch house and pool area. Sam's ranch was between Midland and El Paso, so Ron would bring his carpenter or laborer along, and they would spend several days working on and staying in the house.

Along with other property, Sam also had a house in Ruidoso, New Mexico, where his partner stayed. As Ron was telling me the story, I pictured Sam Vest. He was a well-known figure in West Texas and Ruidoso, a multi-millionaire, third or fourth generation rancher also known for his lawsuits against oil companies. Somehow, it was always his prize bull the oil company had poisoned. Sam was openly gay, and known for wearing pink ostrich skin cowboy boots, a diamond necklace, or other unusual clothing. A friend of mine happened to be an insurance adjuster for the company that insured Sam's holdings and personal belongings. He once told me that Sam never left the house wearing less than $100,000 worth of jewelry. It was odd how Sam had such bad luck with his jewelry, some being stolen, some being lost. After a few years of covering Sam, after numerous claims, the insurance company finally threw in the towel and cancelled him.

As Ron began his story, he removed his shirt and showed me his biceps and triceps. I couldn't believe my eyes. He had gone to a plastic surgeon implant specialist and had these muscle-magazine arms structured with implants. I had no idea that such a procedure existed. Naïve me, I had no idea why anyone would want to do such a thing.

His purpose in showing me his arms was that the left tricep had been damaged. Fluid built up and had to be drained. In fact, Ron brought along a video he had made of sticking a needle into that tricep, draining and measuring the number of CCs of fluid it took to bring the tricep back to its "normal" size. He had to do it twice a day. He stated and showed that it was quite painful to do this.

Of course, I asked how this injury occurred. Here is Ron's story.

Sam, the multi-millionaire rancher, had become infatuated with Ron while Ron stayed at and worked on his house. Ron played along in order to keep the job and get paid. Sam held back payment on invoices in order to make Ron come to his house. But, according to Ron, he would never have sex with Sam. Ron's preference of a partner---and I knew this to be true from what I had observed --- was young, very young, boyish-looking males, preferably Hispanic. Sam was at least ten years older than Ron, and fat. By appearance, he was just an old gay.

At night, Sam would get drunk at the ranch house, and bemoan how he had fallen out of love with his significant other up in Ruidoso; in fact, he couldn't stand him. While Sam took to going to El Paso to visit Ron, Ron took to dodging him.

Nevertheless, Ron was working hard to complete the job on Sam's house. On one occasion, when he had worked all day, he went in to take a shower. When he stepped out of the shower, there was drunk Sam, wanting to have sex. Ron refused and verbally drove Sam out of the bathroom. He got dressed and decided to go back to El Paso. While carrying his suitcase down the hall, Sam pleaded with him to stay. Sam grabbed the back of Ron's left arm and pulled. Ron let out a scream. His left implant had been torn. Ron described his drive back to El Paso as one in excruciating pain. He had been in pain for the last several weeks since the occurrence, and now was having to drain the arm twice a day.

"Glen, I want you to sue Sam for all he is worth!"

"Well, of course, I can do that, but let's analyze how that might play out," I said.

I was stalling for time. My mind raced. *How many people have implants to simulate muscles?* I wondered to myself. Of course, I was aware of the common use of breast implants. In fact, I had handled a couple of cases where the implants had gone awry. But this muscle fabrication was a new one on me, and, after watching Ron drain the pus-like fluid from his left tricep, I could see where the enhancement could be risky.

"Ron, I think the first thing we better do is get you to a doctor."

"I have an appointment next week with the plastic surgeon. Why don't you go with me?" Ron said.

"Okay, where is his office, and what time is the appointment?"

"In Miami, at 3:30 next Tuesday," Ron said.

I don't know how I always walked into these surprise traps with Ron. What would seem quite normal to him and not out of the ordinary would just blow me away. I had assumed the plastic surgeon was in El Paso where Ron lived. Miami seemed like a hell of a long way to go for muscle enhancement, but then, what did I know?

"Well, if we're going all the way to Miami, I ought to take a sworn statement from the doctor about the procedure and the subsequent damage. Do you think you can get him to allow me to do that on such short notice?"

"I think so. I'll call him and make sure," Ron said.

"Okay. I'll arrange my schedule, but Ron, this will be a difficult case to win. I assume there were no witnesses to this incident?"

"Well, no. It's not the kind of thing where you have a crowd watching," Ron said.

"I realize that, but swearing matches are hard to win. A jury doesn't know which one to believe without some corroborating evidence, and you know that Sam is just going to flat out deny this happened."

"I know, but I want you to sue him, anyway. Besides, my workers can testify how he was always hitting on me," Ron responded.

I knew suing Sam Vest was not going to be an easy task. He was litigation-wise and had plenty of money. I couldn't help but be intrigued by the facts, and, depending on how the plastic surgeon described the injury and its possible cause, and depending on how Ron's employees described the atmosphere at the ranch house and Sam's actions toward Ron, perhaps I could put this case together. But then there was Ron; he was either slow pay or no pay when it came to his legal fees. This was certainly a case I couldn't bankroll. It was not a contingent fee-type case. I had a lot of reservations, but Ron was determined. His implants had been expensive. Now, this man, Sam, had caused serious damage in a drunken, horny state.

On Tuesday, Ron caught an early Southwest flight out of El Paso, as I did in Midland. Reaching the hub in Dallas, we met on the Dallas-Miami flight and sat next to each other. Not long after takeoff, Ron said:

"I want to show you something."

He handed me a two-page, handwritten "contract," "letter," some nebulous writing. I wasn't sure what it was.

"What is this, Ron? I don't think I quite understand."

"It's a contract for marriage, just like it says at the top. Can't you see?"

"Sure, I see that it says that. I guess it says that Sam Vest is going to marry you. Is that right?" I asked.

"That's right, but now he has backed out."

"So, when was the 'contract for marriage' created?" I asked.

"While I was working on the house, Sam said he was going to a tax seminar in the Bahamas. He wanted me to go with him. He said he would pay me..."

"And you went." I asked.

"One night while we were there, I told Sam he had to marry me and get rid of his partner that lives in his house in Ruidoso if he was going to have sex with me."

"And he agreed?"

"He did. He was crying and said he loved me and would do anything for me."

"So you wrote up this contract? Whose handwriting is this?" I asked.

"It's Sam's. I had him write it in his own handwriting and sign it, as you see," Ron explained.

"Yes. I do see that."

I looked at the two-page, handwritten "agreement." It was crude, not well written, to say the least. Both Ron and Sam had signed it. It purported to say that Ron and Sam would get married (it didn't say when), that Sam would separate from his partner in Ruidoso (it didn't say when), that Sam would pay Ron a stipend of a hundred-thousand dollars per year (it didn't say for how long), and that Sam would become a partner in Ron's interior design business and fund its operation (it didn't say when, how, or if forever).

As the plane droned on, I sat in silence, looking at the paper. Ron feigned reading a book. I was sure he was waiting for my response. I didn't know how to respond. Clearly, Ron had given me this document thinking it strengthened his case against Sam Vest. Had it not been in Sam's own handwriting and with his signature, I would have questioned its veracity, even suspecting that Ron had fabricated it. I knew Ron's handwriting, however, and this wasn't his. There was no reason to doubt that Ron was telling the truth, that he and Sam, on an infatuated night in the Bahamas, concocted a document promising marriage and monetary compensation for Ron.

"Ron, I don't quite know how to respond. I'm a bit shocked. What do you want me to do with this?"

"I want you to sue Sam for all he is worth. He's backed out. He won't do anything. He won't even pay my invoices for the work I did on his house, and then he ruined this arm. I don't know whether the plastic surgeon can fix it or not!" Ron's voice was rising. People were turning their heads, looking at us.

"Okay, okay, just calm down. Let me ask you some questions. First, who chose the words in this document?" I asked.

"I pretty much told him what to say, but he wrote it down," Ron answered.

"Was he sober when he wrote this?" I asked.

"Well, not really. You know I can't stand drunks. Sam gets falling-down drunk, but he knew what he was doing," Ron explained.

"When was all of this in the document to occur? I mean, you know, the marriage, the money, all that?" I asked.

"As soon as we got back last month," Ron answered.

"Ron, let me ask you something. Sam is just an old, ugly, rich gay. Were you just after his money?"

"Of course. If he wanted me to be with him, he was going to have to pay, and I need the money. What's wrong with that?"

I didn't answer. We sat in silence for a while. I stared at the two handwritten pages. I wondered why Ron hadn't told me about this earlier, why he waited until now, but then, over the years of representing Ron, I had become used to --- or so I thought --- facts being revealed piecemeal. This saga was certainly fitting into that category.

"Ron, I reserve the right to change my mind on what I'm about to say. I need more time to think about this document. I'm not sure about what ramifications there might be," I began.

"Okay, but can you sue Sam?"

"First, this document isn't enforceable. It's vague as to time and performance. It doesn't delineate how, when, or where."

"I don't understand that. What do you mean?" Ron asked.

"Well, for a contract to be enforceable, it has to be specific in every regard. This document is like a general understanding, but it's not specific," I explained.

"That doesn't make any sense. I think it's specific. It says we are supposed to get married. Sam is supposed to pay me $100,000 a year, and pay for my businesses," Ron responded.

I could tell this discussion was going nowhere. It wasn't the first time Ron and I had discussions about the law and its nuances. Ron usually just refused to believe that a given legal principle was the way it was if he disagreed with it.

"Well, let's just table the discussion for now. There may be a way I can use this. I'll think about it," I said.

"I want you to get me all of Sam's money!" he insisted. "If you sue him, he will just settle."

"Look, Ron. Aside from what I've already pointed out, same-sex marriage is not recognized in Texas. This is an agreement to do something that is not even legally recognized in this state's laws. In fact, a literal reading of the sodomy statute probably prohibits it."

"I don't understand. He promised," Ron responded.

"Let me think about it. Perhaps this agreement can be used in your personal injury claim against Sam. I'm not sure how. I'll have to get pretty creative," I said.

We spent the rest of the flight in silence. I was sure Ron was processing what I had said. For that matter, I was processing what I had said. I was sure he was disappointed in my reaction. I suspected that he had anticipated that I would view the revelation of this document with great glee and surprise, surmising it to be the *coup d'etat* against Sam Vest, the rich, gay West Texas rancher. Now, there was disappointment. Through the years of law practice, I was often surprised at how clients would believe that a certain fact, when disclosed, would help their case; actually, it did the reverse.

What was stirring in my mind, my consciousness, however, was something quite different from how I was going to develop the case against Sam Vest. Questions. Numerous questions kept penetrating my thoughts. What was Ron trying to do here? I could understand his anger at Sam for injuring his arm. I had always known Ron to be vain. I didn't doubt that those tricep implants were expensive, and I didn't doubt that the fluid build-up and drainage was painful. Filing suit in retaliation. To me, that didn't fit, even when Ron first told me the story. I had no reason to doubt the story was true, but I also suspected that Sam Vest, eccentric as he may be, would quickly cover the cost of surgical repair, and then some, if approached about the damage he had done in a drunken stupor. I had even suggested that in the initial meeting with Ron a few days earlier. Ron would have none of it. He wanted a large monetary compensation, large enough that we both knew Sam would never agree.

Now this! This marriage contract thing and the disclosure within it that Ron had convinced Sam on yet another of his drunken stupor nights that, for starters, he should marry him and pay him a hundred-thousand-dollars a year. My impression was that Ron's El Paso business, the Salon Red spas and the interior design and decorating business, were on the upswing, popular and profitable. Could it be that he was hitting the same cycle he had run up against in Midland and Lubbock --- apparent boom, then bust? Was Ron just searching for money, a wealthy person to tap through contrivance? Surely, these young business creations of his in El Paso weren't already in trouble. I didn't like the feeling of sitting in moral judgment of Ron on this. I had observed through years of law practice that the lawyer is there to receive the facts as presented to him, and then, to his best ability, not only apply legal interpretation to those facts but to become an advocate for his client.

I placed the marriage contract in my briefcase and looked over at Ron. He turned and looked at me. I laughed as I said:

"Thanks for bringing this to me. I'll figure out how to apply it in your personal injury suit."

I laughed again, only to myself. Hell, if I sat in moral judgment of my clients, I'd have no clients. Courts and lawyers are nothing more than a representation of a dysfunctional society. If everyone were sane and fair and empathetic, one-to-the-other, there would be no need for courts and lawyers.

To add to my belief that we would not prevail in convincing a jury to return a verdict for money damages in favor of Ron against Sam, our suit had to be filed in Monahans, a small town in the middle of West Texas. Under Texas law, a person has the right to defend any suit against them in their home county. Monahans would be the county judicial seat for Sam's home, and Sam's ranch covered most of that county. The citizens of West Texas are generally not gay-friendly, though many a rancher has been gay. This is "redneck" Christian fundamentalist country, but money seldom prevents hypocrisy. Sam Vest was a major economic factor in this part of the world. Piety may be closest to a West Texan's soul, but money is closer to his heart. The people of Monahans probably would not want their economy disturbed.

Later, I developed a social survey for Monahans, and spent time and money having it circulated just the day before depositions were taken so as to have some idea of what kind of jury we might expect, taking into consideration the nature of the parties and the type of issues to be litigated. The survey brought to light that the citizenry may be anti-gay, but Sam Vest was their gay. He had spent plenty of money over the years, not only helping the schools but helping the church building fund, as well. In my opinion, if we tried this case in Monahans, Ron and I might be lynched before the trial was over. Sam's El Paso attorneys were well aware of the lay of the land in Monahans, and ultimately would take our allegations in good humor when the day came that we filed the lawsuit.

As the plane came into Miami International on final approach, I realized we were cutting it close on time. We must quickly catch a taxi to the doctor's office, which happened to be on South Beach. Hopefully, the court reporter I had lined up in order to take the doctor's sworn statement of how this tricep injury could have occurred would already be at the office, waiting for our arrival.

When we arrived at the plastic surgeon's office a little late, I was struck by the plainness of the office, which was located in a plain office building. The staff was quite courteous, but the office was only a reception room and two treatment or examining rooms. There was no art, no paintings or sculptures, and the entire office was a sterile, off-white color. I don't know what I had expected of a plastic surgeon doing this type of work, but I thought the environs would be higher end, perhaps even opulent.

After the examination, the doctor said surgery would be required, and he scheduled it for the following week. He was quite nice and cooperative, and I took his statement. He said it was clear that there had been trauma to the arm, but he couldn't be more definitive. I'm not sure what I was looking for in his statement --- perhaps how the trauma could have occurred --- but I was hoping for more.

By the time we got out of the doctor's office, evening was setting in. Ron had arranged reservations at a small chic hotel, art deco, as it were, which was only a few blocks away. After checking in and dropping off my bag in my assigned room, I went down to the lounge for a drink. I didn't notice, at first, but there weren't any women around.

I had a couple of beers and a sandwich at the bar, then left for a balmy walk around the area. It always feels so good when arriving at a humid coast from dry West Texas. The air heals the skin, and the sinuses open up. Seeing the palm trees and colorful flowers always brings thoughts of living in a place like this. I returned from my walk and ran into Ron in the foyer.

"Ron, I haven't seen one woman in this hotel. What's the deal?"

"It's a gay hotel, Glen. I prefer staying at them when I'm traveling alone."

Well, blow me down, here we go again. I didn't know there was such a thing. I'd never considered myself naïve. As a former DA, I'd prosecuted the worst of criminals, and, in my younger days, was a bit of a womanizer, but the gay world was new to me. I've never been homophobic or prejudiced, but I guess I just did not know the ins and outs of gay society. I did think Ron's inference strange, that he was traveling alone. Hell, I thought I was traveling with him.

Ultimately, I would file a lawsuit against Sam Vest, albeit with a lot of reservation as to how it would turn out.

Ron had his reconstructive surgery, and, apparently, it went well; a day surgery-type thing.

My trial docket had bunched up, and I was meeting myself coming about the time I filed the suit for Ron. He gave me a shock and reason for pause when I filed it.

"Glen, if we don't win the suit against Sam, can we sue the doctor?"

"What do you mean? Why would you sue the doctor?" I asked.

"Well, if Sam didn't cause this, maybe the doctor just didn't do a good job."

I was late for court when the conversation occurred on our cell phones. I didn't have time to pursue the subject further. Suddenly, I had that "oh-oh" feeling in the pit of my stomach. Not only did we have a swearing-match of a case here and evidence of a prior relationship through a so-called marriage contract, but the client was now indicating that he may not know the source of the injury.

Riding the elevator to my court hearing, I called my office to see if Ron's case against Sam had been sent off yet. Perhaps I could take another look at this thing. The answer was that it had already been filed.

Lawyers, seasoned lawyers, are cautious and work hard at protecting themselves from their own client, while at the same time fighting for the client's cause. Self-destruction comes to lawyers who act like Don Quixote and get on their horse blindly. In retrospect, I fall into the latter category. My trial practice had been successful, but I had a strong tendency to believe what my clients told me. On face value, I believed the story they told me to be true. With Ron, it was never easy to get the complete story out of him. Then, suddenly, well into litigation or a particular strategy to accomplish a designed goal, an IED would explode.

5

My self-justification in representing Ron in the Vest case was, in part, ego; in part, intrigue and fascination. While I prided myself on my practice of taking on unique cases, clients out of the ordinary, legal problems that didn't easily fit into the conservative mores of life, I wasn't sure what made Ron tick. I wasn't sure why Sam Vest, with his vast wealth and sprawling land filled with cattle and dotted with oil wells, found it necessary to chase Ron as a paramour when he could buy any lover he wanted. Or, could it be that Ron was fabricating the entire story with the hope of acquiring Sam's wealth, when, in fact, Sam was only being flirtatious?

One thing I knew; the case against Sam was turning out to be a disaster, though Ron insisted we trudge on, that, in the end, Sam would settle for a substantial amount of money. The case took twists and turns irrelevant to the basic issue of Ron's arm, such as arguments over unpaid or hyper-charged invoices on the ranch house remodel, a spit fight over a salon Ron and Sam had established in Ruidoso --- which Ron had failed to tell me about --- and gut-wrenching laughter by Sam's lawyers over the marriage contract. It was not a strong case. Swearing matches, unless it is a female claiming to have been accosted or sexually harassed by a male, should never be taken to court. The promise by Ron that his workmen would testify as to how Sam was always hitting on him while he tried to work never materialized; Ron could never produce them. I thought that might have lent some veracity to his claim. The latent revelation of the dalliance in the Bahamas destroyed any vision of a standoffish Ron, but then, I thought, perhaps the marriage contract could be used to reinforce the claim that Sam ruptured Ron's tricep implant in a drunken rage. Even though it was evident that Ron could not have torn that tricep implant by himself, I came to realize I was pushing too hard to make this case justifiable.

I acquired permission to video the ranch house remodel, and I drove there to do so. As one might expect, the house was a beautiful, rambling ranch-style brick home with a swimming pool ornamented by a large bronze sculpture of an Indian chief looking into the sky. The dining room was elegantly appointed with a chandelier, which Ron had purchased and mounted, a signature mark of his work. Ron loved chandeliers, in part because they were beautiful, in part because they were a high profit item for him.

The living room and master bedroom had been redone. The large, sunken living room faced a grand yet warming fireplace with mounted longhorns above. The chairs and couch were large, overstuffed, and tufted leather. Animal skin rugs, one looking like a polar bear hide, lay on the floor. There were unique combinations of style, from Southwestern to what I would call French antique, though I certainly would not claim expertise. At the same time, there was a mounted buck antelope head and modern paintings on the walls, some bringing out vibrant colors. I suspected these were unusual combinations. Yet everything fit together perfectly well. It was beautiful, it exuded feelings of warmth, it was a place you would like to be. Indeed, it displayed Ron's talent quite well.

Ron hadn't told me about the Ruidoso salon; I'd learned about it from Sam's lawyers. Not only had the salon become popular, it had become a feeder for Ron's interior design work. It was here that he met Jackie Bancroft Spencer and did some work on her house. She was quite pleased, which became the kind of *entre* that leads to other high-end jobs for wealthy people. If it was good enough for Jackie Bancroft Spencer, it was a mark of superiority to use the same designer.

I decided to leave the ranch and drive on up to Ruidoso to take a look at the salon. Setting aside, for the moment, the fact that we didn't really have a case, what I found was a chic, upscale establishment, quite unusual for the little mountain village. The salon was located in a building owned by Sam. Sam's lawyers now made it clear they wanted Ron off the property, pronto.

From what I now saw, it was clear that Ron and Sam had had both a business and personal relationship. This was beginning to look more like a divorce than a personal injury suit, notwithstanding both Ron and Sam having significant others. The problem was that, within itself, Ron's unsubstantiated allegation couldn't rise to the level of a legal claim for damages in regard to his tricep injury. The purported marriage contract was not enforceable, and, therefore, didn't give over to measurable damages. I was really struggling with this case.

Simultaneously, as Ron was completing Jackie's house and getting to know her, his relationship with Sam Vest was ending. While litigation heated up, so, too, did the magnitude of Ron's interior design clientele in El

Paso. He was now high profile with his leased Jaguar, flamboyant billboards displaying his silhouette with lighted sensuality, and the house deal in El Paso he had worked out for himself with a local contractor.

The contractor had originally built the nearly 4,000 square foot house on top of a large cliff overlooking the Western Plains for himself. By the time Ron finished, it was quite striking. The house was a story-and-a-half with a master bedroom and two baths upstairs, two bedrooms, a bath and study downstairs. But it was the living room the visitor first saw. High ceilings lent an air of spaciousness. The fireplace on the far wall was flanked, floor to ceiling, with dark Italian marble that Ron had acquired from a local architect. Windows on either side of the fireplace allowed an open view from this cliffside site across the Rio Grande and the desert mountains beyond. The view was reflective of the hand of a Southwestern landscape artist. Taken together --- the advertising, the Salon Reds, the interior decorating, the impressive house on the cliff --- it appeared that Ron was successful and on the rise.

I returned to Midland to handle business for other clients but feeling less than secure about the case against Sam Vest.

The following week, Ron called and asked me to fly out to El Paso. He would meet me at the airport. He was concerned that someone in the salons was stealing from him. He suspected his female manager but couldn't be sure. He wanted me to inspect the books, do some snooping around, and see why the salons were losing money. To my surprise, Ron had just caught up on my billing, the first time that had occurred in a long while. I told him I would come on out and take a look. I could use the opportunity to drop by Sam's lawyer's office and try to negotiate. I also arranged the taking of Sam Vest's deposition, allowing Ron's to be taken at the same time.

The El Paso International Airport is a Southwestern motif structure where you walk out the front door to your waiting ride parked at the curb. I did that very thing and immediately spotted Ron's Jag. I laughed. He hadn't noticed me because he had his face in his rearview mirror, plucking either nose or eyebrow hairs; preening, as it were.

I spent two days and part of a night going over the books, interviewing people, and just observing activity in the salons. These salons, one in the north part of town, the other closer to downtown El Paso, were, indeed, high-end. Bling, spangle, glitz, and high energy; it was all there. The stylists were perpetually in good humor, smiling and talkative. The spa side had what appeared to be expert masseuses and ladies licensed to perform hair removal, and use cleansing and invigorating facial machines. There were also tanning booths. At one of the salons, I met Lorenzo, a boyish-looking young man, quiet but nice. I soon learned he was now Ron's significant other.

My view of his business, and a rather lengthy interview of his spa manager, brought me to the conclusion that no one was stealing from Ron. The business was poorly-managed, though having every appearance of success. Creditors for supplies had not been paid for months and monthly payments on the machines were behind. The cash flow was good, even great, but it was negative because the overhead and debt service was greater than the income. Beyond that, whenever Ron needed money, he would just drop by and "rob" a few cash registers. He was taking more cash out to support his lifestyle than he realized. His legal issues were mounting, and the hounds were at the door.

As he picked me up from a day's work at one of the salons, Ron suddenly announced we needed to run by a lawyer's office. There, I learned that Ron had been sued by the Verlanders, a local upper-middle class family, over a house redo. To my surprise, I learned that Ron had announced to the lawyer that he wanted me to take over the case, and we would come by the next day to pick up the files. This was all quite a surprise to me, but I noticed the lawyer didn't have any problem at all releasing the file. He almost seemed happy to do it. At this time, I didn't think too much about the new lawsuit. An argument over invoices didn't sound too serious. I would review it when I got back to Midland. Of greater importance was getting to a quiet place where Ron and I could talk and prepare him for the deposition in the Vest case. Depositions were to commence at a court reporter's office at nine o'clock the next morning.

Finally, we arrived at Ron's house on the cliff about the same time Lorenzo arrived in his BMW convertible.

I found that it was not easy engaging Lorenzo in conversation. Perhaps it was because he wasn't used to me, yet. He was friendly but reticent. He clearly liked the splash of being a Salon Red hair designer and of being Ron's cared-for boy-toy, but a conversation of any depth just wasn't happening. I noticed he liked cars, so we talked cars for a while. Without mentioning it, I was more struck by Lorenzo's appearance and his contrast with Ron. Lorenzo had to be barely twenty, slight build, having all the fine features common to Mexican ethnicity --- brown skin, as if slightly tanned by the sun, round dark eyes, high cheekbones, and dark, healthy hair. Ron, on the other hand, was larger, more muscular (even without his transplants), very white, with bleached blonde hair. He was approaching fifty.

I turned to Ron and pointed out that the evening was getting late. We really needed to settle down and prepare for the next day's deposition.

I had never been in a lawsuit with Ron. Let me correct that. I had never gone through depositions and a contested jury trial with Ron. I wondered how he would do, and soon had my answer. While I prepared him, he often seemed distracted. I assigned that to the fact that he had a lot going on. I told him the usual lawyer-to-client prerequisites, like "listen to the question and answer only the question. Don't volunteer additional information." I practiced with him for two hours or more, showing him what a leading question was and how to re-verbalize the question in his answer so as not to be led.

About midnight, I was shown to my room. This was a lovely house. There were many artistic renditions, including paintings and sensuous sculptures, but I noticed that Ron liked to frame pictures he had taken of himself. I assumed he took them himself; at least, many seemed that way. Some were shots taken on trips, on a beach, or some similar setting. Clearly, the dramatically-posed ones had been done by a professional photographer. It appeared that it was not so much that he desired to be a male model as it was that he just liked himself. One could tell that Ron liked the way he looked and was always working on it and dramatizing his appearance.

The next day, by the end of the deposition, it was clear this lawsuit was going nowhere. Sam Vest was just too well-prepared by his lawyers and experienced at being deposed. He acted shocked that such an allegation was being made against him, and flatly denied that such an occurrence had ever happened. He postured that this was a trumped-up allegation in retaliation for arguments over invoices. It's one thing, I suppose, to represent a woman who claims she has been accosted by a sport's star, a Kobe Bryant-type thing, but two gay men involved in a swearing match neither reaches the level of empathy before a jury, nor credibility as to allegations made. It's a who-ya-gonna-believe-type situation. For his part, Ron was absolutely lousy in deposition. He obviously didn't remember any of the preparation from the night before, and often seemed in a state of confusion. The lawyer on the other side ate him up. By the end of the day, it was a relief just to get out of the deposition room. I thought Ron would be upset, but, to my surprise, he acted like there was nothing to it, like nothing bad had happened.

At dinner that evening, he posed questions like, What happens next? When are we going to trial? It seemed odd to me that he would be of this mindset. I explained to him there wasn't going to be a trial, that this was a disaster. There was no way on God's green earth that a jury would bring in damages in his favor, certainly not in Monahans, Texas. With that explanation, Ron never brought up the subject again.

6

My law practice in Midland was small, but it was all I could handle. There is a lot to be said for staying small, efficient, and flexible. Sole practitioners in small towns usually have a Dutch mixture in the types of clients and cases they handle. In a way, it's a little like being the old country doctor. Though the town may be wealthy, as Midland is, the population isn't large enough to specialize in any one field. Divorce or oil and gas law would be the exception.

I particularly liked general practice, however. There was never a chance to get bored, and I was always moving up the learning curve on something. The uniqueness of human interaction and the legal difficulties they produce has always fascinated me. The bread-and-butter of small-town practice is typically defending people charged with crimes, both large and small, a car wreck case here and there, and the ever-ongoing divorce practice. I didn't handle divorces, but not because they weren't lucrative. I just couldn't digest the dysfunctionality of two people screaming at each other, mad enough to kill, and fighting over children who were going to grow up just as screwed up as their parents. It's amazing how much money people will pay to fight over ownership of their kids. My loss. The money was good. I just didn't have the right temperament.

Though I dabbled in various facets of law, a propitious thing occurred early on in my practice.

Midland is an oil town surrounded by hundreds of thousands of oil wells. However, drilling for oil or natural gas and maintaining existing wells is dangerous work. Over the years, education in safety has substantially reduced the deaths and injuries in the oil patch, but it still happens.

One day, a number of years ago, a gentleman whom I knew who owned two drilling rigs came into my office in a panic. He had a rig on contract drilling for an exploration company. The drill stem unexpectedly hit a pocket of gas, and, for some reason, the blowout preventers either didn't work or weren't sufficient. Three men were killed, others injured.

My client explained to me that he had a million dollars in insurance coverage. That wasn't going to be enough; the liability exposure was far greater. Over the years, he and his family had saved five-hundred-thousand dollars, all in CDs at the bank. It was clear that, once the lawsuits started, not only would his savings be lost, his company would be bankrupt. What could he do?

This was my first experience at asset protection and moving a client to offshore havens. It was clear to me that, after the insurance paid off a million dollars, five-hundred-thousand in CDs wouldn't help much; it would be eaten up quickly in attorney fees and litigation expense. I didn't want my client and his family to lose their savings. I immediately went into research-and-design mode, and, after about seventy-two sleepless hours, I felt I had a plan that would work.

The plan I designed was successful, and, although my client went through some grueling lawsuits and eventually lost his company, he didn't lose one dime of his savings.

That early experience would develop into a boutique practice used periodically and sparingly throughout the coming years, but would dovetail into other facets of international practice as Midland's industrial base became more global with the passage of time. There was no way I could have known then that, one day, I would meet a *Wall Street Journal* heiress who would want me to apply such knowledge for a man she wanted to marry. Many years later, I would use this knowledge and its evolution in representing Ron Morgan. There was no way I could have known then that such knowledge would eventually lead to the termination of my participation in the practice of law.

At that early stage, my reputation for knowing how to quietly protect a person's assets sifted through the community, and every few years, someone would get in a bind and seek out my advice. As far as I know, my little systems for saving a client's assets always worked. I never advertised that I had knowledge in this area, as I saw some lawyers do. I abhorred those self-proclaimed experts who advertised seminars on the subject. That struck me as most foolish. When a client comes to you with this type of problem, usually the horse is already out of the gate. You are dealing with a very sensitive situation, and the last thing the client needs is a lawyer who goes around high profiling about how great he is at hiding money. I did attend a few "asset protection" seminars over the years. I found most of their recommendations too convoluted, too cumbersome. At some point, the client must go on with his life, without depending on a lawyer. His financial plan can't be so complicated that he's unable to administer it, himself. For me, it was never about how much money I made in this area of practice. It was more about the study of the law and learning applications that worked for clients. It provided a certain satisfaction.

Confidentiality and the silent working of a plan for my client became the mantra whenever the occasion arose. I could not have been clairvoyant to realize the importance my knowledge of international business and banking would have in representing Ron Morgan, or being a confidante to a lady by the name of Jackie Bancroft Spencer.

7

Over the course of two years, I made numerous trips to El Paso. Ron seemed increasingly dependent. I could sense his fear of failure, a recycle of his Midland experience. In the Day Spa, he had a partner who was a doctor. They began to argue over costs of running the Spa, and who was to pay the overdue lease payments on the dermatage machine. I negotiated the dissolution of the partnership. At Salon Red #2, Ron was certain the manager was skimming the cash register. I developed a cash-flow analysis, which showed Ron was taking more cash out of the register than he realized. He still believed the manager was stealing from him. At the bank where he was behind on monthly payments, I renegotiated a loan. On another occasion, I tracked down some missing paintings Ron had taken on consignment from a widow in an estate sale, and re-consigned them to an art dealer. The list went on and on. Not only was I handling legal matters, I was troubleshooting managerial matters. Although Ron's businesses were booming, he couldn't get a handle on them. He was too scattered and forever starting a new endeavor. More and more, I fended off creditors, just as I had done for him in Midland. The cycle seemed the same.

In the meantime, the suit I had inherited from the other lawyer, the Verlander suit, was warming up. After the last deposition experience, I dreaded deposition day. However, that day came and passed. It wasn't a complete disaster, more like confusion than anything else. Ron's invoices and accounting on the job were in such a state of disarray that it was difficult for the other side to get a handle on costs and what Ron charged on the job.

There were two elements to the plaintiff's position. One was that Mrs. Verlander, the Plaintiff, had been overcharged. Ron's agreement was to renovate and update the master bedroom, living room, and kitchen. He was to do this at his cost plus ten percent. The second allegation was that Ron had either stolen or destroyed heirlooms belonging to Mrs. Verlander. She was a short, fat, menopausal woman, clearly unhappy with herself and life in general. It became evident that her husband tolerated and generally appeased her to get her out of his hair. He owned a chain of fifteen Applebee restaurants, and was gone most of the time. The house remodel was one of those things he approved to give her something to do. Following his usual format, Ron and the client flew to Dallas Market and shopped for a couple of days picking out things she liked, while he tried to appease her vague tastes.

As it turned out, the remodel project took longer than estimated, which created growing tension between the Plaintiff and her husband, and then Ron. The remodel required removing several walls, and re-plumbing. Ron had difficulty with the contractor, fired him, and had further difficulty finding another. Delay, delay, delay in a disheveled house under construction. The husband was getting particularly tense with cost overruns. What was supposed to cost about one-hundred-thousand dollars was now around two-hundred-thousand, but Mrs. Verlander had made changes.

In June, the husband and wife left on a month's vacation to the Caribbean. The husband instructed Ron, in no uncertain terms, that he wanted the job completed during their absence. He was tired of coming home, when he did come home, to a house that looked like a war zone, and having to listen to his wife's incessant complaints. He seemed a nice enough guy, but when he put his foot down, there was no disputing his demands.

Indeed, Ron did put on the final push in the clients' absence, and the project was completed when they returned from their vacation. The wife went into such shock and rigor she had to go to the hospital. She described her home as being totally destroyed. It was nothing like what she had been promised. Not only that, many of her "heirlooms" had just randomly been removed, apparently thrown away or stolen. Ron's reaction was one of surprise and disappointment. He thought the husband and wife would be ecstatic with the completed remodel. As for heirlooms, he wasn't aware that anything but a bunch of junk had been thrown away.

I acquired court approval to inspect the house. I thought it looked quite nice. Actually, I had never seen any of Ron's work that wasn't outstanding. Whether this was what Ron and the lady had discussed, I had no way of knowing. One thing was for sure: the lady was definitely unhappy. Ron's position was that she was unhappy in her marriage and had projected that unhappiness upon him. In fact, he had located the husband's mistress and insisted I interview her. He felt that would be the end of the case.

I did try to interview the lady, but she would have none of it. I subpoenaed her for deposition, which really pissed off the husband. Up to this point, he had been something of a bystander, happy that his wife had a distraction with her lawsuit against Ron. Now, he dug in his heels. As for the mistress, her deposition produced nothing relevant to the case. She knew nothing of the house remodel, and could have cared less.

I didn't like the way this case was going. It didn't have a good feel to it. I had assumed we could negotiate the disagreements and settle out the case, but this Mrs. Verlander was a professional complainer. It became clear this was her stage, she was in the spotlight, and playing to the hilt the spurned housewife taken advantage of by a manipulative interior decorator. Legal cost for her was no factor because her husband would pay the bills; that was his penance. Nevertheless, I felt that, at some point, reality would set in, we could quantify the alleged damage, and Ron could settle out.

8

It was during the period of litigation on the Verlander case and attempting to solve Salon Red problems that Ron requested I ride with him to Ruidoso. He had closed the salon there. Actually, Sam Vest had closed it since it was his property.

"I need to get my things out of the building, and I want to make sure Sam doesn't bother me," Ron said.

"I can do that," I responded.

"I want you to meet Jackie, anyway. We will stay at her house."

"Who is Jackie?" I asked.

"She is this wealthy lady that I have done some work for. She has built this outstanding performing arts theater out in the foothills from Ruidoso and wants me to decorate it," Ron explained.

"When will we be back?" I asked. "I promised to produce a bound volume of all the invoices to Mrs. Verlander's lawyers."

"We'll come back tomorrow night, but it's important that you meet Jackie."

"Okay, but I'll follow in my car just in case you decide to stay longer. I've got to get back to Midland and comply with the Verlander discovery demands," I explained.

I thought it odd that Ron wanted me to meet this lady named Jackie, but then, the business with Sam Vest had to be brought to a close. If Ron had business to discuss with Jackie, it was a nice way to handle two things at once.

The drive from El Paso to Ruidoso is actually a nice two-and-a-half hour drive, partly through winding mountain roads and tall pine trees with a periodic glimpse of snow caps above timberline.

We arrived at Alto Village, a country club community of Ruidoso, before dark. It was wonderful to leave El Paso's oppressing heat, to be here to feel the coolness of mountain evening air and soak up the smell of the pines. As we drove alongside a golf course fairway, deer grazed next to the road in complete peace.

We pulled into Jackie's driveway, and Ron used a clicker to open the garage door. I noticed that he was quite at ease as we entered the house, yet unannounced, through a door in the garage.

As it turned out, we were in the lower level of a ten-thousand square foot house. It held two large bedrooms with separate bathrooms, a very large-yet-comfortable den with fireplace, soft leather couches and chairs, a poker-type card table, and a wall filled with racing ribbons, trophies, and celebratory horse racing pictures. Ron assigned me one of the bedrooms. I had yet to meet Jackie, or, for that matter, A.N., her husband.

After about an hour of entertaining myself and becoming accustomed to the downstairs surrounds, Ron returned from upstairs and suggested that we go up and meet Jackie and A.N.

As we entered the large living room created even more spacious by its full window view of a snowcapped mountain, Jackie stood up and approached me. She was a tall woman, immaculately dressed and groomed, yet not ostentatious. She reached out and shook my hand. I noticed its size and strength. She was most gracious, but I could tell that she was inspecting me, sizing me up. A.N. remained seated. I knew he was in ill health, though he didn't appear to be. I had no way of knowing at the time, but, in a year, he would be dead. On this night, he was courteous but reserved. He had little to say.

Jackie was prepared to take Ron and me to the club for dinner. Earlier, she had talked to Ron by phone, and knew the time of our arrival. A.N. did not care to go to the club for dinner, opting to snack at home. Before we left, Jackie insisted that A.N. agree to play golf the next day. He did agree, and seemed to look forward to it. I would learn later that evening in dinner conversation that Jackie and A.N.'s life together had very much revolved around playing golf. They were avid aficionados of the game.

Alto Village has two country clubs. Dinner that night was at the smaller, cozier one called Kokopelli, the name of the mystical Anasazi flute player. The dining room, not one of those huge, cold, formal dining rooms so often found in country clubs, fit the club's ambiance. Well-appointed in Southwest motif, with a warm bar and fireplace at one end and an open glass view of the veranda and links at the other, it seemed a good place to get to know each other.

The wait-staff came to cognizant attention as soon as we entered. They knew who Jackie was, and it was clear Ron had been there before. When we were seated, Jackie asked:

"Would you care for something to drink?"

I was hesitant. Ron seldom drank alcohol, actually didn't like to. I was looking to him for my lead.

"Ron, what are you going to have?" I asked.

"I'll have some iced tea," he said.

"I'll have the same," I responded.

Jackie ordered a vodka and grapefruit juice. Again, she was pleasant. Again, I had the sense that she was sizing up the man Ron had brought along as a dinner guest. I wondered what Ron had told her about me, but I quickly reminded myself that Ron was not the great communicator. Perhaps I was a surprise guest. Surely not.

"Ron says you are a lawyer," Jackie suddenly said. "I don't like lawyers."

"I don't like them much either," I admitted.

"There is one here that I tend to like. His name is Mike Line, but, most of the time, they just want my money."

I sat quietly. That seemed to be the end of that subject. I hoped it was. To his credit, Ron jumped in and changed the subject.

"What is next on the theater schedule?" he asked.

"The Glenn Miller band is coming. Sometimes, it is pretty good," she answered.

"I understand you built a beautiful theater for the performing arts," I said.

"Yes. That's my little gem, the Spencer Theater. Have you been there?" she asked.

"No. I haven't had the pleasure. In fact, I don't believe my wife and I have been to Ruidoso since it was completed."

"Oh. You must come up for a performance. We shall take you," Jackie said.

So the evening progressed ever so tentatively. That evening, I felt as if I were on trial with Jackie, to be accepted or not. Just as our dinner orders were placed gently in front of us, Jackie abruptly jumped up and headed toward what I assumed was the kitchen.

"What happened? What's wrong?" I asked Ron.

"Oh, the chef didn't cook something to her liking. She's going to straighten him out," Ron answered.

"Does this happen often?" I asked.

"Occasionally. Jackie can be very particular," he answered.

Jackie returned to the table, gracefully sat down and said:

"That's not the way you poach sole. He knows that."

Shortly, a new plate was placed before Jackie, clearly, one to her liking. She left no scrap.

It actually was a pleasant dinner, and, although I didn't feel fully at ease, I did find this lady most unusual and interesting. Nothing about her was boring or commonplace. There was a certain anticipation, excitement, as to what might happen next. I have observed that, when you are going through the get-acquainted stages with a person, they will tell you things about themselves that they want you to know, things that define them as an individual, a person, a special person. It's the beginning of their personal narrative. Mentions of children, schooling, how they got to where they are, for instance, are important to them and they want you to appreciate their lives and to accept who they are. Not so with Jackie. In time, when she would ultimately become comfortable with me, even then I would have to pull personal facts from her. But on this night, even though she didn't follow the usual path of telling me about herself as we were getting acquainted, there was an energy about Jackie whether she was talking about her horses or the theater.

As we drove into the garage at Jackie and A.N.'s, I was glad to be turning in for the evening. I was tiring from a long day of fighting off creditors for Ron in El Paso, the drive up to Ruidoso, and then to dinner, meeting a lady I understood to be important. However, that's not the way it works at Jackie's house for an overnight guest. You have a choice: either a game of bridge or Rummikub. Or you might get by with suggesting Gin Rummy. Since I don't know how to play bridge (Texas Law School didn't provide a course), I agreed to learn Rummikub. Jackie absolutely loved the game and seemed to get a kick out of how stupid I was at learning its nuances. The evening wore on.

As we all retired to our respective quarters, Ron and I settled in for a little talk in the downstairs den.

"Quite a nice lady, Ron."

"Yes, she is. She is hugely rich," Ron responded.

"What is the source of her wealth?" I asked.

"You know The *Wall Street Journal*?" he asked.

"Sure," I said. "It was required daily reading in economics in undergraduate school. I've taken it off and on for many years."

"Well, she is one of the heirs," Ron explained. "She doesn't even know how much money she has."

"Whereabouts is her theater?" I asked.

"We'll take you out there tomorrow. I have to go there, anyway. She wants me to decorate it. I want to do it in Chihuly glass."

"Well, I won't show my ignorance by asking what Chihuly glass is, but if I know you, Ron, it's expensive."

"Jackie paid twenty-three million dollars to build the theater---cash."

"Wow! Must be some place. I look forward to seeing it," I said.

With that, we turned in, and, as always when I'm in the mountains, I slept like a baby.

As I walked upstairs the next morning to see where Ron was, I smelled fresh bacon frying and followed the aroma to the kitchen. To my surprise, there was Jackie, in her robe, standing over the stove preparing a splendid breakfast of fresh fruits, coffee, bacon, eggs, biscuits and fresh jam. The windows were open, bright sunlight streamed in, along with the feel of brisk mountain air. Ron was sitting at the kitchen table, having an animated conversation with Jackie about various decorations for the theater. A.N. sat, reading the paper. I would come to learn that, when you spent the night at Jackie's house, she made breakfast for you the next morning.

After breakfast, we drove out of the pines of Alto Village to the steppes at the foot of the mountain. From a distance, we could see a gleaming white, tall, modern structure cutting the blue sky. The closer we got, the more magnificent it became. It was the Spencer Theater. It sparkled and glistened with steel and glass and silica reflection, artistic cuts and angles going in different directions. It was indeed impressive.

The staff, as I was introduced to them, were all friendly and upbeat. It was easy to see how this structure, with its modern stage, backstage, boardrooms and kitchens, could have cost twenty-three million dollars. It could easily have cost more.

After Jackie, Ron and I parted company, I headed out of the mountains in a different direction, toward my home in Midland. With windshield thought, I began to reflect on the extraordinary introduction to this lady, Jackie Spencer. It wasn't clear to me why I had been introduced or brought into the home as a guest for the night. Of course, I was just trailing along behind Ron while we handled different things. Somehow, it seemed more than that.

As I drove, I tried to describe how this lady looked, how she moved, how she acted. When I got home, I knew that I would want to describe the experience to my wife and tell her about Jackie. I was surprised at just how difficult it was to produce that description. I didn't know it then, but, after her death many years later, I would see a movie in which the great actress Meryl Streep played Julia Childs. It was surreal. I would cry out, "That's Jackie. Look, that's just like Jackie." The tall woman bending in uncertain ways, with a smile and a swoon of a noise, the way she made eye contact and then looked off. Was this striking similarity because both were tall, big-boned women, or was Meryl Streep's depiction more than that? As I watched this movie, I would be dumbstruck, thinking of Jackie.

For now, as I drove towards home, I was finding a description of this woman most difficult.

9

The next six months seemed to pass quickly. Back at my home base in Midland, I had called in a well-known trial attorney from Austin, John Judge, to help on a tanker-truck rollover death case. The opposition, Dallas insurance lawyers, had stonewalled critical facts about the inherently dangerous design of the tanker-trailer, running up the costs on discovery as the case reached intensity. It was time to call in Judge who was known for his aggressiveness and ability in such litigation. This eased the burden on me of too much going on at once. But, at the same time, a client with a drilling mud company in Caracas was having trouble with the "Feds" over retrieving some confiscated money --- about a million dollars --- and tying up his importation of drilling mud. The Verlander lawyers were not letting up on Ron's case. Alleging we were hiding evidence, they filed Motions for Sanctions to hold us in contempt of court. My little staff burned the candle at both ends, and I felt like a fireman running to extinguish one fire after another.

At some point, I received word that A.N. Spencer had died. Apparently, Ron had been of great help to Jackie in A.N.'s final days. Her children's absence during this period made me wonder. Jackie had three children by Hugh Bancroft, Jr., a direct heir to The *Wall Street Journal* and Dow Jones Publishing empire. At the time of his death from a brain tumor, he and Jackie had been married just five years and had three children. The three were ultimately raised by A.N. and Jackie. I thought it odd that they hadn't been more help in A.N.'s final days but that Ron had served that purpose. I saw A.N. only once after my introductory night at Jackie's house in Ruidoso. It was pretty clear that she was in charge, handling his demise, and that Ron was there to help. I would later learn that this was not a close family. Perhaps in earlier days it had been. Now, there was tension.

The Verlander lawyers had reviewed the two-volume set of indexed invoices I put together reflecting remodeling costs. As a result, they subpoenaed the Dallas Market wholesalers for depositions at the Market Center. This struck me as interesting. Surely, they could see that everything on those invoices, from a cobalt-blue chandelier, to sconces, to furniture, was there in the house. Nevertheless, Ron and I planned to be at the deposition. I had prepared an outline of my questioning of the supplier after the Verlander lawyers finished their interrogation.

The Dallas Market is world-renowned and covers just about every facet of clothing, art, and furnishings one could think of. Our depositions were scheduled to take place at a high-end wholesale furnishing store on the fourth floor.

As Ron and I arrived, everyone had already assembled: the Verlander lawyers, Mrs. Verlander, herself, the court reporter who would transcribe the deposition, and a very nervous store manager. The two volumes of invoices I had prepared were sitting on the table. Ron and I sat down, the manager was sworn in to tell the truth, and the questioning began.

After introductions and preliminary warm-up questions had been asked, the questioning progressed something like this:

Verlander lawyer: "Mr. Smith, as manager of this store, do you handle all invoicing for its sales?"

Mr. Smith: "Yes, I do."

Verlander lawyer: "And have you made sales to Mr. Morgan, sitting here at the table?"

Mr. Smith: "Yes, I have."

Verlander lawyer: "On more than one occasion?"

Mr. Smith: "Yes. Mr. Morgan has been a client on numerous occasions for several years."

Verlander lawyer: "Are you familiar with Mrs. Verlander, also sitting here at the table?"

Mr. Smith: "Yes, I remember her from being here in the store with Mr. Morgan."

Verlander lawyer: "Were you the one that waited on them on that occasion?"

Mr. Smith: "Yes, of course. I recall that Mrs. Verlander fell in love with the cobalt-blue chandelier, and I assisted her and Mr. Morgan with quite a list of items."

Verlander lawyer: "In preparation for today's deposition, I asked that you bring a list of the items purchased. Did you do that?"

Mr. Smith: "Yes, sir. I did."

Verlander lawyer: "I also asked that you bring a copy of your store's invoice to either Mrs. Verlander or Mr. Morgan, for every item on the list. Did you do that?"

Mr. Smith: "Yes, sir. I did, but there are no invoices to Mrs. Verlander. Our clients are the designer that bring their own private customer to the store. We invoice only the designer-client."

Verlander lawyer: "Mr. Smith, let's start with that cobalt-blue chandelier. I show you what has been marked as 'Ex. 144' from Vol. 1 of the invoices supplied to us by Mr. Morgan's lawyer. It appears to describe a cobalt-blue chandelier, quantity one, and states the price at twelve-thousand-eight-hundred-and-ninety-six dollars. Can you identify the invoice of 'Ex. 144?'"

Mr. Smith: "Well, I'm looking at it, but, no, it's not our invoice."

Verlander lawyer: "Mr. Smith, it's on your store's letterhead. How could it not be your invoice?"

Mr. Smith: "I don't know, sir, but my signature is not on it. I sign every invoice that goes out of this store for verification."

Verlander lawyer: "Well then, Mr. Smith, can you produce the invoice that went out of this store for that cobalt-blue chandelier and signed by you?"

Mr. Smith: "Yes, sir. I have it right here, along with all the other invoices requested."

Verlander lawyer: "Mr. Smith, I see that your invoice is for eight-thousand-six-hundred-and-ninety-five dollars, and that the description of the chandelier is identical to the one marked Ex. 144, but the one you are showing me has a signature on it. Is that your signature, Mr. Smith?"

Mr. Smith: "Yes, sir."

Verlander lawyer: "Mr. Smith, can you explain why Ex. 144 purports to be on your letterhead but without your signature?"

Mr. Smith: "No, sir, I cannot. We do invoice our clients, and it is typical that our designer-client then adds his or her cost of business in their invoice to their customer."

Verlander lawyer: "So you lend your blank store letterhead for that purpose?"

Mr. Smith: "No, sir. Absolutely not."

Verlander lawyer: "But, Mr. Smith, isn't it common that interior decorators bring people to this Market on the premise that they can buy at wholesale, get a special deal?"

Mr. Smith: "Perhaps, but I have no control over what a client may or may not tell his customer."

And so the questions went, invoice after invoice. After about two hours, the Verlander lawyer passed the witness. The questions I had prepared weren't of much use, now. I mustered as much false pride as I could and said, "We shall reserve our questions for the time of trial."

Each party packed up and rushed to the elevator to catch our planes. Ron and I arrived last in line, so we were facing the elevator door at the front of the elevator as we boarded. As the elevator took its own sweet time descending to the first floor, I could feel Mrs. Verlander's and her lawyers' smirks on the back of my neck. I could have sworn I heard a snicker.

On the way to the airport, I said to Ron:

"Why in the hell didn't you tell me you were fabricating those invoices?"

"That's the way it's done. We all do that," he said, as if nothing of importance had just occurred.

"Do you realize that you've just walked us right into an ambush? How do you think I'm going to handle this at trial?" I asked.

We arrived at the airport, got on the plane, and flew back to El Paso. I was fuming. Not a word was said between us. It didn't seem to bother Ron; he was as nonchalant as ever.

Again on my drive from El Paso to Midland, windshield thoughts raced through my mind. Ron had lied to me, not overtly, but by simply not telling me everything that was going on. It was becoming a pattern. At first, I was embarrassed and angry. My thoughts turned to withdrawing from the case.

Then, realism set in. Lawyers don't just withdraw from a case; judges don't let them --- and certainly not at *this* stage of litigation.

I ruminated on the amount of unpaid legal fees that were piling up on this case. Settlement was out of the question. Mrs. Verlander had blood in her eyes, and the ostentatious manner in which Ron lived belied the fact that he was broke, past broke. The Verlander lawyers probably felt they could acquire a large judgment at trial. I didn't doubt that. They also probably thought they could collect the judgment. I did doubt that. There was no money to be had, only debt and unpaid bills.

10

Early in my relationship with Jackie, indeed in one of the early visits to Ruidoso, we were having dinner and she complained of the treatment she was receiving at the racetrack, Ruidoso Downs. I knew from seeing the racing trophies in the downstairs study that, over the years, Jackie had been successful with her racehorses. According to Jackie, her horses should be winning, yet they were not. Her two-year olds were of the finest breeding. Their times were the best in practice. But when it came to race day, they didn't win. Jackie felt that, at the beginning of the race, the competing jockeys worked together to block her horse out. She also suspected that, since her trainer was a woman, the other trainers were taking advantage of her.

As dinner talk progressed, I mentioned that Jackie's suspicions were within the realm of possibility and that, early in my law practice, I had periodically defended jockeys for track violations. My first employer out of law school owned racehorses and raced at this very track, Ruidoso Downs. I had seen some of the games that could be played to fix races or, at least, to gain an advantage.

Jackie was quite shocked to learn of my experience. She wanted to know what I could suggest to remedy what she was experiencing. She pointed out that she didn't have proof, but she was no fool either when it came to racing horses. I empathized with her. Establishing proof in horse races was most difficult. Establishing an atmosphere of prevention worked far better than trying to catch the thief after the race was stolen. Jackie became both excited and animated as our discussion progressed. She wanted to know what I would suggest to establish this air of prevention before the next race two weeks from then. By the time dinner was over, we had agreed that she would acquire approval from the track steward for two representatives from my office to attend the pre-race jockey meeting. These representatives would be introduced as observers.

I have three boys. The oldest is a state trooper out of Houston. The youngest, Cuatro, was my office manager, and my middle son, Sean, was working on a special assignment at my office. They're big boys, well over six feet, and two-hundred pounds. Aside from football, Cuatro had fought in the Tough Man contest as a hobby. They are whom I assigned to attend the pre-race jockey meeting at Ruidoso Downs.

I did not attend; I had a conflict to handle in Midland. I was later told by a third party that these two boys looked like giants in a room full of jockeys. I was also told that, somehow, they were introduced as law enforcement, which, of course, they were not. Cuatro was quoted as saying, "Glad to meet you. Now, boys, we are going to have a fair race."

Not surprisingly, Jackie's horse won that day. From then on, I was her go-to-man.

In the years to come, as I would attend the Jockey Club with Jackie and Ron, I observed a certain aura of admiration and overheard statements like, "That's the man that straightened out the track for Jackie." Perceptions are what they are, and rumors justify exaggeration. Such was the case with this small saga. But Jackie took great delight in it.

11

Back in Midland, I was working on other cases and trying to set the Verlander case aside in my mind. While working on the truck rollover case, I received a call from Ron. It was a Friday. He had just been indicted for forgery.

"Forgery! What the hell is that about?"

"I don't know. They say it has something to do with those invoices," he said.

"Have you been arrested?"

"No, but I just heard about it," he answered.

"Stay put. I'll call you right back."

I called the DA's office in El Paso County. Sure enough, the Verlander lawyers had talked an Assistant District Attorney into taking the invoices before a grand jury and getting an indictment. They were playing hardball and using their political influence. As bad as the civil litigation facts may have looked, this was not a criminal case.

In Texas, district attorneys and judges are elected. On occasion, either because of campaign contributions or political power, a district attorney or judge follows the influence of the lawyers or law firm before them. Those who have money and put it on the candidates can call in favors later. It's a bit like politics in Washington, only it's the way law is handled in Texas. Ron's civil case had just taken on new meaning.

I spent the next month filing motions in the forgery case and going to El Paso to argue them. Thank God, the court and judge were not the same as in the Verlander case. Because the young Assistant D.A. who had played ball with the Verlander lawyers had never before drafted an indictment for forgery, my Motion to Dismiss based on defective indictment was granted. The indictment was thrown out.

No sooner had the forgery indictment been dismissed than the judge in the Verlander case set the case for trial in three weeks. I filed a Motion for Continuance. It was denied.

The weeks passed quickly. I had scrambled for every trial strategy I could think of to get through this thing. I was encouraged that, at least now, the opposition couldn't impeach my client with a forgery indictment, though I wasn't naïve enough to think this wouldn't be a tough trial. The Dallas Market deposition had been devastating, but I had worked with Ron on his testimony. Perhaps he could soften the blow. Ron's only chance at defense, and to mitigate damages for double-invoicing, was to convince the jury that these were clerical mistakes and a customary practice in the interior decorating business. It was true that the Verlander contract was not of this nature and there should be a remittance, but a remittance in the nature of an accounting. This was not and should not be a case for damages based on emotional trauma and fraud. It was a case of mistake. Now these people were trying to extract undeserved compensation. Our argument was not that strong, but it was all we had. Could Ron handle it? I didn't feel confident.

Two weeks before jury selection, I arrived at Ron's house in El Paso, only to find out he had been arrested the night before and had been home just a few hours. He immediately suggested that we go to a restaurant. It was apparent he didn't want to talk about this at the house.

After being seated at the restaurant, I asked:

"Ron, what on earth happened? Surely, they didn't use that dismissed forgery indictment to arrest you."

"No. It wasn't that. I have a friend that I meet who comes across from Juarez. Lorenzo doesn't know about him. We were at a theater and the police raided it. They arrested a bunch of people," Ron explained.

"But why?" I asked.

"They just don't like gays," he answered. "I paid a fine, and they let me out, but I had to spend the night in jail. It was horrible."

With the Market deposition experience still fresh on my mind, I decided not to pursue the subject. I would go down to the Municipal Court the next day and see what it was all about. The more pressing need was to get Ron ready for trial, which is where I directed our conversation throughout dinner and into the evening at his house.

The later it got and the more I tried to prepare him for cross-examination, the worse he did and the more he wanted to talk about other things. We really had no defense. Our only shot was to mitigate the damages by going through each invoice and providing explanations where we could, and making charge adjustments where we couldn't. I was attempting to change this from a fraud trial to a suit on accounting and getting the charges right. Ron would try to explain the overcharges as an error on the part of a billing employee who did not know this was a cost-plus-ten-percent job. Two days before trial, it looked neither good nor credible.

The next morning, I took a look at what Ron had been arrested for. He gave me a piece of paper with the charging officer's name on it, but it had been wrinkled up and I couldn't quite make out the charge. When I asked to see the officer at the P.D., the desk sergeant directed me to the vice-squad department. The officer met me at the door.

"How do you do, Officer, my name is Glen Aaron, and I represent Ron Morgan."

"I see; I am Officer Guerrero. Please come in."

"I'm from Midland, but I come out here to handle Ron's civil business. When I got here last night, he told me he had been arrested and spent the night in jail," I explained.

"Yes. I have the file here. There were actually five individuals taken into custody."

"What were the grounds for arrest?" I asked.

"Are you familiar with the Ritz?" he asked.

"No. I guess not. What is the Ritz?"

"It's kind of an underground theater downtown which shows pornographic films. Mainly gays meet there. There is nothing particularly wrong with it, but there is often low-level criminal activity --- dope, theft, sex, assault, and brutality, on occasion," the office explained.

"I see. What was Ron arrested for?"

"We are plain clothes, of course. Periodically, we do a sweep through the theater with infrared vision to see what's going on. Your client was sword fighting with another guy," Officer Guerrero explained.

"Sword fighting! What is that?"

Officer Guerrero laughed. He looked at me like I was either ignorant or a complete fool. The subliminal thought hit me that he was probably right. What the hell was I doing here?

"You know that your client is gay, don't you?" Officer Guerrero asked.

"Of course," I said, as if indignant.

"Well, sword fighting is where two guys rub the heads of their penis together. It's usually a prelude to the next step."

"Never heard of it," I said with naïve surprise.

"The couple next to them was already into the full sex act. We gathered them up and arrested them, and then caught a pickpocket on the way out."

I left the police station, my head ringing. God! Where had I been all my life? Sword fighting? How could that be fun? It didn't bother me. It just seemed odd.

What *did* bother me was that Ron had paid a fine to get out of jail. That meant he had pled guilty. There is no other way, that's just the way it works. Oh, he could have pled "not guilty," but he wouldn't have gotten out of jail until a judge set bail which meant he would stay in jail until sometime the next day. By pleading "guilty," and because it was a low-grade misdemeanor, he could pay a fine and get out of jail.

But the repercussions were far greater than just paying a fine and pleading guilty to a low-grade misdemeanor. In Texas, this little deviance is called a crime of moral turpitude. Although irrelevant to the charges of fraudulent invoicing, because of the guilty plea it would be admissible on the grounds of Ron's character, credibility, and whether he was capable of telling the truth. It's called impeachment. I could almost see the expressions on jurors' faces as opposing counsel asked Ron, under oath and on the witness stand, about "sword fighting":

"Mr. Morgan, do you sword fight regularly?"

"Mr. Morgan, on this night a few weeks ago, were you sword fighting with your significant other, the young man you live with?"

"Mr. Morgan, how often do you go down to the Ritz?"

I could see it all now, opposing counsel filling his sanctimonious chest as he prepared for his *coup de grace*:

"Do you feel that you are being honest with your partner when you have these little flings, Mr. Morgan?"

"Oh? You do? Is that the same standard of honesty you measure when you double-invoiced my client?"

In Texas procedural law, a plea of "no contest" to a crime prohibits evidence of that crime in a collateral civil trial. If I could convince the judge that Ron had meant to plead no contest instead of guilty, the situation would be defused as to the damage it could do in the Verlander trial.

I raced over to the justice court and asked to speak to the judge. The clerk immediately started the third degree, took an hour to find the paperwork while I sat on a wooden bench in the hall. As she handed me the case file papers, she bluntly told me that the judge wouldn't do anything, that I was wasting my time. Judges can be sacrosanct in their demeanor and in their thinking. In Texas, a justice of the peace is not required to be a lawyer. Most often, they think of themselves as an arm of law enforcement rather than arbiters balancing the scales of justice. This judge looked at me with some degree of disgust, described the Ritz as a den of iniquity, and my request to change Ron's plea to "no contest" as unconscionable. In other words, "Hell, no!"

Less than two days before jury selection, I began to think I could not put Ron on the stand in this case. He had proven in the Sam Vest depositions that he was unable to handle cross-examination, no matter how much I worked with him. In this case, I could see that the Verlander lawyers had already set him up for perjury between the inconsistencies in his deposition and the revelations of the deposition of the Dallas Market wholesaler. If they were willing to go to the lengths of acquiring a forgery indictment, I had little doubt they would do the same on a perjury trap. I was sure they were waiting with Rottweiler breath to get him on the stand. By testifying in his defense, Ron was sure to walk into one of the traps they had laid. No matter how I coached him, he was bound to screw up under oath. Certainly, he could sit at counsel's table and not take the stand, but the Verlander lawyers would just call him as an adverse witness and no doubt begin their cross-examination, asking about activities at the Ritz.

More and more, it looked like it would be better for Ron not to be at the trial at all. I would hang in there and control the damage as best I could. I didn't doubt for a minute they had used private investigators to track Ron's activities, as well as investigate past interior decorating jobs and interview prior clients. If there were more unhappy clients out there, I figured I would see them at trial.

I have observed through years of practice that people are not generally aware of the trial lawyers' extensive use of investigators, spies. Nothing is private. Most people walk about in a haze with no thought of being observed, followed, or even believing that they would be. It wasn't beyond possibility that there were pictures of Ron and his Juarez friend sword-fighting. My first knowledge would be at the trial when opposing counsel would present Ron, on the stand, with the pictures and ask him to identify the parties. A law firm with enough stroke to control an assistant district attorney and manipulate a grand jury for a quick indictment without my knowing it could certainly have hired a private eye to tip off cops at the

Ritz. The Verlander lawyers had already shown a propensity to put Ron in the pen by pushing the forgery indictment. God only knew what would happen if they really did establish perjury. If that happened, the forgery indictment would be corrected and resubmitted to the grand jury, along with a count of perjury.

I had never before advised a client to absent himself from trial. I had read where famous people such as Howard Hughes had been sued numerous times but hadn't appeared in court, themselves. Was it possible in this case?

When I got to Ron's house, I was pumped up to discuss this possible strategy with him. He needed to understand that the Verlander lawyers were probably aware of his little escapade and had perhaps even instigated the raid/arrest. I didn't know. He needed to realize it would come out before the jury. He needed to know about the perjury trap they had carefully crafted. He needed to realistically face his inability to handle cross-examination, particularly cross-examination based on the deposition testimony of the Dallas Market wholesaler.

With these thoughts whirring around in my mind, I walked into the living room. I was instantly struck by the feeling that something was going on. Ron was sitting on the couch in a rather stiff posture. From the corner of my eye, I saw that Lorenzo had ducked into the kitchen, which was adjacent to the dining/living room area with a connecting door. Ron motioned me to have a seat. I sat down. It was silent for a few minutes, and I wondered what I had walked into. I looked over my shoulder and caught Lorenzo peeking around the corner of the door.

"I have been spending a lot of time in Ruidoso helping Jackie since A.N. died. You know that. You have been up there enough times to know how demanding she is," Ron began.

"Yes. She definitely knows what she wants and doesn't want," I responded.

"She wants us to get married after we finish the theater, and to travel the world." Ron made the statement as if he had just noted a commonplace article in the morning paper.

"But…" I stammered.

"Lorenzo is hiding around the corner. He's crying. I want you to explain that this is just a convenience. She's going to pay me to do it. Nothing will change. I will still be here most of the time. I will take care of

Lorenzo. No need to be upset."

I wanted to say, "But what about the trial? It's not looking good." I started to say, "I can't talk to Lorenzo about this. What do I know about such things?" Before I could regain my composure, Ron said:

"Jackie is going to let me have some money, and I can get caught up on your fees. She also wants to talk to you about some contracts we need with Dale Chihuly."

"Look, Ron, I can't…"

"I'll be back in an hour. I'm late for an appointment. Talk to Lorenzo. I'll be right back." Ron swished out the front door, the first time I had ever seen any hint of an effeminate trait in him.

On the other hand, Lorenzo tentatively hung onto the kitchen door, filled with emotion and somehow looking to me for calming counsel on how everything could be all right. How odd. I thought I was here to try a lawsuit.

12

By the time a trial lawyer reaches mid-trial, he knows everything there is to know about his opponent's character, their defects, the dysfunction in their lives, what makes them happy. Everything. The opponent's lawyer knows the same about his client.

I had tried hard to protect Ron from the Verlander lawyers. He didn't seem to realize what thin ice he was walking on. It was my duty to make it all go away. Only it wasn't going away. I had decided that Ron would stay away from the trial. Initially, this caught opposing counsel off-guard and my strategy appeared to be working. The character attack they had planned wouldn't work if they couldn't first put Ron on the stand.

Mrs. Verlander had just finished direct examination by her lawyers, and, of course, she did well. She had been well-prepared, cried at just the right time about her heirlooms, and talked innocently about how her dream of a beautiful house had been destroyed. Her bagged eyes stared at me without blinking as counsel passed her to me for cross-examining.

If looks could kill. This woman was filled with hate. I knew that she hated much more than Ron Morgan or the remodel job. She hated her life, and I was the enemy. She wanted to lash out in hormonal attack. It was all she could do to restrain herself. I knew, as I paused before commencing cross-examination, that if I could just touch that raging nerve, push that button, the venom would spew through the entire courtroom. I wondered, as I moved my gaze to the jurors, could they see the innate meanness of that social piranha? Or did they see a modest, fiftyish woman who had been deceived and taken advantage of by my client?

As it had many times before, the thought passed through my mind that there had to be balance in this drama. Yes. Ron had deceived this lady on invoicing. No. Her house had not been destroyed; in fact, it was beautiful. But it was a house of unhappiness. I knew that, deep down, her husband hated her, and she, him. She stayed for the money, and there was plenty of it, thanks to the chain of sixteen restaurants he had developed from scratch over a dozen years. When did the marriage fall apart, I wondered. When did he start sleeping in a different bed? When did she learn to manipulate him simply for material gifts on the promise to forestall divorce? Ah! divorce. Such a nasty word. Too expensive to initiate, it is its own living hell. There would never be a time when he would be free of this woman. There would never be a time that her hate and resentment would be sated.

After two hours, I brought my cross-examination to a close. It had been intense. Stress factors were high for both me and opposing attorney, and for the witness. For numerous reasons, the trial had not gone well. From the moment of revelation that Ron had fabricated invoices, the best we could hope for was mitigation of damages. But one thing this jury now knew, at least, was that she was not pure as the driven snow. She had her own style of greed. It showed from the witness stand.

A court clerk handed me a note at counsel's table. I discreetly unfolded it, thinking it would reference some research, some point of law, from my paralegal. I looked down so as not to be obvious to the jury. The note coldly and simply said, "Your father just died."

I sat there for a few moments. My body labored with delayed shock. I rose and said, "Your Honor, I need a recess." Without waiting for permission or response, I left the courtroom. In a witness room, in private, I broke down. I was literally drained from the trial. Now this. My mind flooded with scenes from my life with my father. Scenes like when he taught me to fish as a boy, and how he played catch with me for hours on end.

Gathering what little emotional stability I had left, I asked the judge for a two-week recess to take care of my family and bury my father. The Verlander lawyers objected, but the judge begrudgingly gave me a week. It was a dark time.

13

After returning to trial, I began to question the decision not to have Ron present. If I heard "and this defendant doesn't even have the guts to come up here and explain himself to you, ladies and gentlemen of the jury" once, I heard it twenty times. In my mind, I justified the decision: What do you do with a client like Ron? Just feed him to the wolves?

The Verlanders closed their case-in-chief. I put on two interior decorators to explain the customs in the business and that probably no fraud was intended. I put on a CPA who reviewed the invoices and quantified the overcharge at a much lesser amount than Mrs. Verlander was alleging. I put on a licensed estate liquidator to give an estimated appraisal of what Mrs. Verlander called her "priceless heirlooms," which pretty much turned out to be junk. My trial strategy was not selling. I could tell by looking at the jurors' eyes.

After the case was turned over to the jury, they stayed out less than five hours. The judge read the verdict. I knew it would be bad, but this was really bad. I almost fell through the floor.

The jury found three-hundred-thousand dollars in actual damages, and one-million dollars in punitive damages for fraud. As I closed my briefcase, Mrs. Verlander passed by my table and snickered as she said:

"You are a sorry SOB for defending that man. We aren't through with him yet!"

I had never felt so low. I was still struggling with my dad's death, the hurt of loss, the feeling of guilt that I was not there to hold his hand in the last moments, to assure him that it was all right to let go, that the family was strong and we would take good care of Mother. Now I was here, here in this border town of El Paso, in this cold and unforgiving courtroom. I had just experienced the worst case loss of my career, and now I had to go explain it to my client.

I felt a tightening in my stomach, acid in my throat. I was supposed to call Teresa and Cuatro at my office to let them know how the trial came out as soon as the verdict was rendered. I wondered, Do I do that now, or do I try to explain this catastrophe to Ron? I was sure this would be the end of our relationship. Perhaps that would be best. I would like to have known more about the lady Jackie, how different she was, how unusual.

I walked through the courthouse hall, my leather heels echoing through hollow chambers. The thought came to me that I hadn't been paid for the work on this trial, unsuccessful though it was, and probably I never would recoup my expenses. How could I have been such an idiot as to walk into a situation such as this? Lawyers are supposed to take care of themselves first, but then, I had never been particularly good at that. I seemed to get so wrapped up in cases that I failed to see collateral issues of the client.

I had to shake these thoughts.

I had to call the office.

I had to talk to Ron.

I had to keep walking.

I could do any of these things at that moment. Instead, I opted to drop by the Central Café and Bar a short distance from the courthouse in downtown El Paso. I ordered a double and tried to lick my wounds. After about thirty minutes, I realized it wasn't helping. I headed for the house of Morgan on the cliff.

When I walked through the front door, I must have looked like a retreating Confederate soldier. I sure felt like one. At first, I was encouraged that Ron wasn't there. In the face of utter defeat, one looks for any sign of relief. Of course, this only prolongs the agony, and the agony was great. I've never been good at self-justification. I could have demanded this was all the client's fault. I could have been incensed that the client caused this fiasco by not being straight up with me about dual invoicing. I could have postured all manner of self-defense. But I didn't feel that way. I felt that I had failed, that somehow I hadn't done my best. Good lawyers take bad facts and make them work. Clients seldom come with good facts. If the facts are good, what need do they have for the lawyer?

Ron came in from the garage. I didn't wait for a greeting.

"Ron, we got trounced!" I said.

"How do you mean?" he asked innocently.

"They brought back a verdict of three-hundred-thousand dollars actual damages, and a million for punitive damages for fraud," I responded.

"Oh? So, what does that mean?" he asked.

"It means we lost, and lost badly. It means you have a judgment against you for that amount."

"Oh," he said flatly and without exclamation. "Jackie wants us up to

Ruidoso, tomorrow. She wants to play golf. Did you bring your clubs?"

"No, Ron. I didn't bring my clubs. I can't go to Ruidoso, tomorrow. I've got to get back," I said.

"She will loan you a set. It's important. Let's go to dinner. We'll talk about it."

At dinner, a high-scale restaurant, Lorenzo, Ron, and I sat and discussed Ron's plans for the future. I tried to reflect on the devastation of the Verlander verdict. He appeared to shrug it off. Lorenzo sat quietly, as he usually did. Lorenzo was difficult to read, but I had the feeling that he was quite concerned about what we had talked about earlier, this bizarre marriage idea. Indeed, the thought astounded me. Earlier, I had been overwhelmed with the Verlander suit, unable to focus on it. In fact, I had discounted the idea as one of Ron's fantasies. Why would a 72-year-old woman want to marry a 50-year old man --- and a gay man, at that?

As dinner was served and the salad plates removed, Ron brought up the subject again.

"When we meet with Jackie tomorrow, she wants to talk to you about doing a contract with Dale Chihuly for glass for the theater."

"You mentioned that once before, Ron. Who is Dale Chihuly?" "He is a famous artist in glass. I'm going to do the entire theater in glass. It will be absolutely stunning," Ron answered.

"I haven't done work for Jackie. I would think she had dozens of lawyers," I said.

"Oh, she does. She hates them all, but I told her I want you to work on the things I do. She is going to pay me ten percent. Tomorrow, she is going to let me have some money, and I'll pay you."

"You mentioned something about marriage just before the Verlander suit started. I talked to Lorenzo here about it, but didn't know much. What's that all about?"

"When I finish the theater, we're talking about getting married. Jackie wants to do a lot of traveling, and wants me to go with her. She's going to pay me to do it," Ron explained.

"For God's sake, Ron, why marriage?" I asked.

"I don't know. She's from the old school, I guess. She doesn't want to be traveling and living with a man she is not married to."

"But, Ron, you're gay. She's not. She's older. You're not. It seems rather strange."

"Not really. Nothing will change, except I will be making a lot of money. I will stay with her for about a year, get all the money I can, then divorce her."

The conversation went silent. I really didn't know what to say after that.

The next day, I would go to Ruidoso and I would play a round of golf with Jackie, if she wanted to. I wanted to hear her side of this, if she would tell me.

14

Ruidoso is a mountain village nestled in the Southeastern New Mexico Rockies, known as the Sacramento Mountains, and close to two huge mountains, Capitan and Sierra Blanca. Sierra Blanca is the spiritual center of the Mescalero Apaches who were defeated by the U.S. Army in the late 19th Century, and, ultimately by treaty, the mountain of Sierra Blanca was deeded to Mescaleros. A portion of the mountain was developed as a ski resort known as Ski Apache, a popular winter destination for all levels of skiers. The Inn of the Mountain Gods, an upscale resort and casino on the Mescalero reservation, lies at the far western edge of Ruidoso.

Beginning in the summer of the late '40s, New Mexican and Texan ranchers would meet in Ruidoso and match their horses for racing. Through the last half of the 20th Century, the area to the eastern edge of the village developed into a nationally-recognized racing downs and full-scale horseracing industry. Ultimately, that area transformed into its own village known as Ruidoso Downs, and segregated from the village of Ruidoso, itself.

After the Verlander trial, I again followed Ron to Jackie's house at Alto Village. Alto Village, with its upscale living area, two country clubs, and golf courses, is the kind of place where residents travel around in golf carts. There are no shops. Shopping is done in Ruidoso. The living is quiet and easy, nestled in the coolness of the pines with pet deer roaming at will and fascinating bird species flitting about. It is the summer home of the wealthy from Eastern New Mexico and West Texas. Driving through it, I had the feeling that, if you had the money, living couldn't get much better. These were not people climbing the mountain of financial success. They had already reached the top. The stress of Corporate America was down below.

The sun had set behind the mountain as Ron and I pulled into Jackie's driveway. Again, we entered the large split-level dwelling through the garage to its lower level. It was almost as if this were our territory and we were accepted. Indeed, it had become Ron's territory, and he was accepted. I was just along for the ride, or to perform whatever service that may be requested.

Ron and I were running late. We deposited our belongings in our respective bedrooms, washed up a bit, and headed upstairs. Jackie met us in the spacious but comfortable living room. She was anxious to get to the Kokopelli for dinner.

As we entered the dining room, I again noticed how the staff nervously snapped to attention, their smiles and greetings forced. I wondered how they talked about us when they returned to their humble abodes at night after work. I was struck by that same feeling at the Theater at the time Jackie and Ron introduced me to the staff on an earlier trip.

Dinner was quiet. There was no outburst by Jackie this time to straighten out the chef on how to poach sole. I was frustrated that the dinner conversation didn't come close to the subject of marriage, or even what Jackie wanted me to do regarding the Theater. I would later learn, through many overnight visits, that Jackie preferred to wake up refreshed in the morning, cook breakfast, herself, and everyone sit around the breakfast table to discuss business. This evening's discussion was totally consumed with her frustrations at the racetrack, the perceived ineptness of her trainer, and the mystery of why her horses were not performing better.

I sat quietly and listened, somewhat surprised at Jackie's knowledge of the ins and outs of equestrian racing. There seemed to be a lot of blame going on, and Ron helped at every step of the way. He was good at that when gossiping about someone not present. I knew that Jackie had been successful at racing. A large bronze trophy of a horse named Strawberry Silk was on display in the downstairs study where Ron and I stayed. Jackie Spencer owned that horse. It had won the million-dollar race, the All-American Futurity at Ruidoso Downs.

Sometime later, I would hear how Strawberry Silk had won the All-American Futurity in 1989 under the direction and training of the most successful and famous quarter horse trainer ever, Jack Brooks. Even qualifying for the All-American Futurity is next to impossible. Jack Brooks won the race eight times. No one has ever come close to that feat.

That night, the night of winning the All-American Futurity, Jackie held a celebratory gathering at the Country Club. All the social elite of Ruidoso were there. As Jack Brooks and his assistant trainer arrived, they learned they had been fired. No reason given. Jackie simply said:

"You're fired. But instead of the ten percent I owe you, you'll get twenty percent."

Brooks is a quiet, gentle man. Having worked for Jackie in training

Strawberry Silk, he knew, just as anyone who ever worked for her knew, not to ask "why," not unless you wanted a royal ass-chewing. Jackie seldom --- actually never --- gave a reason for her decisions. So, Jack calmly accepted the statement "you're fired" but he had two comfort zones even though he would miss Strawberry Silk. One, he was to receive two-hundred-thousand dollars instead of one-hundred-thousand. Two, horse owners a mile long were lined up to hire him.

Jack Brooks came to be called "Mr. All-American," and, in 2004, would be inducted into the American Quarter Horse Hall of Fame. In his career, his horses would make more than nine-thousand-five-hundred starts and earn more than thirty-two-million-two-hundred-thousand dollars. He never knew why Jackie fired him. No one did. It was just vintage Jackie.

About six months later, she learned that the wife of the assistant trainer was suffering with a melanoma. She wrote out a check for fifty-thousand dollars and mailed it to the family in Oklahoma City. No note. No explanation. Just a check for fifty-thousand dollars. I was just getting to know Jackie and hearing such stories. There were many. In time, I would experience my own.

We returned to Jackie's house after dinner. She pressed for a post-dinner game of Rummikub. I just couldn't muster the energy. I was gassed from the Verlander trial and ruminating on how we would handle the fiasco of that huge judgment. I begged off and went to bed. Ron's duty was to play Rummikub, bridge, and golf --- which he was just learning --- any time Jackie wanted to, which was often. I didn't know how that came to be, whether it was an agreement in some confidential conversation, or whether Ron just realized this was the way it was to be; he would always be at Jackie's beck-and-call for these entertainments.

A.N.'s role through all those years of marriage had been to serve as companion, to play golf and card games, to be present at horse races and social functions, to stand to the side while the limelight shone on Jackie. I had heard stories that he was a dedicated country doctor, gruff and short-tempered with his patients, yet a patient stepfather to the Bancroft children. He was not ostentatious while he quietly served as this wealthy woman's husband. There was never doubt about his commitment, though I wondered how this played out in A.N.'s mind. As I drifted towards sleep, I thought of how different, how opposite Ron's service would be.

The next morning dawned. Bright sunshine streamed through the pines, birds chattered --- some sang --- and I smelled breakfast cooking upstairs. I had slept hard after finally escaping the depression of defeat.

I entered the kitchen just as I had on prior visits, and as I would in the years to come. There stood Jackie at the stove, whipping up a delicious breakfast. Ron sat at the table, sipping on a fresh-squeezed glass of orange juice. They were engaged in animated conversation.

I sat down. Jackie brought me a cup of coffee and a glass of orange juice.

"Good morning, Glen. How did you sleep?" she greeted.

"Couldn't have been better, Jackie. Thank you. I needed the rest."

"You should have stayed up and played Rummikub with us. Ron needed some help," she laughed.

I watched her move around the kitchen in her robe. It was always striking to me how large a woman Jackie was. She wasn't fat. She was just tall and big-boned. For a girl growing up in the '30s, she must have really stood out; people were smaller then. Even now, her size was impressive. As she sat down at the table after serving Ron and me, her plate of eggs, bacon, biscuits and jam in hand, she said:

"Well, first things first. I have a tee time for eleven o'clock at the Alto Country Club. Perhaps I can beat you this time."

"My father was a scratch golfer. I learned from him, though I was never as good," I responded.

"Well, it doesn't make any difference. We will have a good time. Ron is just learning, but he's getting better. We'll have lunch on the break after the first nine."

"Sounds good to me," I said.

"Now, let's talk about what Ron wants to do with the Theater. That's my little jewel out there. I want the large foyer, the upstairs gathering area and the board dining room to look spectacular. Right now, it's far too plain, and Ron has some great ideas," Jackie explained.

"What can I do to help?" I asked.

"Apparently, this is going to cost several million. I want you to help negotiate with the artist, Chihuly, and make sure we get what we want and not taken to the cleaners. Then there's this other thing. I don't have the money to do this right now. I just bought three new colts for over three-hundred-thousand. I want you to call my trust lawyers in Denver and get the money for the Theater. Also, I'm going to pay Ron ten percent, and I'm going to let him have some money now."

"I'll get right on it," I said.

I had no idea how to call the Denver trustees and demand money. At the moment, I didn't know who Dale Chihuly was, or how to negotiate a contract with him, but what I was coming to understand was that Jackie didn't care for the minutia. I couldn't tell whether detail produced anxiety, or whether there was just no tolerance for it, but one thing became very clear after a few attempts. You just didn't go there. Jackie knew what she wanted, and it was up to you to produce the results. That's what she was paying for.

Our golf game was delightful. I was amazed at how well this 72-year-old woman swung the club. She was quite good, particularly her short game, and she was intent on winning. As we sat in the golf cart tallying our score after each completed fairway, she made it clear that she enjoyed playing with me. While Ron chased balls in the rough, we got to talk, one on one.

I was interested in her life, how she came to be. I had to be careful not to be intrusive. She was sensitive to that. I apologized for being curious, but I explained that I had not met anyone like her before.

Jackie told me she was married to Hugh Bancroft, Jr. for five years, and they had lived in Capitan. New Mexico, on the other side of the mountain, had three children during that time. When he died, he left her one of the wealthiest women in America, although she didn't realize it at the time.

"Why Capitan?" I asked. "In 1948, there was almost no one there. Why on earth did you move from Denver to Capitan, New Mexico?" I asked.

"Hugh wasn't happy. He had the romantic idea of being a rancher in New Mexico. I was just out of school. It sounded exciting," she answered.

Though in the years to come, I would have many visits with Jackie and would ask her questions, I learned her history only in bits and pieces. She was never easily forthcoming. I saw that it wasn't so much that she minded telling me about herself; it was her intolerance for the minutia thing. A short revelation here, a very brief history there. That's all you got. For now, it was clear that the subject of questions about family was closed. We went on with the golf game. The woman loved chasing the ball.

That evening I sat with Ron in the study/den on the lower level next to our bedrooms.

"Ron, we've got some serious issues to discuss, and I need information and decisions from you. I can't just keep guessing and not knowing what's coming down the pike," I began.

"What do you mean?" Ron asked.

"I think you know what I mean, but I'll give you this. You're very creative. I've seen your work, and I can see why your clients, most of your clients, like your work. Seems to me we operate from different sides of the brain. You're creative, in the cloud. I'm more lineal."

"I don't know what you mean," Ron retorted.

"Well, let's start here. That Verlander verdict was a catastrophe because I couldn't put you on the stand as a result of the D.A. indicting you for forgery, and the sword-fighting episode you got yourself into two weeks before trial. Now, it seems you are going to be making a pretty good fee. I don't know what ten percent of this Chihuly thing is, but it sounds like a lot."

"It is. I could make three- or four-hundred-thousand," Ron answered.

"Well, here's the problem. You just lost a verdict for a million-three. These were damned good lawyers on the other side, and I bet they are just as good at collecting on a judgment."

"Well, what should we do?" he asked.

"I can stall this thing for a while, file a motion for new trial, appeal, things like that, but, ultimately, they are going to tie up every cent you get, and they'll try going after Jackie if they think she is giving you money," I explained.

"Can't you hide the money?"

"I probably can, but it will require your taking bankruptcy, again, and setting up a trust outside the bankrupt estate. Jackie can pay the trust whatever you earn, but the trustee is still going to have to find a way to get the money to you."

"Can you do that?" Ron pursued.

"I probably could. I need to do some research when I get back to the office. Who you pick as trustee is going to be important. They need to be sensitive to your situation. They need to be flexible but understand that they will be walking on thin ice on occasion, and they need to know how to take your money offshore without a trace."

"Well, I guess that's what we better do," Ron answered.

"Who are you going to want as your trustee?" I asked.

"I don't know. Who do you suggest?" Ron asked.

"I don't know. Your closest friend? Your closest relative? It's got to be someone you can trust, someone who can learn the nuances of the situation. It's not like we can go down to the bank trust department and say, 'We need a trustee.'"

"Then you have to do it. You have to be the trustee," Ron said.

"I don't know, Ron. That would solve the problem on one hand, but many a lawyer has gotten in trouble trying to serve as a trustee," I said.

"Jackie's trustees are lawyers in Denver. Why can't you be my trustee?" he asked.

"I could. It's not illegal or anything like that. Let's just table it for now. Digest what I've said, and we can talk about it later. Now, tell me how to contact Jackie's lawyer/trustees in Denver and request that money she wants for the Theater decoration."

The next morning, after breakfast and further discussions on Chihuly glass art and what to expect from the Denver trustees, I crawled into my car, headed out of the mountains for the flat prairie of my home, and began windshield time.

My father's death in the middle of the Verlander trial, and all that went with it, left me drained. I looked forward to getting home for some TLC from my wife. Representing Ron had required a lot of nights away from home, and the potential demands of a Jackie/Ron relationship might require more. Thank God, Jane, my wife, stayed quite busy in her own profession. She was chair of the sociology department at our community college. My legal assistant, Teresa, and my office manager, Cuatro, were stressed out at the office, I knew, trying to keep the ship from sinking in my absence. That always happens when I'm away, locked down in a long trial.

My mind, however, kept coming back to this lady, Jackie. How intriguing she was. How different and unique her personality. There was a sensitivity there, absent the false front one finds on the face of so many in high society. Jackie seemed to present herself more with the attitude "what you see is what you get." Yet, at the same time, there was sternness, almost authoritarian.

I decided that when I got home, I would get my work done, but I needed a diversion. I would research the history of The *Wall Street Journal*, Hugh Bancroft, and, to the extent that I could, Jackie's life. One day, you are a newly married ranch woman, the next, your husband has died, and you are suddenly one of the wealthiest women in America. I was enamored with the thought of such a transformation. To the extent she would allow me, on occasions to come, I would ask Jackie about her life and family. I didn't realize it at the time, but this new hobby, historical research and Jackie's most interesting life, would last over the course of the next five years.

15

To understand who Jackie was, I knew I must first understand the history of the Bancroft family, bluebloods of Boston. Jackie told me stories, but those stories only enhanced my research of the Bancrofts. You may wonder, Why the Bancrofts? Because Jackie married a Bancroft, and that was the source of her immense wealth. It was important for me to get a feel for that wealth, to understand its nature.

If it were not for those millions, there would be no story of how a 75-year-old *Wall Street Journal*/Dow Jones' heiress came to marry a 52-year-old gay man. If Jackie had not been rich, there would have been no Ronnie Lee Morgan worth mentioning, and certainly no story to tell. There would have been no performing arts theater, dripping in Chihuly glass, nestled outside Ruidoso, New Mexico, with its arched steel and glass view of the magnificent Sacramento Mountains. If there had been no Jackie, there could have been no four-year, forty-million-dollar spending spree by Ron. Indeed, there would have been no need for my legal representation or companionship, nor would there have been need for my legal career to come to a disastrous end.

In time to come, I would observe a haunting thread linking the fate and the heritage of Hugh Bancroft to his son and, ultimately, to Jackie Bancroft in a way she could not have foreseen. The saying goes that when a person dies, their death was timely or that it was untimely. Which was Jackie's? I would have time to pick the puzzle apart in the not-too-distant future, but some puzzles are not meant to be put back together, for the edges are frayed or a piece is missing. What remains is the insatiable desire to make sense of it.

In those years after Jackie's death, I would reflect with glazed stupor on how I had come to know Jackie for the last five years of her life, of how she had had a strange effect on me. I would think about what I had observed of the people around her in those years, their character and character defects, and how they acted differently, often kowtowing in her presence.

To steal a phrase, the rich are different, and there is a difference between Eastern "old money" and Western "old money." The most obvious difference is that Eastern money is older. In 19th Century Boston, for example, to be somebody, somebody of worth, you must be in the society of the Peabodys, Lowells, and Cabots. There is a famous ditty about Boston being the home of the bean and the cod, where Lowells spoke only to Cabots, while Cabots spoke only to God. The Bancrofts were of this kind of aristocracy.

Jackie was born into elitism but of a different sort from that of Hugh Bancroft, Jr. In America, the socially elite, the wealthy, take on some of the same trappings, but there is that difference between the East and the West. Hugh Bancroft, Jr. came from the Bostonian blueblood, the "my-people-came-over-on-the-Mayflower"-type thing, while the uppercrust of Denver society, where Jackie was raised, is more earthbound, coming from Western adventurism. Denver wealth often arose from gold or silver mining or wildcat drilling for oil. While an East Coast elite may think of Western wealthy society as being on a certain par, it was, nevertheless, crass, an undercurrent that made it not quite acceptable in the East. At least, this is the way it was for the 19th Century and the first half of the 20th. It even exists to this day, to some extent. Eastern society strove to emulate European aristocracy. Western elitism meant only to be rich.

Western society is more cavalier. First, it takes money, lots of it. From there, you're not likely to be rejected. Who you are related to, where you came from, or how you made your money are of little importance; probably none. Hugh Bancroft, Jr. came from old money, inherited wealth. Jackie came from the Western idea of wealth, and not nearly the kind of wealth engendered by the likes of The *Wall Street Journal* and the Dow Jones publishing empire.

But no matter where the wealth springs from, a common thread runs through both. Those who have the wealth, the money and the trappings of riches, must be careful, alert and cautious. They're required to develop a certain Machiavellian knowledge and sixth sense. They're also required to adopt a certain calculated coldness, always being on guard without appearing to be. An entourage surrounds them. Within that court are the "wannabes," those who would do anything, give anything, perhaps even their own soul, to be wealthy. They're the predators who encircle the rich; always promoting, always scheming. Perhaps this is what causes the rich to be different, but I think there is more to it than that. In a way, the wealthy are like a herd of wildebeest surrounded by scoundrels.

I have had many opportunities to observe this phenomena. My

observations were not judgmental. I have no desire to judge. Observing has intrigue for its own purposes. Born of humble beginnings in West Texas, though work has taken me to many parts of the globe, I have always been a true Southwesterner. I wouldn't live anywhere other than West Texas or Eastern New Mexico. I have always been drawn to and enchanted by the Chihuahuan desert, the Davis Mountains, the Rio Grande, and the Sacramento Mountain Range of Ruidoso, New Mexico.

Because I live in an oil-producing center, I have had the opportunity to advise, represent, or work for those building fortunes by their own sweat, blood, and risk-taking, as well as for Eastern families like the Bostonian Wainwrights or Kennedys seeking to expand their already-extensive and well-established wealth through oil exploration and investment. My life has secretly been that of an observer --- of human beings, of man's struggle against other men, and their inhumanity one to another, against physical elements as well as societal stratification, of greed, envy, manipulation, and even crime.

So, by the time I came to represent Jackie's last husband, Ron Morgan, and met Jackie, herself, my sense of observation was keen, honed by years of experience in trial practice, investment banking on foreign soils, and just the general advent of life. Not only were a person's outward actions of intrigue to me, so too how they thought and what brought them to their way of thinking. The real compensation in serving as Ron's lawyer and secretly advising Jackie, as she double-checked her own lawyers' advice or circumvented them altogether, was to observe these two separate and totally diverse minds, to reconcile some meaning of how Jackie Bancroft Spencer and Ron Morgan got together. That was the seminal thought, the initial question in my mind, as I was brought into this fold.

It seemed to me that, to understand Jackie, I must understand Hugh Bancroft, Jr. But to understand what brought him and Jackie together, I must know who his father, Hugh Bancroft, was, and how he came to own The *Wall Street Journal*. I began a path of research.

16

Returning to historical research when I wasn't practicing law was a welcome diversion. I wanted to learn how the Dow, Jones Publishing Co. and The *Wall Street Journal*, the seed of this immense trust wealth, began. I had read the *Journal* many times, admired its broad completeness in financial reporting, and had even used it as a "textbook" in economics class in college. Now, I wanted to feel what society was like at the very beginning and who these men, Charles Dow and Edward Jones, were, how they came to start such a reporting service and publishing company. What I learned was very intriguing.

Charles Dow was a young man in the 1870s. America was rich with natural resources. New York had become the financial center of the world. Earlier in the century, the legal fiction of the corporation had not yet evolved. Populists like Andrew Jackson observed with deep anxiety the mysterious abstraction that would evolve into a legal character as an artificial person, immortal, with limited immunity, protected shareholders from liability of the corporation's acts. But by the 1870s, tycoons like Cornelius Vanderbilt had not only defeated such populist fear of monopoly and aristocracy, they had developed a trading center in New York that would come to be known as the New York Stock Exchange.

In the decade in which Charles Dow began his career as a young financial reporter, Wall Street stock trading was mature and brutal, commonly using tactics of bear raids and price manipulation. There was no transparency, nor were there governmental regulations protecting the investor. For example, in 1870, Vanderbilt's railroad reign culminated in his acquisition of the New York Central and Hudson River Railroad. He created one of the largest corporations in American history. He did this by merging the Hudson River Railroad with the Central, but only after a fiery stock fight. For any young reporter, Wall Street was rich with intrigue and secret trading, not to mention a constant shifting of cause and effect as market values changed from one day to the next, as private fortunes were won or lost.

If financial history has taught anything, it is this: on the one hand, markets and the banking industry are not capable of regulating themselves, while, on the other hand, it has taught that too much governmental regulation stifles entrepreneurship. That history is borne out by the panics of 1819, 1837, 1857, 1873, 1893, the Panic of 1907, the Great Depression of 1930, and the Great Recession of 2007. Charles Dow's first experience with extreme market variations was the Panic of 1873, which threw this country into a severe depression. Banks failed everywhere, and greenbacks became worthless. While some Wall Street wizards were convinced that gold was the only acceptable medium of exchange, other groups pushed Congress for the unlimited coinage of silver, which had long been regarded as the currency of the common people.

The battle over silver versus gold currency raged at the center of American politics. In the midst of this battle and intense period, Dow's reporting on money matters at The *Providence Journal* proved his astuteness in understanding currency and stock markets.

A milestone in the currency battle was the 1873 law known to proponents of silver currency as the "Crime of '73," which abolished the use of silver coins and replaced them with currency based exclusively on gold. That created an abundance of silver on the market. As a result, pro-silver forces campaigned to restore the coinage of silver. The old ratio called for sixteen times as much silver in a silver dollar as there was gold in a gold dollar. The battle between gold and silver was the battle between the industrialist and the farmer, the wealthy and the poor. These battles were every bit as bitter in ideological differences as those we fight today.

The farmer may have wanted silver coinage back --- and they would get it --- but it would be the wealthy tycoons, the entrepreneurs, who would own the silver. They would travel to the mines, inspect them, buy them, then sell stock in them back East, for profit. During this time, young Charles Dow was assigned to accompany a group of Eastern businessmen traveling to Leadville, Colorado, to get a firsthand look at the booming silver industry. These were the men who knew corporate profit, and who knew how to tie up commodities like silver.

In an elegant and well-appointed train, some of these extremely wealthy men traveled to Leadville. Perhaps this reporting assignment was a crossroads to success for Charles Dow, for it was here that he met some of the movers of industrial America. He spent much of his time in the "hotel car" interviewing, taking shorthand notes on his cuffs, and, in fact, demonstrating his acumen, while gaining the confidence of these men. When he later moved to New York from Rhode Island and worked for the Kiernan Wall Street Financial Bureau, he would have no trouble gaining access to the city's financial leaders. His honesty and ability to keep a secret had already won them over.

Edward Davis Jones, a younger friend of Charles Dow, came on board the Kiernan Wall Street Financial News Bureau at Dow's recommendation. Soon, the two proved to be an excellent team: Dow as an idea man, while it was said Jones could dissect and analyze a financial report "with the speed and accuracy of a skilled surgeon."

In 1882, the two opened their own financial news agency, the Dow, Jones & Company, Inc. Their original headquarters was in a small back room in the basement of Henry Danielson's candy store on Wall Street. The story is told that this fledgling news agency scored its first beat with a story on the Standard Oil Trust, a company notorious for secrecy. Its trustee, testifying before Congress, characterized Standard Oil as having "two purposes, two principles: making money and making no noise about it."

Dow, Jones persisted in trying to find out what Standard Oil's John D. Rockefeller was up to. Jones succeeded in interviewing William Rockefeller, John D's brother and a New York Representative. Jones was amazed when Rockefeller said to him, "Why don't you send your bulletins down to Eighteen Broadway?" That address was Standard Oil's headquarters at the time. As if that weren't enough, Rockefeller's next suggestion was even more exciting: "Would it mean anything in particular to you to get a little advance Standard Oil news?" The young paper was off and running.

Aside from its strict principles of honest reporting in a period when stock scams were abundant, Charles Dow and Edward Jones's decision to start a financial newspaper could not have been better-timed. This was the seminal period of the founding of The *Wall Street Journal*.

"As this nation has seen, again and again, the period after a bust is an expanding boom. The panic of 1873 was a far memory. The 1880-1890 decade was one of remarkable national growth and expansion. The population jumped by thirteen million, including five million immigrants. More railroad mileage, 69,000 miles of it, was built than in any other period; we still use most of it, today. There was vast growth in the packing industries. Production of iron ore, wheat and flour, lumber, steel, and coal expanded exponentially, and the South was on an economic rise."

The Boom of the '80s may have been a perfect time to open a new financial news agency, but the boom-times could not last. The Panic of '93 hit with the failure of the Philadelphia and Reading Railroad, amid a subsequent wave of selling on Wall Street. Part of the problem was that the British and European banks that had financed the American railroads demanded payment in gold for the stocks and bonds they were unloading. Bank failures led to foreclosures on mortgages to farmers. The stock market collapsed. Within the year, bankruptcies spread to five-hundred banks and fifteen-thousand businesses. The depression of 1893 reduced the national income by ten percent, driving millions out of work. The unemployment rate rose to twenty percent. The collapse of prices on farms further inflamed feelings among workers in industry. Food lines swelled and charities in large cities were overwhelmed. By the end of 1893, six-hundred-forty-two banks had closed their doors, twenty-two-thousand-five-hundred miles of railway had gone into receivership, and an estimated one-fourth of American industries had gone out of business.

The *Wall Street Journal's* columns carried stories about railroad rates, problems, earnings, and stock market fluctuations. The *Journal* expanded the list of companies it reported on and presented them alphabetically in categories --- rails, telegraph and telephone, land, banks, mines, U.S. government securities, coal and iron, gas and electric, and railways.

But Dow, who had studied financial cycles for some time, finally devised an ingenious barometer for the relationship between stock market trends and general business activity. He believed the stock market as a whole was a reliable measure of overall business conditions within the economy, and one could accurately gauge those conditions and identify the direction of major market trends. He first used his theory to create the "Dow Jones Industrial Index" and the "Dow Jones Rail Index." Today, it's called the "Transportation Index." These were originally compiled by, and reported in, The *Wall Street Journal."* The theory was that, if the industrial average followed the same pattern upward with the Rails, a significant market shift --- a bull market --- was taking place. The reverse also held true. If they followed each other down to new lows, the market was termed bearish. Since these two averages represented two major areas of investment, it was Dow's belief that, unless they both shifted in the same direction at the same time, the move could not be considered critical. One-hundred-plus-years later, that theory is still in use, though it has been tweaked many times by technical analysts.

Dow was the innovator, the decision-maker, in the partnership.

Edward Jones was also a smart analyst, but of a different type. He could look at the financial reports of a company and quickly determine its financial health. He also had the knack for directing sales of the *Journal's* advertising department. Both the *Journal* and the Dow Jones Indices had become a success.

But over a seventeen-year-year period of investigative business reporting, growth, expansion, simultaneously trying to make ends meet for the paper, both Charles Dow and Edward Jones withered under the pressure. Publishing, as it was then and is now, was a brutal business. In the last few years, Dow and Jones argued over policy. In the summer of 1899, Edward Jones decided to retire.

This period, between inception and the turn of the 20th Century, is rich with stories of finance and politics and how the *Journal* reported on it. But the fast pace had also taken its toll on Dow. His health began to fail, and he desperately wanted to retire, as well. The years of squabbling between partners had left its scars.

In 1902, Charles Dow traveled from New York to Boston to meet with Clarence Walker Barron to tell him that he would like to sell Dow, Jones and The *Wall Street Journal*. Barron was a shrewd negotiator cut from the cloth of J.P. Morgan, nineteen years his senior and always his role model. They had both attended Boston's English High School. Barron, already a successful publicist, knew from age fifteen that he wanted to be a newspaperman. He had lifted himself out of the poverty his parents had experienced in fleeing the Great Irish Potato Famine of 1847. Throughout his life, he was fascinated by and modeled himself after J.P. Morgan. He relished covering J.P. Morgan and did so favorably. "The market's symbol of optimism, the bull, was adopted to represent J.P. Morgan, whose body, voice, and temperament are very bull-like, indeed," Barron once wrote.

In reporting the economic panic of the early 1890s --- caused in large part by railroad over-expansion --- Barron reworked his earlier metaphor by heralding Morgan as "the nation's Prometheus. By taking control of bankrupt railroads through voting trusts, J.P. Morgan has saved the country single-handedly."

In June 1887, after eleven years as financial editor of the *Boston Transcript* where he had increased circulation by fifteen percent due to his reporting, Barron founded his own company, the *Boston News Bureau*. Its purpose was to disseminate news of the Boston and New York stock exchanges. It began modestly, but, by 1896, Barron's news-service boasted five-thousand-one-hundred-twenty-three subscribers. He was off-and-running. With each passing year, through hard work and shrewd business management, his prosperity increased exponentially. In 1902, when a tired Charles Dow came to talk about perhaps selling the Dow Jones Publishing Co. and The *Wall Street Journal*, he was no match for a voracious Clarence Barron.

While Dow was intelligent, he was not a born trader. Barron was. He sensed that Dow was desperate to sell, so he acted as if he had little interest. Ultimately, Barron almost stole the company in the trading process. He paid one-hundred-fifty-six-thousand dollars for Dow, Jones and Company and the Dow Jones Ticker Service. One story says that, in order to purchase The *Wall Street Journal*, Barron had to borrow money from his own family. I doubt this story. It doesn't fit with Barron's bombastic nature, on the one hand, nor the timing of his successful ascension with the *Boston News Bureau,* on the other. Taking into consideration the differences in personalities and emotional strength of the two parties at the time, it is more likely that Barron traded Dow so hard that he bought the company with virtually no cash down, and a series of personal IOUs pegged to the *Journal*'s future profits, as recorded history seems to indicate.

Barron learned everything there was to know about the history and operations of the country's leading corporations. Just as J.P. Morgan was ruthless in Wall Street finance, Barron was ruthless in his field. In building a well-disciplined financial news reporter, he was no easy boss. His policy was to "ride" his men until they were broken in to suit him. He successfully launched two news bureaus from Boston, and, by the time Dow let it be known that he wanted to sell Dow, Jones & Company, Barron was the most likely buyer.

Clarence Barron was an unusual and interesting man. Though he was not born into Boston elite --- far from it, in fact --- he was possessed of business acumen, knowing what to do and how to do it, with perceptual timing. He had a strong work ethic, seemingly never to tire, and he paid close attention to overhead and kept it low, particularly when it came to payroll. While Clarence Barron pulled himself up by his own bootstraps, making the *Boston News Bureau* a success, he lived in Mrs. Jessie Waldron's boardinghouse, the stately Marlboro Street townhouse not far from the Boston Commons. By the time Dow approached him regarding the purchase of Dow, Jones and Company in 1902, Barron had achieved financial success. Two years earlier, he had married Jessie Waldron, and, to demonstrate their new family status and his business success, the Barrons purchased a mansion in Boston's exclusive Back Bay section. The mansion boasted twenty-six rooms, eighteen telephones, a library, an elevator, and a staff of twelve servants.

Barron was, by nature, obsessive. His new obsession was sailing. He purchased the ninety-seven foot yacht, the "Hourless," and sailed it throughout the Northeast. At five feet five inches and somewhere around three-hundred-fifty pounds, the white-bearded Barron dressed the part of yacht captain in a commodore's uniform of gold-braided blue blazer, white trousers, and captain's hat. His nature in sailing was no different from that of running a financial reporting news service. He would stand on the bridge and exhort his crew of eighteen, driving them to more exacting service.

In the years he had lived in Jessie Waldron's boardinghouse, he became dependent on her. In fact, in order to have her undivided attention, he drove her other boarders away, thus becoming her star boarder. Often, he listened to her advice, as he had done after Dow approached him to buy Dow, Jones and Company. He once said, "This woman has a surprising ability to suggest just the right action. We sit well into the night, talking about my business problems. After hours of listening, Jessie quietly says, 'Well, Clarence, it seems to me you should do this...'" When he agreed to buy The *Wall Street Journal* and the Dow Jones Ticker Service, Barron, much too obsessed with sailing to manage that New York business, initially turned the New York job over to his wife, who was not obsessed with sailing. He saw her as a woman with business acumen who should have the opportunity of running her own business. For Jessie, it meant commuting from Boston to New York to run the *Journal*. For Barron, it meant having more time to sail his yacht.

On occasion, I asked Jackie about *Wall Street Journal* history, its early years. In the beginning of my research, I particularly wanted to know more about Charles Dow, Clarence Barron, and Hugh Bancroft. Jackie wasn't much help. She, of course, knew who Dow and Barron were, but she didn't know much about them. For me, I was fascinated with this period of American history, and particularly about how these men became the publishing successes they were. Jackie knew more about Hugh Bancroft but didn't seem to care much about his history, either. There were occasions, however, when leads she gave me assisted me in my historical research. From those leads, the stories she told me, and historical references I found, the early history as to how the Bancrofts arrived on the *Journal* scene became more clear.

On one of my visits, Jackie and I sat at the Kokopelli Country Club waiting for Ron to arrive. We looked out over the fairways, expecting to tee-off when Ron arrived. It was a clear mountain day, brisk thin air, and abundant sunshine. The pristine mountain view seemed so far removed from the hustle of Wall Street. It seemed even further removed from this early history of The *Wall Street Journal*. As I looked at Jackie, I had that odd, ethereal feeling of "how did all that come down to this?" From Jessie Waldron Barron running The *Wall Street Journal,* to Jackie Bancroft waiting for a golf game in the mountains of New Mexico.

I mentioned the feeling I was experiencing. Jackie said she had often had the same feeling. My mentioning it brought up the subject of Jessie Waldron Barron. Jackie found it amusing, and I agreed, that it must have been unusual for a woman, in that day and age --- the turn of the 20th Century --- to head up a major financial newspaper. It was not a woman's world then. Surely she encountered different kinds of resistance. It couldn't have been easy.

Jessie was Bostonian and had a large mansion to prove it, but now she spent much time in New York. Running The *Wall Street Journal* was no small task. Both daughters had married; the eldest, Martha, to Horace W. Endicott of the then-Endicott shoe fortune. Later, daughter Jane married Hugh Bancroft. Soon, Jessie would turn to her new son-in-law to help her. While Jessie commuted between Boston and New York, the demands of management required that she spend most of her time at the *Journal*. While there, she stayed in a three-bedroom suite at the Waldorf-Astoria.

Jessie was a good manager but not a browbeater like her husband. While it was successful, the *Journal* had myriad growing pains: how much to charge for advertising when print costs were constantly rising in a period of inflation; usual problems of bill collection, even though sales were high; and how to service and deliver to an ever-growing circulation.

In time, Clarence would retake the helm. Before he finally left his beloved yacht to do so, Jessie brought in her son-in-law to help with the fast-growing, rapidly-expanding *Wall Street Journal*. As Hugh Bancroft left Boston and came on board, a huge and vast publishing fortune began for the Bancroft family. Simply by existing, generations of Bancrofts would live within the *Journal* 's largesse.

An interesting man, Hugh Bancroft graduated from Harvard in 1897, at seventeen, then went on to Harvard Law School. His father, a major general of the Massachusetts National Guard and Chairman of the Boston Elevated Railway, captained the famous Harvard rowing crew of 1879. Hugh had also been on the Harvard rowing crew in his senior year.

Many books detail Eastern blueblood society. While New Englanders were more apt to copy the British custom of "to the manner born" destined by birth to observe certain patterns of behavior, usually associated with good breeding and high social status, New York society was different. There, social rank, social station, or social status were indeed based on behavior, proper speech, and manners, but it was more about how one participated in society.

In 1889, Ward McAllister, a prominent New York socialite, was given the task of deciding who should be invited to a centenary celebration of the inauguration of George Washington. His list included the names of four-hundred people whom he considered to be true elite, the crème de la crème. That list quickly became known as the "Four Hundred" and was accepted as the top in society, a heady place to be. The *grande dame* of the Four Hundred was Mrs. William Astor.

To be prominent as a New York socialite, a person must, of course, be wealthy. Equally important, that person must be refined in the manner in which he or she presented him or herself. And the *grande dame*, herself, must approve of the socialite. In 1904, Mrs. Astor raised the number of those accepted to eight hundred, though the coterie was never referred to as the "Eight Hundred."

The general public, the masses, the hoi polloi, were beneath and below the elite. They did not possess the breeding, the ancestry, or the money to be part of high society. Western wealth, *nouveau riche* like Molly Brown of Colorado silver and gold fame, was looked upon with some degree of horror. The "new rich" may have arrived with newfound money, but they most decidedly were not of the gentility. Instead, they were viewed as persons of odd behavior, crass, and something to be tolerated, if need be, and not accepted in higher society.

On the other hand, the Bancrofts could rightly be called "true Massachusetts bluebloods." They represented the high Boston Tory faction and were among the first settler families that founded Lynn, Massachusetts, in 1632. Arriving on a ship that landed ten miles north of Boston, the Bancrofts were among the pilgrim migration from England that imbued New England with its strong sense of morality and self-reliance. During the fifty years following, the family was the sole exporter of sugar and tobacco for the Massachusetts Bay Colony, a trade that made them immensely wealthy. Sailing was part of the blood that made theirs blue. For these 19th Century bluebloods, horsemanship competitions, both sow and jumping, was both admired and required. It has been said that, in this tradition, if you cross an estate on foot, you are a trespasser; if on horseback, you are gentry. This was the life Hugh Bancroft was born into.

Over the years, the family's Puritanical background morphed into either the Congregational Church or Anglican Episcopalian. They became reliable contributing stalwarts of the Republican Party. Positions they held were often ceremonial; after all, money was not a problem.

Upon graduating Harvard Law School in 1901, Hugh first worked as a bank officer, then served as Assistant District Attorney of Middlesex County. One would assume the position as a prosecutor was not ceremonial. But, then, one would also have to assume that the period from 1902 to 1907 was not an era of crime, as far as Middlesex County was concerned.

It was after this prosecutorial gig that Hugh Bancroft's life, at least his professional life, would change forever, though his love of horsemanship and competition never changed. He married Jane Waldron Wallis, Clarence W. Barron's stepdaughter, on June 15, 1907. From all accounts, Jessie Barron, Jane's mother, quite liked and admired Hugh. Clarence tolerated but did not like Hugh. After all, they were not cut from the same cloth. Clarence was in semi-retirement --- in his mind, he had given The *Wall Street Journal* to Jessie to manage --- mainly sailing around on his yacht. Thus preoccupied, he didn't really know his new son-in-law that well. However, the day would come when great tension would exist between the two men after Clarence retook the *Journal* management

But this was 1907. The Panic of 1907 hit the country and Wall Street. Jessie invited Hugh Bancroft onto the board of directors, and to help her manage the company. That was quite a jump --- from young criminal law prosecutor to the board of directors of the leading financial news magnate of the country --- indeed, the world. In all likelihood, Hugh was in over his head. His background was in neither finance nor publishing but, rather, gentility and ceremonial pursuits. Here, amidst financial panic, he was, in essence, co-managing a discipline that encompassed both finance and publishing. From the time of Clarence Barron's purchase of the Dow Jones and The Wall Street Journal, to the Panic of '07, Wall Street and the country had experienced a boom. Booms are easy to manage; everything you do seems brilliant. Now, it was bust --- and it would be the true test!

In 1912, virtually all Dow Jones' profits had vanished. The Journal's circulation dropped from its high of eleven thousand to seven-thousand-five-hundred. Barron left retirement and burst onto the scene in bombastic style. In Western parlance, he immediately started "taking names and kicking ass." He ran things hands-on and with a heavy hand, at that. His personality exhibited impatience and unreasonableness. He had gained success by learning and earning through natural intelligence and hard knocks; failure was not an option. The self-made Barron, whose father had been a lowly-paid dockworker, had pulled himself up by his own bootstraps. Though not a Massachusetts blueblood, his success sent a dig to blueblood society when he married Jessie Waldron, legally adopted her two daughters, and purchased the mansion on Boston's Back Bay section. He said, "It's a fitting tribute to American free enterprise that I, a virtual waif thirty years ago, can now mingle with the Cabots and the Lowells."

When he arrived in New York to take over Dow, Jones, Barron was forty-six years old. With an untiring, iron hand, he ran the Journal. His most significant contribution: to broaden its geographic reach. The initial step, linking the New York paper with his Boston and Philadelphia papers, paved the way for the Journal's eventual emergence as a national business daily. Within eight years after purchasing the newspaper, circulation more than doubled --- from seven thousand in 1902, then to eighteen-thousand-seven-hundred-fifty in 1910. Now, circulation had dropped back to the seven-thousand-five-hundred level. That was not acceptable.

A week after Clarence Barron retook the Journal, Hugh Bancroft was banished to Boston and given the position of head of the city's transit authority. For the next several years, he pursued his hobby, his true love, equestrian competition.

As for Clarence Barron, timing was everything. Matters were getting complicated in Europe. Industrialists were positioning themselves to profit from war. Clarence traveled to Europe, reporting on the war and clearly seeing that, in spite of President Wilson's protestations to the contrary, America would soon be there. He returned to New York early in 1917, just weeks before President Woodrow Wilson convinced Congress to authorize America's entry into World War I.

Historically for America, wars have been a wonderful thing. They cure panics, recessions, depressions; and they provide a post-war boom. During the build-up to WWI, businesses flourished, manufacturing weapons, war materials, and supplies for England and France and, to some degree, Germany. Dow Jones experienced an upsurge in profits. By 1917, the *Journal's* circulation had climbed to twenty thousand, and Barron earned a salary and dividends exceeding one-hundred-thousand dollars annually. The *Journal,* a powerhouse of financial news and distribution, was back.

For about a ten-year period, Hugh Bancroft remained on his estate in Cohasset, Massachusetts, with his wife, Jane, and their three children, Jessica, Jane, and Hugh, Jr. They lived the genteel life of estate management and social contribution. He wrote financial and legal articles for Barron publications and other news sources. He was particularly incensed by the exorbitance of estate taxes. Being of inherited wealth, he felt the government had no right to tax what one received by inheritance. He devised ways to circumvent inheritance taxes through pre-death investments, then wrote about them. On numerous occasions, he also spoke on the subject.

Hugh spent much of his time on his estate with his horses, teaching dressage to his young children and competing in equestrian jumping and show. He was an excellent horseman, as his father before him and his father before him. A special bond exists between the gentry and their horses; they are like family members and referred to at dinner and in private conversations almost as if they are human.

Though somewhat passive, Hugh Bancroft was an intelligent man. Reared with fineness of manners of what to say and what not to say, he never had to scrape and fight it out, as his father-in-law had done. In this regard, Clarence Barron had a certain disdain for his son-in-law. There existed certain dichotomies: On the one hand, Clarence's personality, the pure capitalist who believed anyone in America could make it if they worked hard enough and applied themselves; on the other hand, Hugh's more compliant personality, self-described as a victim of inheritance taxes though he still had ample money to live well. On one side was Clarence Barron with his bombastic, assertive personality and trading savvy; on the other, Hugh Bancroft, more permissive, more cerebral.

Barron had arrived at the point in age when he realized someone would have to captain the ship. Either that or it would fall back into the inefficient, non-competitive publication it had become in 1912. Even though he apparently didn't think much of Hugh as a businessman, in 1921, he brought him back into Dow, Jones. It is not clear why. Was it with the hope that Hugh could handle the task? Or was it to get the Bancroft family to New York so he could see more of his grandchildren? Whatever the reason, in Barron's mind, it became clear that he would have to go outside the family and the *Journal* itself to acquire the leadership needed.

Barron did just that. In 1923, at the age of sixty-eight, he found his successor in Kenneth ("Casey") Hogate of the *Detroit News*. Hogate immediately impressed Clarence Barron by gaining access to Henry Ford and setting up an interview. Hogate also delighted Barron because of his build. Like Barron, he was short and fat. But Hogate's talent is what most impressed Barron. He was innovative and understood what publishing was about. Clarence Barron appointed Kenneth Hogate managing editor of The *Wall Street Journal*. Thus began the *Journal's* policy to seek out the very best, the most talented to manage and run The *Wall Street Journal* That policy would continue until after the turn of the 21st Century.

After turning management over to Hogate and seeing that the choice was a successful one, Clarence Barron basically returned to retirement, speaking on the benefits of capitalism and supporting the Republican Party and Herbert Hoover's candidacy for President. In October 1928, he died. Interestingly, in 1926, Barron had caused Hugh Bancroft's name to be removed from the newspaper's masthead. No one seems to know if there had been an argument, or if Clarence just decided Hugh didn't deserve that honor. Nevertheless, a week after Barron's death, Hugh Bancroft's name reappeared.

The time was the twilight of the Roaring Twenties, though no one was conscious of its impending demise. The economy was in a boom, and stock speculation was rampant. While Hugh had spent his time railing against inheritance taxes, the *Journal* continued the contest between the taxpayer and the Internal Revenue Service that began the very moment Congress passed the income tax amendment in 1913. Through what might be called "social Darwinism," the wealthy became allies. It didn't matter whether riches were inherited from a sugar/tobacco monopoly, a la Hugh Bancroft, or from discovering mines of silver and gold, a la Molly Brown. Social class was set aside to fight together in the political arena. The age of greed in the Gatsby style was under attack in America. To many, the redistribution of income was un-American.

Then the Crash of '29. Seemingly overnight, there was such a change in paradigm that the longstanding fight against inheritance taxes and progressive income tax was of little importance. The wealth of many, earned or inherited, vanished. Thirty percent of the workforce was unemployed. There was no demand for goods because there was no money and no jobs. There was no supply of goods had there been a demand. No longer was there a fight over redistribution of income. There was no income. Watching the stock market or how a certain company was doing made little sense, unless you just wanted to guess at whom the next executive would be to jump out a window.

Through inheritance as a result of Clarence Barron's death, Hugh Bancroft was hugely wealthy. He and his wife owned fifty percent of the Dow, Jones and The *Wall Street Journal*. If he had been wealthy before from old blueblood money, it was no comparison to the wealth he now inherited. That is the way it was, anyway, until just two years later, the stock market Crash of '29.

Kenneth Hogate may have been managing editor by the time of Clarence Barron's death, but Hugh Bancroft became the paper's spokesman. The paper had been hugely profitable in the late '20s. Joseph J. Ackell, an employee, invented a system that made the *Journal* a national newspaper. By sending a "master copy" of a *Journal* issue from New York, where it was made up, to several plants strategically located throughout the country, the *Journal* could be printed and distributed in those other regions.

The year 1928 was a great one. By the summer of 1929, circulation of The *Wall Street Journal* had risen to nearly fifty thousand. Its News Service, popularly referred to as "the ticker," continually reflected the optimistic mood on Wall Street. The paper charged eighteen dollars for a yearly subscription, and seven cents per copy at the newsstand. The Company's other properties, such as *Barron's Financial Weekly,* were also doing well.

As summer morphed into autumn --- and ever closer to the doomsday stock market crash of October 29, 1929 --- Bancroft lived in denial of any market problem. His and Jane's future couldn't have looked rosier. Telltale signs of market problems surfaced in the summer of '28, but they were concealed by a series of bull rallies of overextended trading, which come at the end of boom times. People, in general, and Wall Street gurus in particular, felt that the market was immortal, that it spoke the truth. Investors continued to believe that they would be the lucky ones. If the chips fell right, they could amass a fortune in one day. Transactions were executed on the thinnest of margins.

The *Journal* had built its reputation on speaking the truth and maintaining the voice of conservatism, but Hugh Bancroft wore blinders. He had not been trained as a market analyst, though he followed the market closely. He and his staff did continue to editorialize, however. On August 21, the *Journal* urged investors:

> "Stock derived further powerful impetus on the up side yesterday
> from the establishment of simultaneous new highs in the Dow-Jones
> industrial and railroad averages at Monday's close. According to the
> Dow Theory, this development re-established the major upward
> trend...The outlook for the fall months seems brighter than at any
> time in recent years."

Throughout September and November, as the market sounded small tremors, the *Journal* shook them off as small ground reverberations with the subtle message to investors to keep buying.

September 5:

> "Substantial recessions took place in the principal trading stocks
> yesterday representing the first technical correction (emphasis mine)
> of importance. Many commission house observers had been
> expecting such a development, and advices to take profits gave
> impetus to the selling movement throughout the morning. "

October 22:

> "The market had a very bad break, the most severe in a number of
> years. There may be some stocks that are still selling too high on a
> basis of selling price times earnings, but on the other hand, there are
> a number of stocks that are now selling at alternative levels...There is
> a vast amount of money awaiting investment."

October 26:

"Beyond indicating the trend there is no idea here of prediction. Conditions do not seem to foreshadow anything more formidable than an arrest of stock activity and business prosperity like that in 1923."

October 28:

"The recent break was due to the position of the market itself. It came when money was 5%, with a plethora of funds available for lending purposes, normal inventories, corporations, flush with surplus money, sound industrial conditions and so on.

"It is because of the fact that the slump was due to the market itself that the storm has left no wreckage except marginal traders forced to sell at a loss."

The next day, October 29, 1929, the grimmest in Wall Street's history, was what we now call the Stock Market Crash of '29. It was no earthly reverberation. It was an earthquake.

But this was the last quarter of '29 and the publishing company was awash in money. Throughout financial publishing history, every crisis in the stock market results in an upsurge of interest in financial news. Well into the following year, the *Journal* flourished, its circulation rising to fifty-two-thousand. Investors may have been broke, but they were starved for any glimmer of hope. They searched every Dow, Jones publication for that glimmer, hoping for a market rebound.

Bancroft tried to satiate their desperate appetite. Under the November 22, 1929 *Los Angeles Times*' headline "Hugh Bancroft, Financial Publisher, Finds No Evidence of Panic or Depression in Current Situation," he was quoted as saying, "Nothing in the nature of a business depression impends," and "the total national income in 1930 will closely approach the high level established in 1929."

Bancroft refused to accept the toll of the bell. In trying to reassure the financial public, perhaps he was trying to reassure himself. He exhorted this was a temporary phenomena. He sought comfort in Republican cohorts, as powerful voices at Treasury and the Fed argued that this financial crisis was a necessary corrective and would be short-lived.

"Liquidate labor, liquidate stocks, liquidate the farmers, liquidate real estate," Treasury Secretary Andrew Mellon advised President Herbert Hoover. "It will purge the rottenness out of the system." Indeed, it did, along with causing the starvation and early death of tens of thousands of people. But, at the same time, Hugh Bancroft editorialized that the liquidation should not be called a "panic," and that nothing in its nature portended a business depression. He tried to differentiate this sell-off from previous panics and recessions. After all, the statement of condition by the Federal Reserve indicated strength in the banking structure. He advised a comeback was certain, and the comeback would be soon.

It's difficult to say at what point hope becomes denial. It is equally difficult to say whether Hugh Bancroft was optimistic about the future --- hopeful, or in denial when he led Dow, Jones to undertake the construction of a brand new building. In 1931, they moved from 44 Broad Street to temporary quarters, and then, on the fiftieth anniversary of the company, in 1932, to a grand new plant. The celebration was there, but behind the façade lay a desperate Hugh Bancroft. Advertising in the paper had all but disappeared, and circulation tanked. People weren't interested in financial news anymore. It was all bad. Truthfully, no one even wanted to hear about it.

Bancroft went into depression. He and The *Wall Street Journal* had backed Herbert Hoover in his bid for re-election. The thought that a Democrat might win was hugely depressing, even more depressing than the current economic state of the nation. Republicans saw Roosevelt as the end of wealth, the end of business. Roosevelt had bonded with Randolph Hearst and his newspapers, while the *Journal* tried to convince voters the market was experiencing only a temporary adjustment on behalf of Hoover.

Hoover was defeated in 1932; Roosevelt was elected. In Bancroft's view, he had lost everything. The once-substantial cash reserves of the *Journal* were gone. The new building and continued operations had created a mountain of debt. To even acquire advertising clients, the *Journal* issued what it called "due-bills," essentially bartering rooms, food, drink, or transportation for advertising. He grew less and less inclined to go to work or make business decisions for the company. He frequently stayed away from the office, and, when he was there, he seemed discouraged and upset. Fortunately, Casey Hogate kept things going.

By the end of that prognosticated year, reality set in. Hugh Bancroft knew he had been wrong. There was no clear path to profit, and he, like so many other wealthy persons, had lost his, or so it seemed. The following year, he retired from the paper, and on October 17, 1933, at the age of fifty-three, he died.

Hugh Bancroft was a highly-intelligent, if not brilliant, man. He had entered Harvard at age fourteen, graduating *summa cum laude* after three years. Then, he accomplished his master's degree, and from there went to Harvard Law School. By the time he was twenty-one, he had three degrees from Harvard. The Bancroft family was very proud of Hugh. It is said that, as soon as he opened his mouth at the dinner table to speak, which wasn't often, his father would make everyone hush up, afraid he wouldn't catch every word. Hugh was a truly cultured gentleman, having been raised in Bostonian elite society, as well as an accomplished sportsman, winner of many equestrian events.

But the very wealthy do not have a shield against problems of mental health any more than the average person. It could be said that, in 1933, not much was known about depression, so help was not available. But that is not correct. Freud had accomplished his work, and even as Hugh Bancroft was in his final depressive state, his daughter, Mary, was beginning to work with Swiss psychologist Carl Gustav Jung, continuing for some four years on her own psychological issues. So, help did exist. But in the 1930s, there was also a social stigma in admitting or showing any such weakness. Hugh Bancroft was untreated. He suffered greatly.

One year out of law school, he married Mary Agnes Cogan. A year later, October 29th, 1903, he lost the love of his life when Mary Agnes died in childbirth while bearing a daughter, Mary. Between that death and 1907, he lived with his parents. He worked at various jobs, including the assistant district attorney position in Middlesex, Massachusetts, but mainly he buried himself in equestrian pursuits -- dressage, steeplechase, and fox hunts. He paid little attention to Mary, almost as if she were too painful a reminder of her mother. Much of the child's early rearing was left to her paternal grandparents, in the midst of clan warfare between the Irish Catholic Cogans, Mary Agnes's parents, and the English Congregational Bancrofts, and the constant wrangling over the grandchild.

In 1907, Hugh married Jane Wallis Waldron, and began a new family: daughter Jessie in 1908, then Hugh, Jr., and Jane. Jane and her sister had been adopted by Clarence Barron, so, when Hugh married Jane, he married into the Clarence W. Barron family. I say the "Clarence W. Barron" family because Clarence was authoritarian and overbearing. The self-made man of wealth didn't care that much for his son-in-law, who was born with a silver spoon in his mouth.

One can see how Hugh Bancroft, predisposed to depression and periodic lapses of self-esteem, would have struggled with the early death of his first wife, a baby girl he didn't know how to relate to, and, ultimately, an overbearing father-in-law who was also his employer and boss. Then, when Hugh finally did have the unfettered management of The *Wall Street Journal* and Dow Jones Publishing, it seemed all was lost in an economic depression he adamantly refused to acknowledge.

As autumn began in 1933, the mental depression Hugh was experiencing was too much. From the Boston Public Library, he took a book on poison gases. He purchased ingredients for the gas he intended to make from different places throughout the city on the pretext that he wanted to get rid of an infestation of rats on his property at Cohasset.

On a dank October day, at his estate in Cohasset, Massachusetts, at the age of 53, Hugh Bancroft took the last right of man. He entered the small blacksmith shop adjacent to the stable, where so many of his beloved horses had been shod, closed the doors, stuffed cloth around them and the windows, and lit a fire in the forge. The medical examiner called it suicide by coal gas poisoning. Hugh Bancroft, in deep depression, had committed suicide. His daughter, Mary Bancroft, was living in Zurich, Switzerland with her husband at the time of her father's death.

Mary Bancroft reported that, in her father's life, he had several "nervous breakdowns" which were hidden from public, and even family knowledge. He would lapse into a depressive state, isolate himself, and, for weeks on end, he would speak to no one. Someone had to constantly be with him so he wouldn't "harm himself." Then, all of a sudden, he would snap out of it. As his daughter reported, the sun would break through the clouds again. He described what his depressions were like, how at such times he felt that he was balancing precariously on the edge of an abyss, overwhelmed by a desire to throw himself into it and "finish everything, once and for all."

17

Having researched this early history of The *Wall Street Journal*, I was learning more about the Bancroft lineage, the source of Jackie Bancroft Spencer Morgan's vast wealth. And now it was the source of what was becoming my client Ronnie Lee Morgan's substantial wealth. He may have been Jackie's third husband, but I wanted to know about her first husband, Hugh Bancroft, Jr. Who was he, really? What was he like? He must have been about twenty-four when his father committed suicide. How did that affect him?

Before I could answer those questions, however, my research kept turning up interesting facts about Hugh Bancroft, Jr.'s half-sister, Mary Bancroft. This was the child whose mother, Mary Agnes Cogan Bancroft, died in childbirth in 1903. When I learned that, as a grown woman, Mary Bancroft had not only followed journalistic pursuits out of Zurich but that she was a spy for the United States against Germany, I had to know more.

I found that her papers and writings were archived at the Schlesinger Library at Radcliff College. There were twenty-four-and-a-half file boxes, three folio folders, one folio plus folder, two audiotapes, and four photograph folders. She had also written at least two novels of an autobiographical nature. It was going to take some time to get to know Mary Bancroft, but it didn't take long to figure out this was an unusual and exciting woman.

Mary Bancroft's childhood, like that of her father's, was encapsulated with wealth, protection, and elitism. The average person might think how wonderful it must be to be born into such wealth and never want for anything. This usually is a misperception, however, and certainly was not the case for Mary Bancroft.

Born October 29, 1903, Mary began life with only a foretelling of the struggles she would face as a child. Mary's father, Hugh Bancroft, one year out of law school, had married his sweetheart, Mary Agnes Cogan. By doing so, he had stepped outside the bounds of acceptable Bostonian blueblood society. Her mother died birthing her, but, even before birth, the stage of struggles had been set.

The Bancrofts were of English-Anglican heritage, and quite proud of it. Their house on Ware Street in Cambridge was large, and they owned a country estate in Cohasset, south of Boston, with many rooms, many servants, and many fine horses. The family, early Massachusetts settlers, had come from Derbyshire, England. Much of their wealth came from a monopolistic trading right in sugar and tobacco with the Massachusetts Bay Colony that was handed down through inheritance from generation to generation. When a Bancroft married, he or she was expected to stay within English ancestry and its elite class.

Hugh Bancroft had broken that societal requirement by marrying Mary Agnes Cogan. Not only was this still a time in Boston when it was possible to see want ads reading "No Irish Need Apply," but the Cogans were Irish Catholic. It just couldn't get worse in the Bancrofts' eyes. In fact, the marriage created so much stress, Hugh and Mary Agnes were married in neither the Catholic Church nor the Anglican Congregational Church, but in the Cogan house, the home of Mary Agnes's parents. That was just one year before Mary Agnes died in childbirth.

While the Bancroft house on Ware Street was essentially an estate, the Cogan house in North Cambridge was a half structure of three stories, next to the other half structure where someone else lived. The front was almost next to the curb, the rooms small and dark. The Cogans were by no means poor. They were middle-class and had come from Ireland's Country Kildare.

When Mary was born, the tension between the Cogans and the Bancrofts was so high that Hugh's parents hid Mary in a laundry basket and whisked her away to their home in Cambridge so that Mary Agnes's relatives, whom Hugh's grandmother referred to as "those Cogans," would not have an opportunity to raise her as an Irish Catholic. In this situation, perhaps possession was nine-tenths of the law, and the Bancrofts being who they were, no one in law would dare contest their behavior.

This was the beginning. As a newborn, of course, Mary would not have been aware of the rift or the prejudice. As she grew into childhood, however, the domination of Hugh's mother, Mary's grandmother, showed itself for every bit of the dysfunction it represented. She denigrated the Cogans whenever their name came up or Mary requested to go visit. Hugh, himself, had grown up under his mother's strong maternal thumb. Throughout her life, he never let a night pass without talking with her.

From the time Mary was born until Hugh remarried four years later, he and Mary lived at the large Bancroft house on Ware Street with its five acres of lawn and stables in the back. In time, however, Mary came to know her maternal grandparents and longed to know everything she could about her mother and the Cogans. She was proud that her mother had graduated from Radcliff. She was proud that her grandfather Cogan was a member of the Common Council of Cambridge and, for four years, a member of the Cambridge Board of Aldermen. But she was also proud of her grandfather Bancroft who became mayor of Cambridge.

Throughout her childhood and indeed throughout her entire life, Mary was close to her Uncle Joseph Cogan, a graduate of Harvard and Harvard Medical School. But it was her godmother, Aunt Clara Cogan, who remained disturbed at her lack of Catholic religious instruction. As she grew older, Mary became very much aware of the disdain each family had for the other. She felt the tug and pull emotionally, but, most of all, she missed her mother.

When she was almost five, her father married Jane Wallis Waldron, the adopted daughter of Clarence W. Barron, the wealthy financial news publisher and owner of The *Wall Street Journal*. Here again, Hugh Bancroft married outside the Boston "Brahmin" class, so-called for the designation used in India for the upper caste. Boston Brahmin were British Protestant-- Unitarian, Episcopal, Congregationalists, or Methodists. Each were wealthy and portrayed themselves as the landed gentry, part of an aristocratic closed society. They were politically a tight-knit group --- Federalists, Whigs, Republicans.

It is no wonder that, when Hugh Bancroft first married Irish Catholic Mary Agnes Cogan, it brought about such vile distaste from the Bancrofts and strong protectionist feelings over granddaughter Mary that she not become like the lower class. Now, this second marriage by Hugh to Jane Wallis Waldron was more of the same. There was, however, a difference. Aside from Clarence Barron's wealth, he had little use for the Boston Brahmin society. He could circulate within it but with tongue-in-cheek.

Clarence Barron was a paradox. Though a caste society disgusted him, he loved the trappings of wealth. Though his father had been a dockworker, and Clarence had pulled himself up by his own bootstraps, he was, nevertheless, a racist. He once wrote an article on the inferiority of the Mexican people. No doubt he felt the same about black people. He was American and capitalist to the core, and, at the same time, a strong proponent of ethics. In 1920, he investigated Charles Ponzi, inventor of the Ponzi Scheme, which helped lead to Ponzi's arrest and conviction. Clarence

Barron was impulsive and intuitive, and he took no quarter, certainly not from the likes of the Bancrofts.

Mary Bancroft was not his granddaughter but he treated her as though she were. He doted on her, and she loved him greatly. She would later write, "I felt he cared for me and was interested in my having a life that satisfied me, I eagerly followed everything he suggested." As she grew up, he suggested she work in journalism, and as she lived frustrated and unhappy in Cuba with her first husband, and then with her second husband in Zurich, she would write long letters pouring out her heart to "CW" (Clarence Barron). Always supportive, he would write her back.

Mary first married Sherwin Badger, who came from Boston's Harvard-educated elite, and took her to Cuba to live while he worked for the United Fruit Company. They had two children. She hated Cuba and lived segregated from Cubans. She never loved Sherwin and later claimed that she married him in order to quit school at Smith.

After a few years of marriage, she had an affair and fell madly in love with Leopold Mannes, who was also married. They promised each other they would divorce their spouses. The news drove Mary's Irish side of the family into a rage. They could not fathom her marrying a Jew. Ultimately, Mary and Leopold did not marry, but she did go through nasty divorce proceedings, along with the usual fight over who gets the children.

While sailing on the French Line bound for Bordeaux, she quickly became involved with Jean Rufenacht, a French Swiss. Jean was an international accountant and banker, and while still in love with Leopold and rebounding from her divorce from Sherwin, Mary married Jean.

Mary Bancroft had numerous dalliances; even while involved or married to one man, she would have an affair with another. She seemed to be searching for something different, looking for some new excitement, more than anything else.

There is no question that she had been spoiled since birth, doted upon by each facet of an extended family. There was a feeling that, since she had no mother, special care and attention must be given her. Greater nurturing must be given by her Bancroft grandparents, since she was unfortunate enough to have Irish Catholic on one side, while at the same time, her Irish grandparents felt that the other side of the family must be counterbalanced in its influence. Then, along came Clarence Barron who gave not a whit for this class warfare between Cogans and Bancrofts, and tried to attend to every desire of whom he perceived as his adopted granddaughter. She felt piled upon --- feeling sorry for herself that her mother died having her, the pulling pressure from both sides of her extended family. Yet, Mary Bancroft grew to adulthood in the midst of great wealth and elitism. As a young woman, she developed a personality of overblown pretentiousness and often wondered who she really was.

It was in this state of immaturity that she moved to Switzerland with her new husband. There, in Zurich, lived the eminent Swiss psychologist Carl Gustav Jung. She first heard him lecture at the Federal Institute of Technology, then she read his book, *Modern Man in Search of a Soul*. She sought his help as a therapist, and he counseled her for four years. They even became good friends.

While Mary wrote as a freelance writer, often writing about the difference between what German leaders were saying and what they really meant, Allen Dulles had taken note of her writing. As head of the Office of Strategic Services (OSS), America's spy agency, he was living under diplomatic cover in Berlin. These were the '30s, when Hitler was expanding German influence and taking over Eastern European countries.

Dulles crossed the Swiss frontier to meet Mary. She fit the profile he most liked, one that was most like his. She was wealthy and from the upper class where she could look down with a more caustic eye upon the machinations of war and intrigue. Dulles also knew that Jean Rufenacht, Mary's husband, was a well-respected international accountant and traveled throughout Europe with impunity. Mary could accompany him and report to Dulles on what she observed so as to give an on-the-ground observance of Nazi troop movement and social and governmental conditions of various countries.

This opportunity provided what Mary Bancroft had always sought: excitement. Early on, Mary had learned how to be flirtatious, her favorite technique being to show her legs. It wasn't long before Dulles bit on the subtle sexual overtures, and he and Mary became lovers as well as a productive spy team. Mary made great contributions to American intelligence, both prewar and during the war.

German officer Hans Bernd Gisevius was with the intelligence service of the German Army known as the Abwehr. Gisevius, as he was referred to, had written a book, four volumes in German. Dulles brought Gisevius to

Mary, insisting that she translate the volumes into English. The undertaking was monumental and took the years throughout the war to complete.

As usual, Mary was sexually attracted to Gisevius and he to her, but they got past that and made substantial progress. Gisevius would periodically come out of Germany to visit Mary in Switzerland to work on his book, particularly those parts where Mary was not sure what he was saying.

Gisevius's manuscript was dynamite. He described many attempts by various generals and highly-placed civilians to organize a *coup d'etat*. Initially, these conspirators planned to remove Hitler from office and take over the government. Ultimately, they realized that they would have to kill him in order to accomplish the *coup d'etat*. Within this group of conspirators were such men as Dr. Hjalmer Schacht, president of the Reichsbank; Ulrich von Hassell, German ambassador to Romse; Carl Goerdeler, former mayor of Leipzig; clergymen like Dietrich Bonhoeffer; lawyers; labor leaders; professors; a group of young idealists known as the Kreisan Circle, and various military men like Field Marshal Erwin von Witzleben, General Ludwig Beck, and General Franz Halder, chief of the German General Staff.

Amazingly, the conspiracy had the blessings of Admiral Canaris, head of the Abwehr and his subordinate, Colonel Hans Oster, acted as the coordinator of the conspirators' activities. This Abwehr connection gave the conspirators the cover they needed. The Gestapo did not dare to touch the intelligence service of the German Army, and Abwehr members could travel freely.

Of course, history has now well-documented the failed assassination attempt on Adolph Hitler and the attempted *coup d'etat*, code word Valkyrie and used to move troops in support of the *coup d'etat* once Hitler was assassinated. But this was a revelation, as Mary Bancroft translated Gisevius's book. Indeed, it was dynamite information for American intelligence. Even after the failed attempt on Hitler and Gisevius's escape, she continued to work with Gisevius.

Mary Bancroft did a lot of growing up in Switzerland in the war. She served her country well and became an astute interviewer of refugees and those escaping both Germany and Eastern European countries. From these interviews, she learned much about the conditions of German troops and troop movements. On one occasion, she intercepted a German soldier's letter to his wife where he was asking her to send him a spoon, "but there are no more aluminum spoons in Germany. I guess the Russians have mine. But better my spoon than me!" When Mary reported this letter to Dulles, he was delighted to hear about the aluminum shortage.

After the war, Mary divorced Jean Rufenacht. The marriage had been both physically and emotionally abusive. Mary struggled with her male relationships. As a teenager, she once wrote, "I studied a list of boys...I didn't feel particularly romantic about any of them. They were just there, in reserve, like money in a piggy bank, to be used when a need arose for guests at a dinner or house party...I shifted the names around, promoting some boys, demoting others..." Later in life, she would disclose that her true lover, the men she actually felt emotional attachment for, were Leopold Mannes and Allen Dulles.

Mary returned to New York City after the war and immersed herself in local politics and her writing. She broke Bancroft tradition by becoming a Democrat. She worked on Harriman's campaign for governor of New York in 1954, as well as the Adlai Stevenson campaign for U.S. presidency in 1956. Had her father, Hugh Bancroft, been alive, this would have been more than he could tolerate. He would not have approved, perhaps not even forgiven.

Mary Bancroft died on January 10, 1997, at the age of ninety-three. She was no doubt the most colorful of the Bancrofts. Jung described her as an intuitive extrovert. People writing about her in the *New York Times'* obituary used words like "coquettish," "bewitching," "brilliant," "daring," and "restless." One description said that Mary Bancroft was a "woman with...penetrating intelligence, infallible intuition and boundless verve---not to mention legs that rarely failed to draw a second glance."

18

It would be an understatement to say Hugh Bancroft, Jr. was born with a silver spoon in his mouth. But something happened to him along the way, something serious, something the silver spoon could not protect against.

Born in 1909, on the beautiful coastal village estate at Cohasset, Massachusetts, ten miles south of Boston, Hugh, Jr. was brought up in traditional Eastern blueblood aristocracy. The estate employed in excess of twenty servants and was fashioned around equestrian elitism.

From early on, education, horsemanship, and mastery of equestrian pursuits were drilled into the young man, and, indeed, he became accomplished in them. He followed these pursuits into manhood and won numerous ribbons and trophies. Not only has the tradition of equestrian hunting and show been a ticket into the American elite; it's a requirement, a binding thread that runs through the higher echelons of society, an indication that a person has money to mix and associate with the very wealthy, as well as having the rearing and training that gentility requires. Upperclass history is rich in tradition, from Virginia to Massachusetts, from Jefferson, himself, to say, the Bancrofts a century later.

When Hugh Bancroft, Jr. was born, his father and his grandmother, Jessie Waldron Barron, struggled to manage the *Journal* while his grandfather, Clarence Barron, was having the time of his life, yachting. The Panic of 1907 had hit the nation's economy as the New York Stock Exchange fell close to fifty-percent from its peak the previous year. The 1907 panic eventually spread throughout the nation when many state and local banks and businesses entered into bankruptcy. Retraction of liquidity by a number of New York City banks, and a loss of confidence among depositors, along with almost no regulation in financial markets, deepened the panic. The U.S. did not have a central bank to inject liquidity back into the market. The economy struggled for years. War drums beat in Europe, and even though President Wilson had campaigned on keeping America out of the War, it was a way out of economic doldrums.

The *Journal* held true to form, writing articles to bolster confidence of both depositors and stock traders. However, its circulation and advertising income had dropped. In 1912, Clarence Barron left his yacht, or at least his constant obsession with yachting, and returned to New York to take over management of the *Journal*. He sent Jessie and Hugh home to Boston and Cohasset.

Though the Bancroft family traveled from Cohasset to New York frequently, Hugh, Jr.'s childhood and pubescent life was centered around the Cohasset estate. He was raised in both the Bostonian Anglican manner of his father, and under the wing of his famous, domineering grandfather, Clarence Barron.

Throughout the war years, Hugh, Jr. grew up just like any other wealthy, aristocratic child. Though his parents had three children --- Jessie, Jane, and, of course, Hugh, Jr. --- it was granddaughter Jessie and his adopted granddaughter, Mary, who became the apples of Clarence's eye, the ones he doted upon. Typically, it was the eldest male child, the child who would carry on the lineage name --- albeit Bancroft instead of Barron --- who would be the favorite. Not so with Clarence Barron. It has never been clear why he did not hold the father, Hugh Bancroft, in high esteem, but it is clear from recorded actions that he did not. Perhaps this was why Hugh, Jr. was not the favorite. That is not to say he was deprived. Of course not; he was raised in opulence. But children pick up on unspoken attitudes, a subliminal marking, of parents or grandparents, at an early age. Perhaps this was an ingredient of what was to come in Hugh Bancroft, Jr.'s life.

Beyond that, as Hugh, Jr. approached manhood, the culture of America underwent change, such as tensions between what was expected in aristocratic society and temptations of what went on in the middle class. It was the advent of the "Roaring Twenties."

World War I ended by the time Hugh, Jr. was ten. Fifty thousand American soldiers had died. It did not take long, even for patriots, before bitterness and disillusionment spread throughout the country. In the decade to follow, John Dos Passos wrote in his novel, *1919,* on the death of John Doe:

"In the tarpaper morgue at Chalons-sur-Marne in the reek of chloride of lime and the dead, they picked out the pine box that held all that was left of…John Doe…the scraps of dried viscera and skin bundled in Khaki they took to Chalons-sur-Marne and laid it out neat in a pine coffin and took it home to God's country on a battleship and buried it in a sarcophagus in the Memorial Amphitheatre in the Arlington National Cemetery and draped the Old Glory over it and the bugler played taps and Mr. Harding prayed to God and the diplomats and the generals and the admirals and the brass hats and the politicians and the handsomely dressed ladies out of the society column of the Washington Post stood up solemn..."

Ernest Hemingway would write *A Farewell to Arms*. Years later, a college student named Irwin Shaw would write a play, *Bury the Dead*. And a Hollywood screenwriter named Dalton Trumbo would write a powerful and chilling antiwar novel, *Johnny Got His Gun*, about a torso and brain left alive on the battlefield. Ford Madox Ford wrote *No More Parades*. Great unrest surfaced in the general populace, along with great tension between commoners and the elite. There were strikes; there was violence.

Hugh Bancroft, Jr. may have been sheltered in his upbringing, but it would have been impossible that he escape the knowledge of tensions between classes. By the time he was a teenager, culture change had replaced class strife. The spirit of the Roaring Twenties was marked by a general feeling of discontinuity associated with modernity, a break with tradition. This, too, was a holding time for the young man.

At the same time he upheld the patronage of the estate through social events and equestrian competition, the move was on to shed elitism. The middle class was on the rise, and everything seemed feasible through modern technology. Formal requirements were discarded. Women had gained the right to vote and took command of their own bodies. Their fashions were both a social statement and a breaking-off from rigid Victorian ways. They did away with confining corsets and donned slinky knee-length dresses, which exposed their legs and arms. Cosmetics, typically unacceptable in American society because of its association with prostitution, became, for the first time, extremely popular. Older generations labeled the rebellious middle-class women "flappers."

Society was more open, free, and adventuresome. Starting in the 1920s, ballrooms across the U.S. sponsored dance contests, where dancers invented and competed with the new moves. The foxtrot, waltz, tango, Charleston, and Lindy were the most popular. Mass production made technology such as the automobile, movies, and refrigerators, easily affordable to the middle class. Telephone lines were strung across the continent. Electricity was available everywhere.

The workplace changed, as well. Women, brought in by necessity to ramp up war production, now transitioned in large numbers into metropolitan centers for clerical jobs. It was the advent of the typewriter, telephone, and filing cabinet. Hugh Bancroft, Jr. was born in recession, raised in wartime, and reached manhood in the decade of bathtub gin, the Model T, the five-dollar workday, the first transatlantic flight, and the movies. Clearly, he had one foot firmly planted in Victorian aristocracy, while the other ventured into the developing cultural freedom.

One can only surmise to what extent Hugh Bancroft, Jr. was buffered from this social revolution. It must have been difficult to find balance. His family and a few others controlled the means of dispensing information. Historian Merle Curti observed about the '20s:

"It was, in fact, only the upper ten percent of the population that enjoyed a marked increase in real income. But the protests which such facts normally have evoked could not make themselves widely or effectively felt. This was in part the result of the grand strategy of the major political parties. In part it was the result of the fact that almost all the chief avenues to mass opinion were now controlled by large-scale publishing industries."

Hugh Bancroft, Jr. reached the age of twenty in time for the Crash of '29 and to see his father, who had tutored him and raised him in the gentility and comfort of estate horsemanship, become consumed with the economic downfall of the United States and The *Wall Street Journal*, itself. F. Scott Fitzgerald wrote in the article, "Echoes of the Jazz Age":

"It was borrowed time anyway---the whole upper tenth of a nation living
with the insouciance of a grand duc and the casualness of chorus girls."

Sinclair Lewis captured the false sense of prosperity, the shallow pleasure of the new gadgets for the middle class, in his novel *Babbitt*:

"It was the best of nationally advertised and quantitatively produced alarm-clocks, with all modern attachments, including cathedral chime, intermittent alarm, and a phosphorescent dial. Babbitt was proud of being awakened by such a rich device. Socially it was almost as creditable as buying expensive cord tires.

"He sulkily admitted now that there was no more escape, but he lay and detested the grind of the real-estate business, and disliked his family, and disliked himself for disliking them."

As the economy and the *Journal*'s financial problems worsened, Hugh, Jr. continued to live on the estate, successfully compete in equestrian ventures and maintain the Bancroft persona. It must have been increasingly difficult, and, as his father withdrew, he must have felt estranged.

In 1932, romantically on Christmas Eve, he became engaged to Marjorie Dow, a socially-acceptable mate. But a dark cloud was forming. Ten months after that engagement, his father committed suicide in the stables on the estate. Family members, in particular children, often take such tragedy as rejection, thinking it to be their fault. Hugh, Jr. was a young man of twenty-three. There is no way of knowing just how deeply his father's suicide affected him. Nevertheless, the marriage to Marjorie Dow only lasted a few years, ending in divorce in 1936. Hugh, Jr. then began to drift. In the space of five years, events including his father's suicide, his marriage and divorce, and what seemed like limited income for one of his status, led to drinking more heavily.

On Christmas Eve of that year, the year of his divorce, he crashed his automobile into a steel upright of the Summer Street Bridge, near the Army Base in South Boston. Unconscious, he was taken to the Boston City Hospital, and was found suffering from a fractured nose and a brain concussion. He was placed on the hospital's danger list.

Hugh, Jr. had never worked except for a few appointed positions. More than anything else, his occupation was the care, training, development, and competition of his horse stable. In 1940, he drifted into a marriage with Bettina Gray, one that didn't last either, ending in divorce within five years. His first child, Bettina Bancroft, was born on February 12, 1941. The child was four years old at the time of the divorce. Hugh, Jr. was thirty-one.

Literally, there was nothing in Massachusetts to hold Hugh, Jr. there. With the stigma of his father's suicide, two failed marriages, and his tiring of competitions, he decided to head West. Hugh, Jr. was searching, had always been searching; for what, he was not sure. Perhaps the geographical move to the West would bring some meaning to life, some relief; relief he found progressively in the bottle. Not that he was a falling-down drunk; he was not. He was in very good physical shape; tall, handsome. But always there was a dark cloud in his mind. Perhaps, perhaps not, the fact that he did not have to work intensified the cloud. He had nothing to do with the *Journal* but to live off its largesse and semi-annual distributions.

When Bettina was born, Hugh, Jr.'s lawyers advised him to set up a trust that would provide for her and any after-born children and their mothers. Since Bettina was born in 1941, the lawyers called it the "'41 Trust." Thus, his stock ownership in the Dow Jones Publishing Co. and The *Wall Street Journal* was placed in the '41 Trust, which stood on its own, no matter what might happen to Hugh, Jr. All dividends of that stock flowed into the trust.

As Hugh, Jr. migrated to Denver after his divorce from his second wife, he selected an estate firm in Denver to act as trustees of the '41 Trust designed by Boston Bancroft trust lawyers. As it turns out, the Denver firm serves as trustees of that trust to this day, more than a half-century later.

In Denver, Hugh, Jr. lived at the Park Lane Hotel and hung out at the prestigious Denver Country Club where Jackie and her parents, the Frank Orthwein Everts, belonged. It was never clear to me from talking with Jackie if she met Hugh, Jr. at the Country Club in Denver, or back East while at Connecticut College in New London. Nevertheless, she was almost twenty-three, a Denver socialite, a debutante, a graduate of Kent School for Girls in Denver, a recent college graduate, and a frequent golfer at the club.

How long Hugh, Jr. and Jackie knew each other before they married I don't know. Jackie told me it wasn't long. Immediately after her parents announced the engagement in the society pages of The *Denver Post* and held the announcement party at the Denver Country Club, the couple escaped to Albuquerque where they were married. In a sense, it was a whirlwind affair. Jackie would be his last wife.

Today's neurological science knows that a brain can be hard-wired for depression through genetics, or trauma-based because of injury or traumatic experience. Dr. Gabor Mate in his landmark book, *In the Realm of Hungry Ghosts,* writes:

"The very same brain centers that interpret and 'feel' physical pain also become activated during the experience of emotional rejection: on brain scans they 'light up' in response to social ostracism just as they would when triggered by physically harmful stimuli...Addictions always originate in pain, whether felt openly or hidden in the unconscious."

It was pretty clear that Hugh Bancroft, Jr. felt pain. Was it because he was the grandson of a famous and obsessive man and no one could top his accomplishments? Was it because his father had come to see himself as a failure and committed suicide? Was it genetic from his father's suffering with depression? Or did it stem from his brain injury in the car wreck? No one knows. In those days, the course of pain or cause of depression was not an open subject.

Whatever demons Hugh Bancroft, Jr. faced or did not face, his actions indicated that his attempts to flee kept him moving West, seeking solace in marriage.

Jackie and Hugh, Jr. could have stayed in Denver and lived the Denver Country Club life. The eyebrows would have moderated and the new couple would have been accepted. They had plenty enough money to warrant societal acceptance. It was not as though Denver was blueblood country, anyway. This was, after all, Molly Brown country.

Hugh, Jr. wanted to go further West, far enough away to leave behind any comparisons of him with his grandfather or his brilliant father who came to such a depressing end. Rather than stay in Denver society, in 1948, Jackie and Hugh, Jr. rushed to Albuquerque, New Mexico, for a quick wedding on the way to the ranch Hugh, Jr. had bought at Capitan, New Mexico, at the foot of the Sacramento Mountains, along with a house at the edge of the little town. I say little because there couldn't have been a hundred people in Capitan. This was the country of Billy the Kid, Kit Carson, and Mescalero Apaches. Indeed, Hugh, Jr. had gone West and taken his new bride with him.

If Jackie were looking for an adventure, something far different from her conservative pre-school, Eastern education, she certainly found it here. In the late 1940s, Southeastern New Mexico was anything but the lap of luxury. True, the fledgling town of Ruidoso on the other side of the mountain had just held its first horse races, and artists like Gorman were in their very early stages of Indian paintings and depicting Southwest vistas and landscapes. The little town of Carrizozo, with its cattle-loading railroad head, was only thirty miles away. But this was sparse country.

Hugh, Jr. knew plenty about thoroughbred foxhunters, jumpers and managing an Eastern estate; he knew nothing about cattle ranching. He had bought a twenty-section ranch in the dry Southwest. Twenty sections of land in Massachusetts are vast amounts of acreage, but no one there owns that amount of land or anything close to it. However, in the desert

Southwest, twenty sections are not enough for an economically-viable cattle ranch. As Western ranches go, theirs may have been a modest ranch, but Hugh, Jr. and Jackie named it the "Bar Lazy H. B. Ranch." They registered its brand as the "Bar Lazy Left H B," with the brand requirement location being placed on the left rib of the animal. Hugh, Jr. hired Fletcher Hall, one of the best ranch foremen in the area, to run his ranch just as Jackie began to have babies.

This wide-open space was the hard-core ranching center of Eastern New Mexico. There was nothing easy or gentile about it. Carrizozo, just to the north, was an active and vibrant cattle shipment railhead as well as the county seat of Lincoln County. Its population was close to two thousand. With no other town for hundreds of miles around, medical, legal, and shopping needs were all met in Carrizozo. It didn't take long for Hugh, Jr. to fall out of love with ranching and to start looking for other diversions. He wasn't in the East anymore, but the gnawing had returned.

When they arrived at Capitan, Hugh, Jr. was thirty-nine and Jackie was twenty-three. The following year, their first child, Chris, was born, and the next year, their second son, Hugh III, nicknamed "Wink," was born. Jackie had her hands full taking care of babies. As for Hugh, Jr., the desire to "party" had not abated. He'd met a local, rambunctious party guy by the name of Redge Bishop. They spent their time chasing one idea after another; but mainly, they drank.

So Hugh, Jr. was gone a lot, and not much help to Jackie or the "Bar Lazy H.B. Ranch."He spent money left and right, but it was never clear on what. What was clear was that he couldn't make it from one trust distribution to the next. In those days, distributions were about two million a year. It wasn't enough; he couldn't make ends meet. Johnson Sterns, president of Citizen's State Bank in Carrizozo at the time, remembers Hugh, Jr. coming in for a loan months before his next trust distribution to borrow enough to get by on until then. He always brought his buddy, Redge Bishop, with him.

Before Chris and Wink got out of diapers, Jackie had their third child, a daughter, Kathryn. It was 1952. As Jackie struggled with the three children and tried to make the ranch produce a profit, Hugh, Jr. became ill, seriously ill. At first, doctors couldn't determine what was wrong with him. He left the ranch and stayed in the hospital at Carrizozo. On October 20, 1953, he died of complications from a brain tumor. The children were four, three, and one.

Jackie and Hugh Bancroft, Jr. had run off to the Wild West to try their hand at ranching. For Hugh, Jr., it was one more attempt to escape the mental demons that chased him. For Jackie, it was a romantic escape from girl-school discipline and the mandates of debutante society. They'd been married five years, had three children, and a ranch incapable of commercial success. Their assets at the time of his death were these:

56 cows
48 two-year old heifers
6 bulls
27 one-year old heifer calves
21 one-year old steer calves
1 Holstein steer
3 saddle horses
3 mares
1 two-year old horse
1 yearling colt
1 filly

They had recently bought a 1953 Ford pickup and a 1953 Ford station wagon. Probate records listing these assets paint a picture contrary to what one would expect of one of the wealthiest families in the nation, certainly well within the top one-percent of wealth. It seems so unusual. Here was Hugh Bancroft, Jr., a man of Boston blueblood heritage, living modestly on a ranch in New Mexico with his bride, a Denver debutante. This couple could have lived the high life of Manhattan, traveling in limousines to balls and the theater.

Jackie told me that when Hugh, Jr. died, she hadn't been aware of the '41 Trust funded by all The *Wall Street Journal* stock he had inherited from his father. The trust is what ultimately took care of Jackie and his three children by her. She received the proceeds from Hugh's life insurance; he had been heavily insured. Why? With that kind of wealth, one would think there would be no need for life insurance. All Jackie knew at that young age and after that short marriage was that there was a trust. If she needed money, she was to call the Denver trustees and ask for it. To the day of her death many years later, her attitude toward money was, if she needed it, call --- and they had better send it.

Though the ranch was not a commercial operation---thankfully Jackie was well taken care of and not exactly destitute --- Hugh had also left her with three small children. In the four-year course of bearing them, she had met Doctor A.N. Spencer of Carrizozo, New Mexico.

One year to the date of Hugh, Jr.'s death, Jackie and A.N., as he was called, slipped quietly out of Carrizozo and married in a simple, private ceremony. She and the children moved to Carrizozo where A.N. continued his medical practice while Jackie reared her children. Not known for his bedside manner, A.N. was, nevertheless, the respected medical provider for that part of the country.

A.N. came from an illustrious New Mexico ranching lineage. His grandfather, W.C. McDonald, was New Mexico's first statehood governor. Even with that background, he cared nothing about ranching. Jackie, on the other hand, worked with her ranch foreman who ran both the ranch at Capitan and the ranch A.N. owned at Carrizozo. Most of her time, however, was dedicated to raising children and serving on civic committees in the small but vibrant town of Carrizozo. From a first husband who partied and searched for something that could never be found, to the unshakeable stability in a second husband, Jackie had made the right move.

I visited Carrizozo fifty years after Jackie and her three small children had moved there. I walked down its main street, but the people were no longer there. It was cold, and dark came early. Here and there, a few lights came on within a building or a house. Down the street, the wind blew towards me for a brief interval, sometimes diagonally, sometimes not at all. A tumbleweed brushed my jeans on its way to its destination, a destination to nowhere, which is how this street in this windblown town felt---the middle of nowhere. The chill rang through the air along with a feeling of loneliness. What had once been here was no more. It was gone. At the end of the street, I saw only the windblown, lonely emptiness.

Had I walked down this same street fifty years earlier, I would have been greeted by sounds of a bustling cattle business: trailer-anxious livestock awaiting the train to Kansas, the meat packing plant rushing to complete its shipment of beef before the train's scheduled arrival, people traveling from the far reaches of the county to the county courthouse to transact land business, then visit with the banker before leaving. This street, this main street, would be busy with cars, trucks and cattle trailers, and the young people would look excitedly to the week's end of schoolwork and social activities. That had been the Carrizozo of Jackie, A.N., and the three children's time there. Then life moved to the other side of the mountain. There were only memories here now, if one chose to remember them.

For thirty years, Jackie and A.N. lived in Carrizozo and became a vibrant part of that community. The children had never known their father; A.N., the doctor, was their father. They were typical kids growing up in a small town, attending public school until they reached high school. Then they were sent off to prep schools. Not until after their prep school years would they understand the great wealth they had been born into. For that matter, Jackie didn't seem to understand the wealth left to her by Hugh, Jr. In some ways, she didn't display it in arrogant style. Certainly, she and A.N. belonged in the top income echelon of Carrizozo but, by comparison of their wealth to similar wealth in other parts of the country, they lived modestly. As banker Johnson Sterns put it, "Jackie could never connect the dots on money. If she needed more money, she just called the lawyers in Denver and said send it."

Jackie had been a great supporter of the little town. When the kids needed costumes for their school play, she called a theater in New York and said to send costumes. When asked what sizes, she said to send them all. Another time, she bought a Greyhound bus to haul the kids to the ski slope so they could learn to ski. She paid for their lift tickets. And, still another time, she gave the town a nine-hole golf course and clubhouse. She and A.N. played golf on the course almost daily, except in winter.

Over the course of the thirty years she lived in the little town with A.N., Jackie did many things for the town, itself. For several years, she gave the municipality one-hundred-thousand dollars, to maintain the structures she had built for the town. The majority of the citizens were grateful. But, in one city council meeting, a councilman objected. He didn't mind her giving to the city, but he didn't think Jackie had the right to dictate how the money should be spent. That was it! The town never received another dime from Jackie Bancroft Spencer.

In 1984, Jackie and A.N. moved to Alto Village, on the other side of the mountain and on the outskirts of Ruidoso. A.N. had retired from medical practice, the children, raised and gone, chased their own life's sagas. A.N. and Jackie built a beautiful split-level home with an open view of Sierra Blanca Mountain, joined the Alto Country Club, a community of wealthy retirees. There was daily golf, nightly socials, and, on the days she didn't play golf, Jackie had her bridge club, which she enjoyed dearly.

On its surface, this story might have ended here. But, for Jackie, there was something deeper. She had never forgotten her education and appreciation for the performing arts at Kent School for Girls and Connecticut College. Even while raising children in Carrizozo, she maintained her contacts, not only in Boston and New York, but in California, as well. She monetarily supported the performing arts, and she greatly enjoyed attending and watching performances as often as she could.

From young girlhood on, Jackie had had a competitive spirit. In fact, it was so keen that, coupled with her height, it gave an edge, a domineering edge, to her personality. It made no difference the game; Jackie was hell-bent on winning. I played numerous golf games with her, and she was quite a good golfer. She never wanted her competitor to give quarter, but she did everything in her power to win. The nightly games of Rummikub and cards were every bit as competitive. Just like her golf games, they were playing fields that allowed her to exhibit not only her competitiveness but her stamina. She was quite remarkable.

It was that very urge to win that drew her to the sport of horse racing as it had grown and developed in the mountains of Ruidoso. Through the last half of the 20th Century, Ruidoso Downs, an entire equestrian industry and segregated town, developed into a billion-dollar mélange. The trappings of Eastern thoroughbred racing are different from Western quarter horse racing. Aside from shorter, faster races, the accepted attire is cowboy boots, hats and Western wear. Crowds of spectators come from all over the Southwest to watch and gamble. The Jockey Club is filled with the rich and, sometimes, the famous. The emotion is frenetic; the competitiveness is addictive.

When Jackie and A.N. moved to their new home in Alto Village, Jackie was drawn to the idea that she would win in this environment. She could own horses, hire trainers, build her stables at Ruidoso Downs. From the other side of the mountain, her home and ranches in Carrizozo, she had watched Ruidoso and the equestrian development of Ruidoso Downs grow. She was sure she could win. A.N. retired, the children were gone, the ranches were put to rest, and Jackie competed in quarter horse racing. It brought a feeling of energy and excitement. As far as I could tell from how Jackie described this period, this new beginning, she held no remorse for what she had left at Capitan: first with Hugh, Jr., nor the intermediate years in Carrizozo. She neither longed for the nostalgic past nor harbored resentment that this was where she had spent much of her life. What I saw was a lady who didn't live in the past. She was where she was, and it was the present that was on her mind. That's not to say she couldn't get wrapped up in her goals. I have watched people reach success, wealth and power. Later reflection, a feeling of insufficiency, a morsel of disappointment all seem to disturb them, feelings they can neither escape nor explain. I never saw such reflection in Jackie, from horse racing to building a performing arts theater, to ultimately planning a life's end with Ron Morgan. The challenge was of the moment. The past was what it was, worthless for reflection or judgment.

After a session with Ron and Jackie in Ruidoso, one of many that frequently revolved around a theater production, I decided to drop down to the little town of Capitan. I had driven through it on occasion on my way to Carrizozo, Ruidoso's county seat. It's one of those towns that, if you blink, you'll miss it. Though rich in history, it was never large in population. I had met people in Carrizozo who had known Hugh, Jr. or Jackie. I thought it would be interesting to find out if anyone in Capitan still remembered them. They didn't. Of course, it had been fifty years. I did, however, come upon an interesting discovery.

Outside of town is a marked street that runs up the side of a hill. Its name is "Bancroft." I drove up the hill. The road, a road to nowhere, vanished. What could this mean? None of the town leaders knew how the road had gotten its name. I checked the plats and legal records at Carrizozo, and they supplied no clue. Later on, I asked Jackie if she knew of the named road. She didn't. I asked if she might know how or why it got its name. She didn't. It was clear she really didn't care.

1

19

I have observed that coincidence is often indistinguishable from intent. Ron called from Ruidoso and requested Jane and my attendance at his and Jackie's private wedding. The event would be small, gracious, with select and very few friends, Jackie's children and their spouses, though, oddly, not their children. It was to be held at the Ritz Carlton in Palm Springs, California. Ron wanted me there, and, as it turned out, Jane and I were the lone attendees from Ron's side. The date was exactly one year and one day after the death of A.N. Spencer, Jackie's quiet, compliant, doctor-husband of so many years. I saw this to be curious. From my research of the Bancroft family, I knew that Jackie had married A.N. one year and one day after the death of Hugh Bancroft, Jr.

The call from Ron did not surprise me. When Jackie and I played golf a few weeks earlier, I confirmed that, indeed, this 75-year-old heiress was going to marry my 52-year-old gay client. Ron had told me, of course, but I felt the need for confirmation from Jackie.

After receiving Ron's call, I reflected back to the day of the golf game and my conversation with Jackie.

"Jackie, I need to talk with you about something, but I really don't know how to bring it up," I began.

"Oh? Well, I guess the way to bring something up is to just start," she responded.

"Ron mentioned something about marriage, and I am concerned about assets," I said.

"Yes. We are going to get married in a few weeks. I want you and your wife to be there."

"Have you met Lorenzo?" I asked.

"Yes. He has been coming up once a week and doing my hair. He is also helping me with an exercise program."

I left the subject of gay/heterosexual marriage silent, though it was raging in my mind. Clearly, Jackie knew Ron was gay and that Lorenzo was his significant other. She could have cared less. I wanted to ask, "Why on earth do you want to get married? What's wrong with just doing things together?" With Jackie, you had to be careful with what you asked and how you asked it. Over time, I came to learn this aspect of her personality. I had seen and heard about her reaction with others whom she felt had been intrusive. Go too far and the Jackie hammer came down; you were excommunicated from the Jackie court. Just as Jackie had the odd personality trait of blurting out something on her mind, she had a sense of termination for every relationship and it made no difference who you were. In Carrizozo years earlier, when the town councilman complained about Jackie's dominance over the money she gave the town, that was it. The town council never got another dime, nor did they ever hear another word from her. Her way with others caused one to choose their words carefully.

"Jackie, I'm happy for you and Ron. I know you will have good times together, but I need to remind you he has other creditors that will be after any income or assets Ron receives," I said.

"Ron told me you had taken care of that. Of course, he will receive things. I will let him have some money, and he wants to buy this place in Puerto Villarta." Ron hadn't told me about wanting a place in Puerto Villarta, but it didn't surprise me. Placing Ron in bankruptcy, I felt, and designing a trust outside the bankruptcy should give him the protection he needed.

"I believe I have taken care of the problem. I've set up a trust for him. As long as you pay the trust, or place properties in it for him, there should be sufficient protection," I explained.

It became clear that the discussion had come to an end. Jackie wanted to focus on the golf game.

A few weeks after that conversation with Jackie, Jane and I boarded a commercial flight to John Wayne International, rented a car and drove to Palm Springs. We were expected at Jackie's house for drinks and hors d'oeuvres, and for dinner at the club.

Palm Springs and neighboring Indian Wells are rife with country clubs and golf courses. The subterranean waters of the Colorado River allow for massive irrigation of the desert surface, turning it into a Shangri-la of deep rich greenery contrasted with a backdrop of desert cacti and rock. Jackie's club was one of the older, more well-established clubs with multi-million dollar homes and property lines creeping up the desert mountain, plush vegetation, spraying water fountains, and green fairways below.

Jackie's house was a beautiful, rambling Western ranch style, open, bright, and nestled into a desert rock mountain, landscaped in desert cacti and white and red yucca. At its original building, so the story went, Jackie had instructed the contractor to dynamite a niche into the mountain for the location of the house. Shortly after, authorities showed up to explain that it was illegal to do such a thing. Apparently, asking for forgiveness rather than permission worked. Jackie's house was built. That was many years ago. Until Ron came to open up the house a couple months before our arrival, Jackie had not been there for five years.

After Ron showed us to our room, I couldn't wait to take Jane to the garage. On my previous trip there, I had been given the liberty to drive the "Bancroft" around Palm Springs at my leisure. The Bancroft is a beautiful blue coupe convertible with a V-12 engine, designed in Germany at a Mercedes factory by Jackie's son, Wink (Hugh Bancroft III). He had spent several years in Germany designing the car, working with Mercedes' engineers. He planned to bring the Bancroft to commercial market in the U.S. However, it never made it, probably because the cost per unit was too high. Only six Bancrofts were ever manufactured. Too bad. The vehicle drove like a dream.

Jane and I, Ron and Jackie, went separately to the Ritz Carlton for the ceremony. When we arrived, our private group of about a dozen had already gathered in the small meeting room. Ron had made sure the room was well-appointed with flowers and a champagne fountain. A young lady passed among us with hors d'oeuvres. Jackie was lovely in a pale pink silk and chiffon dress. She wore the beautiful yellow diamond ring Ron had given her. Even at that celebratory moment, I couldn't help but find it odd how Ron would give Jackie diamonds and expensive jewelry paid for with money she had given him. He would then be broke and later ask for more money.

But, on this evening, the mood was festive. When the nondenominational preacher showed up, Jackie spent a few minutes with him, telling him what he could and couldn't say. With the twelve of us gathered around, the short ceremony seemed more like a christening than a wedding. At its end, we were ushered into a private dining room for a sumptuous dinner of several entrees, from Beef Wellington to mahi-mahi. The wine flowed freely.

While I sat next to Wink and spent the evening talking cars, Jane sat next to Kathryn, Jackie's daughter from Boston. Both of Jackie's children were most interesting. Wink told me he had been involved in car racing in California for many years, while his trophy wife was consumed with jumping horse competitions. From what Kathryn told Jane, she seemed to live a rather reclusive life in Boston, but she was a lovely person. Her daughter, training in operatic voice, lived in Europe. Jackie's other child, Chris, opposed the marriage and had not been invited.

In the years to come, I would learn of the stress between Jackie and her sons. Though the '41 Trust provided its own generous semi-annual distribution to the children, like their father they were always on the shorts. There was never enough money, and mother was supposed to be the easy tap. Except that she wasn't.

20

Ron had finished decorating the Spencer Theater. Indeed, it looked fabulous, replete with Chihuly glass. Chihuly's creations, renowned for their explosion of colors, grace places like the Bellagio, Last Vegas, the Atlantis in the Bahamas, and Florence, Italy. Each is like a separate painting created as its own reason for being; each piece of blown glass an intricate part of the whole. A completed piece arrived at the Theater in its own special truck, followed by its own assembly team from Seattle. The amazing process could not, would not, be hurried.

The entire Theater structure and interior design was Jackie's "little gem" nestled at the foot of the mountains. Architect Antoine Predock created the structure out of four-hundred-fifty tons of Spanish mica-flecked limestone which appeared more as a sculpture than a building: its crusted lobby jutted like a cut diamond from its north side, a waterfall gently cascading from its very core towards the south. The completed structure cost Jackie twenty-two-million, while the interior design totaled nearly five million and took almost a year.

The contract I was charged with drafting with Chihuly was as unique as he was. Chihuly was not only an artist of massive blown glass; he sketched artistic renditions --- themselves worth a lot of money --- in anticipation of creating a project to show what the future production of the glass should look like and where it should be installed. For our purposes, we attached the drawings to the contract so there would be no question as to how the interior of the Theater would look.

Drafting contracts sounds like boring work to most people, but it is an expertise unto itself. I dare say it is an under-appreciated expertise --- until a problem arises. A lawyer who writes contracts lives in mortal fear that he missed, overlooked, or didn't anticipate a certain possibility, that he didn't see the possibility of a glitch in performance of the agreement. But the client expects the lawyer to be clairvoyant, to protect him against every eventuality. In the contract I worked on and Jackie and Chihuly signed --- it was my first art contract --- there had been one little hitch; other than that, it served well.

When the foyer centerpiece arrived, the twenty-foot tree of blown glass, forest green and reflective of the mountain forests of the surrounding mountains, took several weeks to construct. Jackie had insisted on not coming to the Theater until its assemblage was complete. Then a small celebratory, by-invitation-only, reception of Ruidoso's elite would be held to anoint the occasion, christen the tree, and admire the decorative creativity of the Theater.

In our separate rooms at Jackie's Alto Village house, we dressed for the reception. We were excited. The Ron – Chihuly creation was complete. Ron had worked at the Theater all day, making everything just right. As we gathered to leave for the Theater, I could see Jackie's eyes twinkle in anticipation.

When we arrived, the well-dressed entourage was having cocktails and hors d'oeuvres, engaged in animated conversation. No doubt they reveled in the gaiety of the occasion and enjoyed the beauty of the spectacular glass tree.

We walked in. Jackie greeted no one. She stood like a statue, looking up at the tree.

"Take it out!" she said.

I was dumbstruck. I had no idea what could be wrong. What had happened?

Jackie and Ron went to a private room. The rest of us mingled quietly around the tree. The hushed gathering appeared to be at a loss, not knowing whether to stay or to leave. After what seemed like a very long time, Ron returned to my side.

"What's wrong?" I asked.

"The tree is supposed to be red, not green," he said.

"No one told me," I said in defense.

"That doesn't make much difference now," Ron answered.

I didn't know what that meant, but I had this feeling deep inside me that I had failed, that this was my fault.

"I'll be back in a little while," Ron said. "I'm going to take her home."

He made his way through the gathering, making apologies and easing the situation as best he could. Ron was unusual in this regard. He was quite adept at handling himself socially, and he had a knack for easing tension on a social stage. This elite gathering, this court, was confused. They were not sure whether they had been rebuffed, or whether the tension came from something Jackie had seen. Ron's talent for making people in such gatherings feel at ease was being put to the test.

Gradually, the people drifted away. I spent the next few hours wandering around the magnificent structure. The view through the peaked glass and steel frontage of the mountains beyond would inspire any person entering its portal. The tall, glittering green tree reflecting the sun's light in myriad directions, seemed quite at home. Yet, I felt terrible. How could I have made such a mistake?

I pulled out my briefcase and looked at the contract. Indeed, attached was a rendered drawing of the tree by Chihuly; behind it, a schematic of the parts and proposed assemblage. No mention of color.

In time, Ron returned to pick me up. I was glad to see him. I had been at a loss when abandoned at the reception. I wasn't sure whether to call a cab --- not an easy task in the mountains, I supposed --- or was I to wait? While waiting and trying to ease my mind about the whole episode, I was unsure whether I should return to Midland, talk to Jackie, or exactly what I should do.

"How is she?" I asked, as Ron walked in.

"Well, it's not good. You will just have to make Dale Chihuly exchange it. Jackie wants it to be red," Ron explained.

"But you were in Seattle when a lot of this glass was being blown. Didn't you know the tree was to be red?" I asked.

"I know. I know. You'll just have to fix it, and in a hurry," Ron said.

Dale Chihuly is proud of his work, as he should be. The man is full of energy, always in motion. That green tree cost Jackie a million dollars, and, as far as Chihuly was concerned, it would cost another million if she wanted a red one. At least, that was his initial response. Some of his projects had been absolutely huge. No doubt he had had disagreements with clients before. How could he not? Chihuly didn't really bother himself with such matters. His lawyers handled contract disputes or other disagreements.

I had the feeling of impossibility. Chihuly wanted a million dollars for another blown tree; Jackie wanted the green one sent back and replaced with a red one, at no cost---and she wanted it now! I suggested to Chihuly's lawyers that I fly out to Seattle, sit down with them, and work this thing out.

The Seattle lawyers saw no need for in-person negotiations. Instead, we held long teleconferences with a lot of back and forth. I argued that the contract did not allow for artist discretion, that it was Chihuly's duty to acquire permission before deciding on a color. It was not a strong argument, but it did make one wonder what a court interpretation would be if this thing ended up in litigation.

As we countered arguments and positions day after day, gradually the Seattle lawyers backed off the million-dollar demand. I called Jackie, at first, to give her status reports, but she wanted none of it. She told me to handle it with Ron, and whatever Ron decided would be the final decision.

In one of my conference calls with the Seattle lawyers, I was asked if I knew lawyer Mike Line. I answered that I did. Had he contacted them? Their answer was quite vague, and it left me with the feeling that other negotiations had been going on without my knowing about them. The Seattle lawyers also referred to the Denver lawyers, the managers of the '41 Trust from which all of our funding came. I questioned whether the trust's lawyers had been contacted. Again, I received a vague, roundabout response. I had to wonder how many cooks were in this kitchen of negotiation. I never found out.

The cat-and-mouse game continued for about sixty days. We finally reached an agreement: Jackie would pay four-hundred-thousand dollars for another tree.

Ron signed off on the deal. But it seemed to me that he already knew about it before I explained it to him.

21

With Ron in bankruptcy, we closed the glitzy Salon Red Day Spa and Salon Red styling studio in El Paso. No doubt the Verlander lawyers with their million-plus dollar judgment were surprised to find that Ron had no assets, or what assets he did have were past broke. His lifestyle --- the salons, flashy Interstate 10 billboards, his dress, Jaguar and that of Lorenzo, his significant other --- would lead the casual observer to believe Ron was rolling in money. Because Texas law allows what is called homestead exemption, he did keep his home on the cliff overlooking the Western Plains and Rio Grande.

Jackie gave Ron chunks of money periodically, much of which he placed in the trust I had set up for him. I noticed, however, that, more and more, Ron kept the money instead of placing it into the trust.

I called Ron in Ruidoso and told him that I needed to come up, we had to talk. He told me to take the Lear.

Early on in my relationship with Jackie and Ron and at my recommendation, they leased a Lear jet based in Midland. Prior to that, I had noticed that, when they took trips, they leased a jet out of El Paso, flown by a renegade sort of guy whom Ron had met in his Mexico dealings. What I mean by that is, this was the same guy who, back in the '70s, had flown a helicopter into the New Mexico State Prison yard, picked up an inmate and flown back out. I had taken a couple of trips with Jackie and Ron in this plane and hadn't thought the pilot maintained it well. In fact, after a near-miss at an airport, I recommended that we use my friend Dallas Smith's Lear, in Midland. I knew him to be a superb pilot with several planes meticulously maintained.

The Lear flight from Midland to Ruidoso is twenty minutes and costs about two-thousand-five-hundred dollars. The drive via car is two-and-a-half hours and costs about sixty dollars in gas. Nevertheless, I was grateful for the opportunity. As I did more and more things for Ron and Jackie, they would tell me "just take the Lear."

When he picked me up at the little Ruidoso airport, I said, "Ron, as close as I can tell, Jackie is giving you anywhere from twenty-five- to fifty-thousand dollars a month."

"So?" Ron asked.

"You've got to remember, you are in bankruptcy. It hasn't been finalized. You are supposed to report any income received, not to mention the Verlander lawyers sitting out there with their judgment just looking for any money you might get," I explained.

"I don't care about that. Jackie and I are about to go on a cruise," Ron retorted.

I didn't think that was a relevant response, but conversations with Ron often went like this. I didn't let up, however. Ron had to understand, in the light of the bankruptcy, the importance of how he handled his income, on the one hand, and the Verlander judgment, on the other. The last thing I wanted to do was defend him on bankruptcy fraud. I decided I needed to revisit the matter with both him and Jackie, and insisted that we have that discussion that night before dinner.

As I dressed for dinner in the room I was always assigned, Ron came in.

"Jackie is really reluctant to have this discussion, Glen. She just doesn't want to do it."

"Well, I can't help it. It has to be done. She has to have a clear understanding of how your money has to work," I said.

"But you know how she is. I can't make her talk about it."

"Ron, you go up there and tell Jackie I said there is no choice. The discussion won't take long. It won't be painful. Everything will be all right, but we have to play by the rules."

This was the first and only time I had ever put my foot down with Jackie. I figured there was no telling what Ron had told her about his business situation. With his tendency to gloss over things, she might walk into a situation that even her Boston or Denver lawyers would be unable to deliver her from.

Ron and I waited in the upstairs living room for Jackie to get ready. It was a beautiful Spring evening in the mountains, and the view of the great snowcapped Sierra Blanca Mountain through the arched glass living room window was magnificent indeed. A gentle fire periodically crackled in the fireplace. But for that the room was quiet while Ron and I sat, waiting.

Jackie kept us waiting for quite a long time. I wondered if this was because she didn't want to have this discussion. Or was the delay a bit of punishment for my insistence on having it?

As I sat there in silence, I noticed something I had never noticed before, even though I had stayed at the house many times. This house, well adorned with paintings and art, had not one picture of Jackie's family, anywhere. No picture of her children, grandchildren, or former husbands Hugh Bancroft, Jr. or A.N. Spencer. About the time it suddenly struck me as strange, Jackie entered from her master bedroom, which itself was almost as large as a house.

She was cordial but reserved:

"Okay, Glen, what is the discussion you want to have?"

"I know you have been told about the lawsuit we lost in El Paso, and that Ron has a one-million-three-hundred-thousand-dollar judgment against him," I said. "He also has other creditors after him."

"Yes. I know."

"Primarily because of that judgment, I placed Ron in bankruptcy," I said.

"Yes?"

"When you give Ron money, that has to be reported, and his creditors have a right to the money. That is why we set up his trust. If you pay the trust, my position is that it doesn't have to be reported," I explained.

"Okay," she said.

Jackie wasn't making this easy, but, in time, she loosened up a bit. I had the feeling she understood that whatever she paid Ron had to be paid into the trust. But I also had the feeling she would do whatever she damned well pleased, and resented the machinations of the legal world. She decided she would give Ron an American Express card with a fifty-thousand-dollar limit so he could have money when he needed it, and if he had a trust, fine. She didn't care about it and didn't want anything to do with it.

After dinner, Ron and I retired to the ground level den next to our bedrooms. He opened the conversation by telling me that the trust I set up for him had to produce enough money, enough income, that he could live comfortably for the rest of his life. He was still going to buy things and the credit card Jackie was going to let him have would get him by, month to month, but I had to assure him that I could make the trust earn enough for his future.

"I told you before we got married that I was only going to stay married a year, then divorce her. I can't stand any more of this," Ron said.

"Ron, it seems to me you are both getting something you want. I don't fully understand it, but, for the most part, it seems to be working for each of you. You're just going through a period of adjustment. Take a few days off, and go spend it with Lorenzo."

This idea seemed to ease his stress, though I really didn't know what stress Ron had been under. He wasn't the type to talk about his feelings. In fact, it was often a guess to know what he felt, or what he was thinking. So much of my relationship with Ron through the years was fill-in-the-blank. I wondered if he and Jackie had ever discussed this "stay married for one year" plan, or was this just what Ron had in his mind?

This had not been the first discussion---more like a comment than a discussion --- of how Ron wanted me to handle the trust financially. We had talked on other occasions that typically a trustee would conservatively handle funds, such as CD deposits, bonds, and mutual funds. For Ron, the problem with that approach was it would not throw off enough income to keep him in the lifestyle he wanted to have, post-Jackie.

The other problem was the mass of creditors --- not to mention the Verlander judgment --- sitting there in bankruptcy court. If, in fact, they did attack the trust I had set up to protect Ron's income and Jackie's deposits; and if they were successful at penetrating the body of the trust, the funds would be depleted. By developing offshore companies and using foreign bank accounts, at least we had established another layer of protection.

I had developed the practice of sending Ron a quarterly report on the trust. This would, of course, be expected of any trustee. The uneasy problem I faced was that quarterly reports are obviously disclosures. That is their purpose, to disclose between the trustee and the beneficiary the financial activity within the trust and how the funds are being used. The problem with this standard format of business is that a litigant or a court can cause the reports to be produced. With such disclosures, they would then know how, when, and where to take the assets from Ron.

As the night discussion wore on, Ron emphatically directed that the trust, and the monies placed into it, be invested in such a way that no creditor could ever get to it, and where it would provide income for the rest of his life. He was just as insistent that whatever I invested his monies in, I had better never, ever lose any of it. Of course, these were near-impossible goals to perfect, and I responded to Ron with that thought. I pointed out that the simple thing to do would be for Jackie to make distributions and property conveyances directly to him. That meant we had to report each action to the bankruptcy court. They would then take charge of the asset for the benefit of his creditors. This was the very thing Ron did not want. I explained there would always be the risk that a creditor could attack the trust directly on the basis that it was a subterfuge for Ron's financial benefit. However, I felt the law was on our side on that issue. The trust was a separate entity unto itself with spendthrift provisions protecting against creditor claims. It would make little sense for Jackie to give Ron money or assets only to have creditors seize them if they could break through bankruptcy protection. I explained that I felt we had set up sufficient barriers to protect against that.

The final barrier had to be how the trust invested funds distributed to it by Jackie. Conservative investments like mutual funds would work to some extent, but they certainly would not provide the cash flow Ron demanded. The other problem was that, while they had their place in his portfolio, they were registered securities sitting there for every creditor to see and make designs upon. A good portion of his portfolio, because of the lifestyle he led and the litigation expenses he anticipated when Jackie died, would require riskier offshore investments. These had the potential for high cash returns and would be difficult for a creditor or litigant to identify and seize.

On this night, I told Ron that I felt defensive, that I felt he was either attacking the plan I had designed for him, or that he had some suspicion of me. I felt we had made sure progress at accomplishing his desired goals, but if he knew of a better plan, if he had someone he trusted more, he should go for it. With that, he backed off.

Ron and I were sitting in twin leather-tufted chairs in front of the fireplace in the lower den. We were surrounded by the feel of success. On the table between us sat a bronze replica of Strawberry Silk, Jackie's horse and winner of the All-American Futurity, the richest purse in quarter-horse racing. My discussion about bankruptcy rules, Ron's trust and investments had gone on for a while. The fire flickered out now, and a chill edged the room. Ron had sat quietly during my discussion. I knew that he hated these types of talks. Tonight, I couldn't tell if he was just disinterested or distracted. He neither made suggestions on trust strategy, nor verbalized any disagreement.

What I had not told Ron was that the trust had just made a forty-six-thousand-dollar profit in five months on one investment. It related back to the time of the Sam Vest lawsuit and the trip to Miami to take the deposition of the plastic surgeon.

I had read about an AIDS clinic in Miami that was doing good things. Before flying to Miami, I called the clinic's director to see if I could tour the clinic when I finished taking depositions. He was quite accommodating and said he would be delighted to show me the clinic. Just give him a call when I was ready.

The clinic was packed with patients and, though clean and sterile, the place was cramped for space. The administrator was very upbeat. I could tell he was proud of the work they were doing. I told him I knew the clinic was a non-profit organization, and that I represented some wealthy people who might, on occasion, make a contribution. I did confide that I couldn't promise. My clients generally did not contribute to eleemosynary institutions, but perhaps I could talk to them. What I could do was donate legal work, pro bono, if they had things that needed doing. In fact, that had been in the back of my mind when I read about the clinic, called, and requested a tour.

The administrator was delighted and shared some quasi-legal matters I could help on. He then approached a subject totally unfamiliar to me. This clinic serviced a large clientele of AIDS patients. Some had life insurance policies. They knew they were going to die, and their named beneficiary was no longer significant to them. In some cases, their families had abandoned them because of their sexuality; in other cases, their partner had predeceased them. Circumstances varied. Many of these patients wanted to cash in their policies so they had money to ease their living conditions in their final sickness.

But the life insurance company discount was too deep. Investment companies had taken to contacting the clinic for leads on which patients had life insurance policies, and made a donation for the information. The administrator was concerned about the ethics of such a disclosure, even when the patient agreed. He wanted me to research the practice in light of governmental regulation, and also to read the contract these companies used to purchase the assignment of the life insurance from the patient. Was there anything that took undue advantage of the AIDS patient that the patient should be warned about? I agreed to service these requests for the clinic, and did so in the months to come.

From this relationship, I received a call one day from the administrator who told me a patient had been offered eighty-thousand-dollars by an investment company for his one-hundred-fifty-thousand-dollar life policy. Because of certain special needs, the patient had to have one-hundred-thousand dollars. Did I know anyone who would pay that price?

I thought about it, and told him a trust I represented would buy the policy. Four months later, the patient died, and the life insurance company paid Ron's trust one-hundred-forty-six-thousand dollars.

Why was I not telling Ron on this night of this good news, this profit for his trust? I'm not sure. For one thing, he wasn't in good humor and such news would only be of passing interest to him. For another, he was obsessed with how much he was ultimately going to get from Jackie. A forty-six-thousand-dollar profit on a one-hundred-thousand-dollar investment in five months would hardly be a ripple on the pond to him.

Finally, he said, "I'm going to bed. All I'm saying is that it's hard enough to get money out of Jackie when I want it. Just don't lose it."

He added, "Before you go, I need you to do something. Jackie and I have been to Puerto Vallarta. There is a condo there we want to buy."

"Puerto Vallarta?"

"Yes. We like it. It is just being completed. I'm going to decorate it. I don't trust the real estate agent. I want you to go down there and make sure the title is in my trust."

"Sure. I'll be glad to," I responded.

"I need you to do it tomorrow," Ron said.

"Oh. Okay."

With that, we headed to our respective bedrooms. I knew that Ron always liked to play the "I don't understand" card when he didn't want to take responsibility, but I also knew there was no way he could not understand what we had spent the evening discussing.

The next morning, I headed back to Midland. I wondered if Ron was serious about this divorce thing. He and Jackie had been married about six months, and it seemed to be going well. I realized this was more of an arrangement than a marriage. Jackie had her travel partner, who was required to attend all social functions, play golf/bridge and Rummikub with her. Ron got to travel in complete luxury, spend adequate time with Lorenzo at the house in El Paso, and he was given plenty of money to live on. Why a divorce? I mused to myself. As strange as the relationship seemed to someone like me, it appeared to be working. Perhaps Ron was just going through a period of adjustment. Then, too, just as Jackie was prone to sudden out-of-left-field outbursts, so too was Ron, though it took on a different dictum, vague in its own way. I knew that Ron had a warehouse in El Paso. When Jackie purchased a work of art for him, periodically, he placed it there. I had the feeling Ron looked at this as a kind of savings account. Eventually, he would either sell the things he accumulated, or use them in some design.

As the plane landed and I headed for my office, I reflected on something else Ron told me. His marriage to Jackie was his path to retirement. He wanted to be rich, and he never wanted to have to work again.

What made Ron tick? What made Jackie happy with this relationship? At times, I thought I knew. At other times, my search for deeper meaning was futile.

I told the pilots to get ready to head to Puerto Vallarta. We would leave the next morning.

22

Ron fell in love with Puerto Vallarta, and Jackie didn't seem to mind. They took numerous trips to the picturesque coastal village, which serves tourists and expats from all over the world. Ron had evolved a new characteristic. Perhaps it had always been there, latent under the surface of his personality. Everything he saw that he liked he must own, and, with Jackie's money, he could.

Cash and properties deposited into Ron's trust reached into the millions. It was happening quickly, and I wondered where this was going, where it would end. The first "condo" purchased in Puerto Vallarta cost well over a million dollars. Ron instructed me to place ownership in his trust. I felt obligated to verify that demand with Jackie, and took it upon myself to visit her separately about it.

Meeting Jackie about a desired transaction was never an easy matter. She would be cordial, but without saying so, she made one feel they were intrusive and their questioning was not well-accepted.

This was the atmosphere I found myself in when I inquired how the Puerto Vallarta condo should be titled. I went further, however, because I was concerned about the fast-growing wealth of the trust I had created for Ron for which I served as trustee.

"Jackie, the trust I set up for Ron is becoming quite affluent. I assume that is all right with you?"

"What do you mean?"

"By placing the Puerto Vallarta condo in his trust, along with art purchases and monies already there, the trust will be worth several million dollars."

"I don't really care about that, Glen. Why are you asking me about this?"

"Well, let me be more specific. Is it all right with you to place the Puerto Vallarta property in Ron's trust?"

"Certainly. That probably won't be the last," Jackie answered.

"I have to ask, Jackie. What are your children going to think about these gifts to Ron?"

"My children are spoiled. They each get several million a year from their own trusts, and they are always calling me wanting more money. I don't care what they think. Chris, in Dallas, can't wait for me to die. My money is all he wants, and he'll do anything for it. If Ronnie wants something, he can have it. I don't care if anything is left when I die."

I could tell that Jackie was getting upset and that this was the end of the conversation. I had pushed it just about as far as I could. I had been aware of Jackie's strained relationship with her two boys, not so much with her daughter. On one occasion, I had been sitting at the kitchen table when Jackie had a heated telephone conversation --- argument --- with one of the boys over money. But then, I had also been present when she and Ron had heated arguments over money. Jackie had given Ron an American Express card with a fifty-thousand-dollar limit. I think she thought Ron would use it within reason, but every month, when the bill came, the card was maxed out, and she would have to pay it off.

My position in this unusual relationship became clear to me. Jackie didn't come right out and say it, but she indicated in so many words that I should not be meeting with her behind Ron's back to question the judgment of a transaction. I got the subtle message and felt properly admonished.

It was also clear that Jackie felt quite capable of handling her relationships and her money. If she needed additional money, she would contact either me or Mike Line, the local lawyer, to call the Denver trustee to send more. She was doing this more and more frequently.

In leaving my meeting with Jackie, I headed for Mexican customs at Ciudad Juarez. Ron had fully loaded an eighteen-wheeler with art and furniture to transport to Puerto Vallarta for that new condo. The fact that I had not finished the legal work on the condo closing didn't seem to matter. Neither did the fact that a new issue --- a quandary --- had arisen. At what point, if any, was I to question a decision by either Jackie or Ron? When was an inquiry an asset to decision-making, and when was it being too nosy? Having represented numerous wealthy individuals, I respected the rule of intrusiveness. One may be the lawyer, the CPA, or the doctor, but you are not to cross the line into what is not your business. In representing Ron, but with Jackie relying on me and asking my advice when she chose to, it seemed that the line between advice and intrusiveness was constantly moving. Even at the time of Jackie's fateful voyage, there hadn't been a resolution to that issue.

While I was at Mexican customs in Ciudad Juarez acquiring legal passage for the eighteen-wheeler, I learned that Ron had fired the servant staff at the Puerto Vallarta condo and hired people he liked. This gave rise to a Mexican legal issue --- and the quandary --- I needed to handle. Mexico has strict labor laws about servants and property. Servants follow the property, not the ownership of the property. Americans often think they can waltz in and do what they want without regard to Mexican laws. That attitude is not well received by Mexican authorities. It is true that the rich and powerful in Mexico can get what they want and bypass the law. To do that, one must act according to culture and custom, including jumping through certain hoops and not being disrespectful. In time, I took care of the matter, but it would take two separate trips to Puerto Vallarta.

While I was in Juarez working through the custom's objections on Ron's eighteen-wheeler full of furnishings, Ron asked me to go with him to a client's house to deliver a small sculpture and pick up a payment for the interior decorating work he had done.

I climbed into his Jaguar as we left Mexican customs. I had a pretty good idea where we were going. I had known that, as Ron's reputation for making things look rich and pretty was developing in El Paso, he had met some of the then-*narco-traficante* families and done work for them in Juarez. I had admonished him on the danger of working with these people, but Ron had a blasé way when encountering potential danger. He literally had no opinions about politics, drug wars, or culture differences. To him, they didn't seem to exist.

There is a facade of order in Juarez, indeed in all of Mexico. Having represented companies in the leather industry out of Guadalajara, I was somewhat familiar. For decades, this city of two million has drawn people from both sides of the border with its own brand of intrigue and historical mystery. It claims the invention of the margarita; it is the birthplace of the zoot suit, of velvet painting, of the border factory era, of the most innovative and modern drug cartel, of world-class murder of women and men. Juarez has long supplied Americans with what they wanted --- booze during Prohibition, women at all times, men, young virginal men for the homosexual, opiates outlawed in the United States, acceptance of quick divorces once recognized by the State of New York and other states.

As we left the core of the city, I watched white buses lumber past with the tired faces of factory workers, and indigenous, crippled, and malnourished people begging in the middle of the street. Ron made a wrong turn and we ended up in a dirty, drab barrio, largely unvisited by anyone but its inhabitants. The road was rough and rutted. I could tell most shacks lacked electricity and water. They were put together with a chaos of boards, pallets, beams, rebar, old cable spools, tires, scrap metal, and anything else the inhabitants could beg, borrow, or steal.

"Ron, have you ever thought we could be one of these people?" I asked.

"I hate this place. I made a wrong turn," he said.

"No, Ron, think about it. We could have been one of these people just as easily as who we are."

"I'm going to just turn around and go back the way we came. That's the best way to do it."

"Why are kings without pity for their subjects? It is because they count on never being human beings. Why are the rich so harsh to the poor? It is because they do not have fear of becoming poor. Why does a noble have such contempt for a peasant? It is because he will never be a peasant," I said, quoting Rousseau. Ron didn't hear me.

Finally, we pulled out of the barrio and into "narcolandia," a place where those who have, for the moment, succeeded in some facet of the drug industry build their dreams and live out time until their mostly early deaths. The streets have names like Michigan, Alaska, Arizona, or Oregon. Mansions, narco-mansions, rise up, but the killings constantly create vacancies.

Ron had developed an association with an architect and had decorated several houses. Architects in Juarez come from all over the country to make their wealth from the rising narco-class, a keen market in this city grinding with poverty. Often, the owner vanishes --- sometimes before the completion of the mansion, sometimes not long after. No one asks why. Another simply fills the place of the missing.

I was far more aware of the reality of the narco-class than I would like to have been. Either Ron wasn't aware, or he didn't care. More likely, he had use only for the money. He had complained to me that these clients were always slow pay and he had difficulty getting his money. This was his last job. He didn't need these people anymore. He had Jackie.

We pulled into a cul-de-sac and quickly drove up to a wrought-iron, padlocked gate. A plain-clothed guard, with an automatic rifle strapped across his shoulder, came out from behind a stone pillar. He knew Ron from his work on the house, and passed us through.

We were in the land of "narcotecture," the three-dimensional statement of the dreams of the poor who now prosper. The houses are orange, red, green, yellow, blue, and purple. Their columns rise at porticos and huge tinted windows, some of which are two stories. These mansions rise up in various places. I see one that is three stories of gray concrete with uncovered orange girders. It is a work in progress, maybe six-thousand square feet or more. Next door, workmen install expensive wooden doors on yet another mansion. Large dogs bark from dark places. Men glare. No one is to come here unless they belong here. You feel the eyes from dark places. You know you are being watched.

A maid answered the door. We entered a foyer and faced a spiral staircase leading to the second floor. A non-descript gentleman in his fifties, dressed in slacks and a short-sleeved shirt, came down the stairs. Ron introduced me as we were led into the living room. He placed the sculpture he was carrying in an honored spot, and he and the client went into an adjoining room, while I stayed in the living room.

I sat on an expensive couch and admired the well-appointed room with its high ceilings and majestic lighting through tall, arched windows. The entire room, including the fireplace mantle, was painted in an oil-based white that made one feel angels might descend at any moment. From a lifetime of doing business in Mexico, I knew that was not the case. (I also knew the environment was worsening in Ciudad Juarez as turf wars accelerated.) I wondered how long this *narco-trafficante* would enjoy his surroundings. I mused at who would fill his space when he was gone, how and how quickly, as far as anyone would concern themselves he never existed. That's the way it is in Mexico.

When Ron and I left in his Jaguar, the feeling of being watched returned. I assumed the business between Ron and the client had been concluded. I thought I observed relief in Ron that he would not have to come back to service the narco-*nouveau riche*, not now that he had Jackie.

Our car motored past the giant flagpole erected in the 1990s by then-President Ernesto Zedillo so that a gigantic Mexican flag would gently wash across the face of El Paso. I wondered if Ron ever thought of helping Juarez's poor, starving, and downtrodden, or if he held them in disdain just as his clientele did. I wondered if President Calderon had ever entertained the thought of helping these huddled masses. I wondered why, if I were so concerned, I didn't come to Juarez to help these poor people, myself. I would talk to Jane, my wife, about it.

23

Puerto Vallarta is much as the travel magazines picture it, a Shangri-la on the Pacific Coast of Mexico where tropical mountains drop to the sea. It is expensive and filled with wealthy expats and tourists from around the world.

Ron and Jackie's condo was all I might expect. Nestled into the side of the mountain looking down on the Spanish red-tiled roofs of the town, it had a perfect view of the village and the blue bay below. I've called the structure a "condo" because that is what Jackie and Ron called it. It was about six-thousand square feet, and had a small pool. The living room opened into a sweeping veranda giving the entire place a feeling of openness and light. Ron had outdone himself with the furnishings, sculptures, and art.

A pastime of any visitor, including myself, was to use the telescope Ron had set up on the veranda to look at the boats on the bay and watch what the people were doing on them. On one trip, my friend Dallas Smith, who piloted the Lear, noticed that the roof of a hotel below us was set up with a swimming pool and outdoor bar for parties every night. It seemed odd, Dallas noted, that women were never at these parties, which would have made the telescoping more interesting. We also noticed the hotel's flag mast flew a nation's flag we did not recognize. Watching the goings-on in the town from the veranda had become a fun evening pastime.

Ron came into town and set up several business meetings for us for the next day. On the way to our first meeting, we passed within a block of the hotel Dallas and I had spied on the night before, and I asked:

"Ron, what nation owns that hotel? Dallas and I couldn't recognize the flag."

Ron laughed and said:

"You don't know what flag that is?"

Feeling a bit inadequate for not knowing, I admitted:

"No, I guess not. I thought I knew most of the flags in the Western Hemisphere."

"That's the gay flag. That's a gay hotel," Ron said, still laughing.

"Oh, no wonder there were no women at the pool," I responded.

As time passed, I would make many trips to Puerto Vallarta. Ron was into acquiring property there, which required negotiation and legal work. Because of my frequent travel back and forth, the Mexican government required a Mexican commercial visa of me, which made clearing customs easier. Typically, I traveled in the Lear and taxied to a private part of the airport. Clearing customs in privacy usually took about twenty minutes.

The customs agents and I became familiar with one another. We often joked, called each other by first names or nicknames, and had a good relationship. On one occasion, however, I had taken my grandson with me.

As we deplaned, I noticed that the customs crew was different. We entered the little private port and I presented our papers. The head agent told me we had a problem. I asked what it was, and he said I had presented a copy of my grandson's birth certificate. Did I have the original? Of course I didn't have the original, or I wouldn't have presented a copy. The agent and I went back and forth. He kept telling me he could not accept a copy. I kept telling him he had better figure out a solution, I wasn't flying this plane back to Midland, Texas, to get an original. I glanced over at my seven-year-old grandson, and winked at him. I could tell he was getting worried. Granddad was beginning to raise his voice and was talking in a foreign language he could not understand. He didn't want to be forgotten in a place called "Mexico."

As we talked, I noticed perspiration popping out on the agent's forehead. He sat, looking at the documents. I stood over him. He was agitated and nervous. Finally, he asked if we could step outside for a moment. I said, "Of course." It had gotten quite warm in there.

Actually, he wanted to step away from the subordinate customs agents. Outside, he mumbled that perhaps a "tip" might help resolve this matter. I was well aware of the custom of "mordido," the "bite," in Mexico, and was ready to participate in the custom. In most places in the world, things simply do not work smoothly without it. Even though bribery is commonplace at every level of government in Mexico, one must use tact, never the word bribe or mordido. In this case, tip was the preferred nomenclature.

In the heat of the moment, I made the mistake of reaching into the wrong pocket. When traveling, I always keep my hundreds in one pocket, my twenties in the other. I asked the agent what would be appropriate for a tip, and accidentally pulled from my hundred-dollar pocket. The die was cast, as it is said. The agent's eyebrows raised when he looked in my hand,

and as he gave me a perspicuous nod, I peeled off a hundred-dollar bill. Had I had my wits about me and pulled out my twenties, the bite would have been a twenty-dollar bill.

Through the course of four years, Ron bought several million-dollar Puerto Vallarta properties, some for rental, some with an eye toward resale; all in the name of the trust I had set up for him. This was causing a problem. When Ron initially explained how he wanted the trust to work, or, at least how he envisioned the goal, it was to be an income-generating entity protected from domestic creditors, the IRS, and Jackie's children. Therefore, I envisioned never conducting business in the United States. I had never filed for a tax identification number, nor had the trust filed an income tax return.

However, throughout the first few years of the trust, Ron imported large amounts of art works and furnishings from other countries and warehoused them in El Paso. He also took unreported, large cash distributions into the United States. This was not how to protect oneself within a trust. No matter how I might admonish him, I would find, after the fact, Ron paid no attention and threw caution to the winds. I could never tell, through many aspects of Ron's life, whether he felt invincible or whether he just couldn't perceive risk/reward exposure.

In following the goal of creating an offshore cash-cow for Ron's future, I had established a corporation and office in Belize that headquartered an online casino. Acquiring the software through professional contacts in Vegas and setting up accounting and payment controls took about a year. Belize was ideal for an online casino because broadband T-1 connections were plentiful and the domain name address would be Belize. Additionally, the major Caribbean undersea fiber line connecting instantaneously to the entire world was within a stone's throw of where I had set up the online casino. In the second year, the casino was cash-flowing twenty-five-thousand dollars per month with hardly any overhead.

To diversify the activities and income of the trust, I retained a CPA and Hong Kong attorneys to establish a Hong Kong trade corporation with an office in Shenzhen, China. The trade company served multiple purposes because of the myriad opportunities in China. Its primary purpose was to protect importations of art works, sculptures, and furnishings from all the countries Ron had haphazardly imported into the United States. At least, by using the Hong Kong company, these shipments would not show up in Ron's name. Of course, that would only work if Ron told me about the purchases as he made them, which allowed me to ship through the Hong Kong company. Sometimes he did. Sometimes he didn't. Through the first few years, there were several million dollars in shipments.

Although Ron was as tight-lipped about those details as he was about most other details, it was pretty clear he was stockpiling a high-end inventory for his post-Jackie future. Several years had passed since he told me he would stay married to Jackie for one year and then get a divorce. I'd never brought up the subject again after that night of disclosure, nor had he. That idea seemed to be off the table; all appeared to be about money and lifestyle. Neither were the touchy-feely type. Feelings of affection between Ron and Jackie weren't apparent, nor were deep yearnings of mutual love. Nevertheless, they did share mutual respect and unwritten confidentiality in all matters. It was Ron's position --- not as a job but as a position --- to keep Jackie company and entertained. I couldn't help but wonder: Had that been Dr. A.N. Spencer's position in all those years of marriage?

Ron would return to his house in El Paso, which he shared with Lorenzo, for a short stay at the termination of trips he'd taken with Jackie. Long trips, such as the five-month cruises, took their toll. Ron made up for his absence with stays of a week or two with Lorenzo at one of the casas in Puerto Vallarta. It was clear that Ron didn't want to lose Lorenzo, but it was also clear, at least to me, that Lorenzo had never had it so good and wouldn't find a better ticket to ride if he tried. He was provided with a nice convertible, always new, and adequate spending money. His peers undoubtedly envied his standard of living. While making sure Lorenzo had what he needed or wanted, Ron plied Jackie with diamond pendants, rings, and jewelry he purchased from his jewelry broker in Midland in order to receive his kickback.

Jackie, who had never worn much jewelry before Ron, seemed to enjoy the presents. She knew she would have to give Ron money later to pay for the gifts, but she played the game, seemingly without objection. At times, she got resistant and contentious when Ron became too pushy. His Midland broker would contact him with a story that she had just received a very, very special item from Neiman-Marcus that Jackie would love. It was only a hundred-thousand dollars; a very special deal. On some occasions,

Jackie balked. "Enough!" she would scream.

For me, I continued doing what I was told and played golf once in a while with Jackie. Occasionally, something happened that filled my populace soul with laughter.

While visiting one of the numerous country clubs in and around Palm Springs, Jackie, Ron, and I were warming up on the practice range. One of the young employees from the pro shop hurriedly ran out wearing an embarrassed look. Somehow, he knew my name.

"Mr. Aaron, Mr. Aaron, I'm very sorry. No one is allowed on the course with a collarless shirt."

I was struck dumbfounded in mid-swing. "Collarless shirt?" What was he talking about? Oh! my shirt!

"What? This shirt is not appropriate for golf?" I asked. I thought my nice crewneck shirt was quite stylish for the day's golf game.

"No, sir. I'm sorry. Your shirt must have a collar."

"Really!" I said. "Well, don't get your panties in a wad. Go back where you came from and get me a shirt with a collar on it. Extra large. Charge it to Jackie's account."

As the young man headed back to the pro shop, I wondered what would have happened if he had approached Jackie on some dress-rule violation. She would have probably bought the club and fired the poor soul on the spot. Lucky for him that I was the culprit of the terrible faux pas.

24

On a trip to Palm Springs, Ron decided that the Audi and Jeep Cherokee he and Jackie traveled in at Ruidoso needed upgrading. I wasn't with him at the time, but received a call at my Midland office inquiring about licensing and titling a Rolls Royce. I was taken aback. The idea of purchasing a Rolls Royce to drive around the mountains of Ruidoso would never have crossed my mind. Nevertheless, I wasn't sure how the vehicle should be titled. Ron's trust was becoming more and more exposed, but I certainly couldn't put it in Ron's name, personally. The creditors would be all over that one.

"May I inquire as to the cost of the vehicle?" I timidly asked the Rolls-Royce dealer in Palm Springs.

"I'm not sure I am at liberty to disclose that," came the elitist answer from the other end of the phone.

I have always had difficulty with haughtiness, and I seemed to be running into more and more of it lately.

"Well, if I'm to tell you whose name to put this car in, you will tell me the cost to put on the books," I said.

The sales manager reported that the cost of the Rolls was right at two-hundred-sixty-five-thousand dollars, inclusive of tax and title.

A few weeks later, I was summoned to Ruidoso to attend a performance at the Spencer Theater. The Theater's director scheduled performances once a year. Traveling performances, often out of New York, made their way across the nation to various theaters, colleges, and town halls for the performing arts.

The Theater provides valet parking while attendees wait in their vehicles in the line approaching the well-lit, sparkling building's entrance. Fifty cars must have been lined up in the right lane waiting their turn as Ron, Jackie, and I crept past in the left lane in the black Rolls Royce. The only thing missing was a chauffeur. Ron drove, Jackie sat in the passenger seat, I sat in the back. As we pulled under the portico, the valets rushed to open our doors. I wondered if Oscar attendees ever had this feeling.

On the second floor of the Theater, Jackie had set aside a special place, known as the "Founders Club," for gatherings of the group also known as the "Founders Club." Originally formed to help set up the Spencer Theater Foundation while she was alive, it's where Jackie held court. Later on, the Club's membership grew to include big contributors to the performing arts foundation. On performance nights, the Founders Club, comprised of Ruidoso's high society, came together to basically rub shoulders with Jackie, show off their latest designer clothes, unique jewelry pieces, and most recent surgical tucks or enhancements. Pre-dinner drinks were always cordial. The area included its own kitchen, bar, and dining area decorated with Chihuly glass. Attendees then dined on an exquisite meal often prepared by a European chef.

Talk centered on each person's horse and how it was doing. If doing well, there was still a complaint about something; nothing was ever perfect. Politics were seldom an acceptable subject in these elite gatherings. Everyone pretty much followed the Party line, aware that politicians lived at Jackie's door every campaign season. The closest talk ever came to politics was the perpetual concern over water. "The subsurface water table is dropping and wells are harder to come by." Or, "It seems strange with as much snow as the mountains get." On this particular occasion, Jackie was quite unhappy with George W. All she and Ron got after giving him fifty-thousand dollars was a picture taken with him and a lot of other people when he flew into Albuquerque. No conversation, no nothing. So, superfluous conversations, pasted smiles, and search for acceptance continued until performance time.

By this particular evening, the Chihuly red tree had been installed in the foyer. Jackie opted not to have a special congratulatory gathering for its christening as she had done with the green tree. Everyone agreed that the red tree was, indeed, stunning. Some were bold enough to mention to Jackie that it was even more beautiful than the green tree. Most, however, admired the glistening tree of blown glass, made a few comments to their fellow attendees, and moved on. I could tell that Jackie liked the tree and all the Chihuly art that Ron and Dale Chihuly had installed.

After the performance, I followed Jackie and Ron backstage to meet the performers and congratulate them on a performance well done. This was our usual protocol. Later, Jackie greeted the people as we passed through the crowd at the front door of the Theater on our way out. The Rolls awaited, engine running, valets standing beside each open door.

That evening, when we got to the house, Jackie went on to bed, while Ron and I settled down in the downstairs den. I could tell he had something he wanted to talk about.

"Someone has been sneaking around the house. I think they have been coming in," he said.

"How do you know?" I asked.

"I can just tell, and I am afraid for my jewelry collection," Ron said.

"Well, I need a little more to go on. We can beef up security, but how do you know someone is coming in?"

"Come here. Let me show you something," Ron said.

We ducked into a small cubbyhole room under the stairwell. At the back of the room was a safe.

"I put this safe in here," Ron said as he knelt down, turned the combination and pulled the door open. Inside, there were trays of jewels, mainly diamonds, and, except for a number of watches, most of the jewels were unmounted. There must have been several hundred thousand dollars' worth. I would have preferred not to have seen the safe, nor the jewelry in it.

"I can tell that someone has been in here, and I'm worried. It could have been Sam Vest," Ron said.

This was getting weird. Ron could give me no indication of how he thought someone was coming into the house. Through the years, I had observed a paranoiac streak in Ron; I never knew which way it would turn. Usually, it was bent toward an employee he was sure was stealing from him. This happened frequently. I had also seen him foster this feeling in Jackie on occasion. I was sure Jackie was unaware that Ron had been stockpiling diamonds he was acquiring from his jewelry source in Midland and the one he had worked for in Lubbock when he was in college.

I also knew that safes in homes were a poor excuse for protection of one's valuables. Criminal history is replete with violent individuals entering a wealthy person's home, perhaps holding them hostage. That type of criminal typically has a goal in mind, to gain access and to come away with riches. I had even run across a few such individuals in my career. But their plan is poorly thought out. If the resident shows up unexpectedly or, to the surprise of the thief is already there, violence erupts and either injury or death occurs. The burglar is usually high on alcohol or drugs, which means reason and logic are useless. But then, if you had tray after tray of diamonds, where *would* you keep them?

I didn't discount Ron's concern in view of his high-profile living and the common knowledge that Jackie was a wealthy woman.

This incident brought to my attention that there was literally no protection in place around this house as Ron and Jackie drove in and out, dressed to the nines, wearing expensive jewelry, and riding in progressively more noteworthy automobiles. The house was nestled quietly in the pines; all the better for hostage-taking or burglary. As a result of never finding the slightest evidence of someone stealing from him --- from his first paramour I had met years before to his employees and his now-persistent paranoid suspicions --- I had grown to recognize Ron's tendencies. However, in this instance, while there may not have been anyone sneaking around the house --- there was no evidence in support of it and Ron could not give me a credible example --- I did agree that Ron and Jackie should have greater residential security. I told him I would work on a security arrangement for the house, and if someone were coming around or getting into the house, they would be caught.

In the days to come, I investigated the commercial security firm located in this little mountain village. It proposed the usual: wire sensor tape for windows, code panels for doors that signal headquarters so that security personnel either call the house or send someone in time to see if everything is all right. I was not impressed. At best, these types of systems, regardless of TV advertising, are capable only of telling you that you've been robbed, raped, or killed.

I spoke with the sheriff's department and made arrangements for a regular patrol to drive by the house, to actually drive up the driveway and do a 'walk-around' of the house. They were accommodating not just because Jackie was who she was but because the Theater maintained 24/7 security personnel which paid well. Working there was a nice part-time job for off-duty sheriff's deputies. Even still, I knew this arrangement was not adequate. Anyone could time the patrol, if they so desired. However, it did offer the appearance of authority and law enforcement.

At breakfast one morning, while Jackie was frying eggs, we discussed the security situation. Jackie pointed out that, in all her years of living in these mountains, she had never had a problem; not one. I refrained from pointing out that she had not been married to Ron all those years with the affluent spectacle that followed. Under no circumstance was Jackie going to be bothered by punching in codes at doors, nor did she intend to have her privacy invaded by security measures. In her words, that was as bad as having the robbers. I could see that Ron was backing away from the idea, as well.

Ultimately, I had cameras installed around the house's outside perimeter, and an indoor monitor locked in the closet with the safe containing Ron's growing diamond and jewelry collection. I suggested that we hide a camera that would catch anyone going into that closet. He would have none of it. I knew this was a poor excuse for a security system but it was better than nothing, which is what they had had before. To their good fortune, Ron and Jackie were neither burgled nor robbed.

As I drifted off to sleep in my room that night of the Theater production and my talk with Ron about security, I realized my bedroom door was open to the outside. I liked sleeping that way in the mountains. I liked the feel of the air and the rustle of the pines. I felt sure that Ron's fear was unfounded. Besides, how could an intruder get into that big safe? I mused that, in the past few years, Ron's paranoia seemed to be getting worse. I drifted off to sleep.

25

Two months had passed since I last saw Ron and Jackie. Then he called, excited about a house he and Jackie planned to build across the state highway from the Theater. The house sounded most impressive, but Ron had heard that a major electrical transmission line was scheduled for construction at or near the house's property line. This would be unsightly and destroy the ambiance and view of the house. Ron wanted me to check the rumor out, and, if it were true, stop the proposed construction or require it to be moved to a different location. Beyond that, he wanted me to go to El Paso with him and meet Harry Farah, the architect designing the house.

As I drove into the driveway at the Alto Village house, I was glad to see the open garage door. For some years now, I was allowed to enter the house through the garage to the downstairs bedroom I customarily occupied.

Something was different. At first, I couldn't decide what that could be. The back of the Rolls-Royce didn't look the same. I parked, got out, retrieved my bag and started walking towards the garage. The back of the Rolls said "Bentley." *That's* what was different. This car wasn't the Rolls.

After tossing my bag on the bed, I headed upstairs and found Ron and Jackie sitting at the kitchen table.

"What's new in the garage?" I asked.

Ron looked surprised, as if he didn't know what I was talking about.

"Oh! the Bentley. We traded in the Rolls. The dealership out in Palm Springs gave me a good deal," Ron explained.

I wanted to ask how much it had cost, but I knew better than to probe the issue in front of Jackie; she generally didn't appreciate those inquiries. I also wondered if Ron had put the title into the trust. I didn't pursue that query, either.

It appeared to be a bad time to bring up *any*thing. I had just walked into one of Jackie and Ron's arguments. I had witnessed these arguments before and never felt at ease sitting there during the process. They didn't have many arguments, but the arguments always followed the same format. Ron would want something. Jackie would balk at paying for it. Ron would pout for a few weeks and buy Jackie a piece of jewelry at some point in the pouting time. Jackie would give in.

"Why on earth do we need such a big house?" Jackie asked as I sat down at the kitchen table.

"It's not the size. It's the beauty of the thing," Ron responded.

"No. It is the size. Fifteen-thousand square feet, or whatever you said, is too big. *This* house is too big!" Jackie said.

"Look, I've designed it where it is one story and easy to get around. No elevator to get trapped in," Ron said.

The year before, Jackie had gotten trapped in the elevator in the present house. Ever since, she had refused to use it, though it was difficult for her to climb the stairs from the ground floor and garage where she drove in, to the main upstairs floor of the house. Jackie was in amazing shape, but her knees could not handle stair climbing. The problem initially gave rise to the subject of moving or building another house. Ron was excited about building another house and wanted to put it into the trust. His idea of how the house should be was more grandiose than Jackie's idea of what they needed.

"That house looks too big. We don't need a house that big," Jackie said.

"It will be beautiful. It will be across from the Theater and complement the design of the Theater, and there won't be any elevator to get stuck in or stairs to climb," Ron said.

"That God-damn thing is so big I won't even be alive by the time it is finished," Jackie responded.

The blueprints were large and almost covered the kitchen table, which itself was large. Ron huffed, rolled up the plans and left the room, presumably heading downstairs. As often happens with Jackie and Ron, one went one way, and the other a different way. I never quite knew which one to follow, or, as in the disagreement, what to say.

"I'll go downstairs and see what he's up to," I said to Jackie, or perhaps just to the cosmos. She made no reply as she continued peeling the vegetables she was working on at the kitchen sink, her back to me.

When I walked into the downstairs den, Ron had spread the plans out on the poker table. He was anxious to show them to me. If Jackie wasn't interested, he wanted to show them to somebody.

Indeed, the proposed structure was quite impressive. It was about thirty-five-thousand square feet, with a large, magnificent portico perfectly suited for receiving guests, and a large mahogany double front door entrance. Behind that entrance was a long covered walkway, designed to reflect light in unusual and fascinating ways, and led to the front doors of the house. The rear of the house gracefully edged around a very large swimming pool, uncurbed on one end as if gradually drifting into the water like a sandy beach at ocean's edge. On the far side of the pool were three cabanas, which served as guesthouses, and they, too, faced the large pool of water. The surface of the structures would be the same white Spanish silica limestone the Theater was made of.

"Ron, this is quite a structure. I didn't know you were planning such a thing."

"Yes, it's outstanding, isn't it? I need for you to get the property next to it bought and make sure no high lines are built beside it. Also, we might be able to buy all that acreage across the road and do a high-end development," Ron said.

"Why do you want to do a high-end development?" I asked.

"It will look good with the Theater, and after we build this house, we don't want someone coming in and building a bunch of cheap houses across the road."

"But, Ron, it doesn't seem Jackie is going for this."

"Oh, she will change her mind. It will just take a little time. Tomorrow, I want you to go down to Harry Farah's with me and do a contract with him. I have agreed to pay him one-hundred-thousand dollars for his initial retainer and for drawing up these plans."

The next morning, we headed out of the mountains for El Paso and a meeting with Harry Farah. El Paso is a strange town, certainly not one that will marquee on any travel brochure. There is no place to hide the eye from the failed Mexican state across the border and the millions of malnourished beings living among open sewage in shack huts on dirt streets.

Harry's condominiums sit on a slope of the Franklin Mountains, a dry barren range that knifes into El Paso and forces the city to spread as a "U" around its base. As you travel through its central thoroughfare, Interstate 10, all you see is a wedge of the Franklins plowing into the city on one side, and the acidic air of Juarez on the other side. People spend their lives simply curling around the base of the Franklins, hemmed by the Rio Grande and its flowing raw sewage dumped from the Mexican side, and dairy farm manure and fertilizer from the American side. In recent years, with laundered money from border factories and drugs, mansions have crept up the slopes of the Franklins, some of the big houses on lots so steep they stand on huge stilts, but the mountain itself is pretty much unchanged.

Prior to that day, I had never met Harry, but he and Ron had been friends for some time. Harry, a graduate of Texas A & M and a member of the well-established Lebanese clothing manufacturing family of El Paso, had worked as an architect for many years in El Paso. As I looked at the various structures he was responsible for building, I noticed they were all cathedral-like, large, grandiose structures.

Harry was a delightful character with a large Mediterranean nose, darker skin than mine or Ron's, and he looked very much Lebanese. Beyond his appearance, he was second-generation Texan in attitude and thought, with a quick and delightfully dry sense of humor.

Ron and I drove through vaulted gates and parked at a three-story structure that housed six condominiums. Harry owned this structure, and lived and officed in one of the condos. The whole place was unorthodox, a combination of high-end living and architectural design. Several work houses and a yard, where marble and various types of stone were cut, sold, or built into some interior structure, sat at the far end of the parking lot. The whole place occupied the lower side of a desert mountain, with a view of El Paso and Juarez beyond.

Harry was bent over a drafting table as we walked in.

"Did you bring my check?" was Harry's greeting as we walked into his drafting room.

"Not yet, Harry. You haven't done anything to deserve a check."

This type of banter, I would soon learn, was constant between Ron and Harry. Indeed, it was Harry's way of conversing with anyone he liked. The check they referenced was the one-hundred-thousand-dollar initial retainer for designing the new house and overseeing its construction.

"Well, hurry up, Ron. Also, tell your girlfriend I need a check for four-hundred-thousand dollars immediately. I ordered marble from the quarry I use in Italy. It will look fabulous throughout the foyer. The quarry wants their money."

I would also soon learn that Harry's reference to "your girlfriend" was an inside joke. Harry was gay, too, and this was just part of his wit.

As I sat and listened to Ron and Harry go over changes in the plans and some of the problems they were already running into, I could tell this project had been in the making for awhile. I had just left an argument between Jackie and Ron the day before about whether the house should even be built. Now, here we were, in Harry's office. Clearly, Ron had already committed to a half-million-dollar expenditure, if you only counted Harry's retainer and the purchase of the Italian marble. Not only that. I was supposed to go out and commit to property purchases and enjoin an electrical company from building transmission lines near the property. I knew from years of experience with Ron that the "cart-before-the-horse" theory didn't register with him, but this was taking it to a new level.

I decided to venture forth and ask Harry:

"How much is this house going to cost?"

"Not much," he answered. "A little over eight million. I guess. Who knows?"

26

Juarez, El Paso's sister city, or, perhaps better to say, El Paso's dark sister, was experiencing a rash of brutality, rape, and murder of women. No one seemed to know why. Since the passage of NAFTA (North American Free Trade Agreement) in the '90s, American manufacturing plants had sprung up along the Texas-Mexico border, mainly at Juarez because of its easy access to Interstate 10. This had created an influx of people from all over Mexico as they heard about jobs with American companies (*maquiladores*) in Juarez. Many of these laborers were young women who not only wanted a job but a new way of life away from where they were born and raised in Mexico. Most parts of Mexico have the "baby factory" mentality when viewing its female population. There was a certain aura of independence and promise of a higher standard of living if you migrated from your Mexican village to Juarez to obtain work and a new way of life in an American factory.

Unfortunately, it didn't turn out that way. The average pay for *maquiladores* labor in Juarez was around fifty dollars a week, but somehow the word hadn't gotten back to the Mexican villages in Central Mexico that it cost more than that to live in Juarez.

The people kept coming, Juarez kept growing, and the crime rate kept rising. No one seemed able to get to the bottom of it. An enduring fact in Juarez is that there are no facts. Stories float across the city, stories of murders, of executions, of rapes and robberies, stories of men protesting and women holding vigils.

Years later, at the bridge linking Juarez and El Paso, a memorial would be erected to murdered and vanished women, pink ribbons fluttering in the breeze, each ribbon bearing the name of a soul lost to life. Many women were never found or even known of, so no ribbon fluttered in the breeze for them, similar to the American memorial, the Tomb of the Unknown Soldier. In Mexico, if you are lost or broken, that is your fate. It ends there.

At my home in Midland, it is the evening custom for my wife and me to settle down with a glass of wine and share the respective events of our day. Jane is not only a social scientist but a historian of women's rights.

One evening, the subject of what was happening to women in Juarez came up, and we wondered what was being done. What could be done? Were there human rights' organizations on the ground? I was able to tell Jane about Esther Chavez, a woman whom I had heard of. Somewhere around 1999, she founded "Casa Amiga," a shelter for abused women in Juarez. That first year she handled 250 clients, but the yearly admissions had grown into the thousands. I didn't know a lot about it, but I promised Jane I would look into it further. Maybe I could even get Jackie to make a contribution.

In the days following, I reflected on some of the things I had learned about Jackie and how she had helped people through her life and in her post-Hugh Bancroft, Jr. days.

In Carrizozo, that little New Mexican town where she lived, the children wanted a boxing program, so she bought them a professional ring. They wanted to bowl, so she built a recreation center. Ruidoso children wanted to ski, so she underwrote their annual lift tickets. One time, she toured a camp for troubled boys, and the bus she was touring in broke down; she bought the facility a new one. Then there was the time she read about a local child desperate for a liver transplant. She helped pay for it, and thereby saved his life.

I felt sure that, if I told Jackie the story of the women of Juarez, she would help. I had noted that, for the last several years, certainly since I had known her, there had been no philanthropic efforts. But those years had been filled with building the Theater, A.N. Spencer's final illness and death, and then, of course, along came Ron. Nevertheless, I promised myself I would tell Jackie about Esther Chavez and Casa Amiga in nearby Juarez.

27

Jackie had a good heart. She would help people when it occurred to her that a person or group of people needed help. This was particularly true through the first half of her life. She felt no calling to leave an inheritance to her children. She felt their preoccupation with money had made them selfish and narcissistic, particularly true of her son, Chris, in Dallas.

I once asked her if she knew the history of Andrew Carnegie. She told me she knew who he was but she didn't know much about him. I told her he had espoused that the accumulation of wealth was "one of the worst species of idolatry." He declared, "There is more genuine satisfaction, a truer life, and more obtained from life, in the humble cottages of the poor than in the palaces of the rich." He wrote about how his vast fortune should be left, and mused that it could be left to family members and heirs --- a step harmful to the recipients --- or he could permit the state to tax the estate away and use the money for public purposes.

A third way was the most appealing to Carnegie --- establishing a mechanism in the form of endowments or foundations in which surplus wealth could be administered "for the common good." Philanthropy, he argued, should help those who helped themselves, or perhaps it could endow libraries, parks, recreational places, works of art and public institutes to help people in body and mind.

In 1901, Carnegie sold his steelworks for two-hundred-fifty million and retired. He died in 1919, having left three-hundred-fifty million for philanthropic endeavors, from Carnegie Hall in New York City to the Carnegie Institute of Washington, the Carnegie Endowment for International Peace, and more than two-thousand-eight-hundred libraries.

Jackie listened with uncommon patience to my historical review of Andrew Carnegie. I had once given a speech on his life, so these facts flowed easily for me.

The discussion had arisen as Jackie complained about her children. I gathered there had been an argument on the telephone about money. Her complaint was not to me directly. It was more an expression of frustration mailed into the ethos. But, as she began to internalize on my review of Andrew Carnegie's philosophy, she told me that she knew there was such a philosophy, and she didn't disagree with it. She felt she had been philanthropic by contributing to politicians she believed were good men, and setting up the foundation for the Spencer Theater, and she had helped many people on instantaneous occasions.

I assured her I was in no way criticizing her or the good she had done. Her complaint about her children had reminded me of the life of Andrew Carnegie, and I suspected he had had similar problems in his life. It seems a common human malady that, when a parent has substantial wealth, the offspring see it as their source of livelihood and even life itself, rather than seeking self-reliance. Jackie told me she felt her boys had attempted to be successful in business. Wink had taken a turn at manufacturing automobiles, while Chris made investments as a venture capitalist. But none of this would have been possible without Bancroft inheritance, and when they failed, they always looked to her for more money.

Jackie went on to say she didn't know how long she would live. She had experienced several health problems in the last several years. It was difficult to know how much life was left. She wasn't in fear of death, and was mostly into taking life one day at a time. She wanted to continue traveling, playing golf, and enjoying life right up to the end, whenever that might be.

I felt that Jackie had been quite candid with me, which I appreciated. I'm not sure why I appreciated our talk. I guess if you do work for someone directly or indirectly, it lifts some of the burden to feel you actually know them on some level.

I felt that, but later realized I hadn't made the point I wanted to make in my spiel about Andrew Carnegie. Aside from the money, the thing that made Carnegie's money work for good was that he or his lawyers had set up a system, endowment systems, an organization that gave life and endurance to his philanthropic goals. Perhaps the Theater foundation could be enhanced for the good of performers or performing students beyond just contracting for traveling performances. Some of Jackie's early gifts to benefit children were so wonderful, perhaps a system could be set up that would be enduring.

I never got there in the discussion, and, really, I felt that Jackie expressed it: It was time to enjoy her life for the pure sake of enjoyment.

But as I left that discussion with Jackie, I couldn't help but reflect upon the opulence Ron had created with both Jackie's money and her permission. Millions of dollars of Chihuly glass, trays of diamonds and jewels, a warehouse full of art, sculptures and furnishings, a Rolls-Royce and a Bentley, all came about in a span of four years, and now we were building a house costing millions of dollars. I had once heard Jackie make a flippant remark. "Oh, Ronnie is just having fun." I wondered if Jackie thought that was all there was to it.

I was intrigued by a correlation I saw between Hugh Bancroft, Jr. and Ronnie Lee Morgan. Hugh, Jr. was always running from something. By studying his life, one could entertain several possibilities as to what he was running from, but it was clear he was perpetually trying to escape. Ron, on the other hand, was always running towards something --- a new or side love affair, the next purchase, the next business idea or project. It was setting the strategy for the next acquisition. There was never a belief system or philosophy.

I once read about "The Hedonic Treadmill." Consumers, the theory goes, routinely escalate their purchases, hoping new stuff will make them happier. Indeed, a new car feels wonderful, but sadly, the feeling lasts for only a few months. You get used to driving the car, and the buzz wears off. The consumer looks for something else to make him happy. Ron had come to the point where he could hardly finish one purchase before obsessively running to the next, not realizing how short-lived the happiness of the last purchase would be.

I was sure this must be what I had read about, The Hedonic Treadmill.

How this all started had become a muddle in my mind. I had my own life, my law practice outside of Ron and Jackie's activities, but this thing had mushroomed into something far larger than I could ever have expected. Was this a bad thing? Was it a good thing? Before one of their cruises, Jackie said, "I'm having the time of my life!" Indeed, she did seem to be enjoying herself. She didn't really seem to care that much about Ron's spending sprees and grandiose ideas. Sure, they had periodic arguments about money. I guess every family does, and, as most families do, they would come to resolution.

Nevertheless, it was overwhelming to me how two people could get two million dollars every three months and be broke by the sixtieth day. It was the same with Jackie's children and their trust distributions. A few million a quarter just wasn't enough. One could say it was a family tradition, but, as far as I could tell, running short on money had not been a consistent problem for Jackie --- until she met Ron. It was the syndrome of lack I could never get used to, that, even with all this money, the pervasive stress that more was needed.

28

The Lear stretched out over the Caribbean as we left Miami for the Bahamas. I looked down on the aquamarine vastness of the ocean below, and marveled once again at just how swift this aircraft was. We had left Midland that morning with Dallas Smith piloting, and a co-pilot sitting in the right seat. We often traveled at forty-five thousand feet, and at speeds that made commercial aircraft below us look as if they were moving at a very slow pace. The Lear was limited to Western Hemisphere travel but offered great flexibility in management of offshore enterprises. When it came to Hong Kong and its sister Chinese City, Shenzhen, we used the monotony of commercial flight.

Cuatro, my son and office manager, traveled with me. He had developed as my back-up on international business. There were times when teleconferences or e-mails could not adequately handle a situation, and an in-person, troubleshooting trip was necessary, instead. The problem may involve personnel employed in a business we operated for a client, or the problem may relate to a governmental regulation such as a licensing problem or permit requirement. Such problems required face-to-face diplomacy and one of us would have to dispatch to ease the matter.

The same held true in banking matters; a one-on-one, in-person meeting with the banker was required. The banker had to know we were the ones authorized to handle the transaction; verified *bona fides* were always required. Offshore banking is not one-stop, American drive-through banking. You have to know what you are doing in order not to risk your client's deposits. The banker on the other side of the transaction must reach a comfort level that you are not someone from the U.S. Department of Treasury, or an investigator from his own government seeking to make the bank a token casualty to exemplify the island's "get tough on tax havens" policy.

This trip was about banking. Ron's trust had funds that needed to be "parked" for a while until it was time to repatriate them. It was not a situation of tax evasion; that was not the intent. The goal was to stabilize the funds while the Verlander lawyers conducted aggressive post-judgment discovery procedures, both in the bankruptcy court --- which had jurisdiction over Ron --- and in the court of original jurisdiction where judgment had been rendered.

Privacy is a hard thing to come by. It is non-existent online, and use of the telephone for offshore banking purposes reveals a foreign number that can be followed. In terms of privacy, cash is unrivaled. It is highly portable, it is accepted worldwide, and, best of all, it does not leave behind a trace. Once issued, there are no records of transfers. It is a "bearer" instrument, which simply means that whoever holds cash is presumed to be its rightful owner.

It was the turn of the century, the new millennia, and I was aware the United States had initiated a goal of "cleaning up," in essence, abolishing tax-havens in the Caribbean. Over the years, I had used the Cayman Islands, the Bahamas, and Panama, as far as the Caribbean was concerned. Large corporations, such as Fortune 500 companies, primarily used Bermuda, tactfully referred to as an "offshore financial center" instead of a tax haven. Major corporations can evade American taxes by shifting their domicile. American citizens, however, are taxed by their home country, no matter where in the world they live, or where in the world they make their money. I have observed that, in some respects, corporations have more freedom and flexibility than individuals. That is why it is important to work within the shield of corporate authority.

Even though the principles of offshore banking for corporations are similar to those for individuals, Uncle Sam went after private banking. Now the Organization for Economic Cooperation and Development (OECD), with some thirty member countries, had joined the game and brought pressure on Caribbean governments to clean house in the private banking sector. I wasn't sure what we would find as we contacted the bank I had used in the past, but they knew we were coming. After a cautious meeting to determine the bank's stability, we could make a decision about making a deposit at that time.

Banks in the British offshore havens of Europe, Jersey, Gibraltor, Isle of Man, and Guernsey are used for privacy purposes, though Swiss banks are far more efficient; however, distance creates inconvenience. All of these havens had recently been targeted by the U.S. and the OECD, as well. If the Bahamian bank didn't prove satisfactory, we would return to Panama, which has one hundred-sixty-two banks in Panama City, many of whom are worldwide banks, including the Bank of China. The Bank of China requires a "gratuity" --- we Americans call it a bribe --- but, once it's paid, they are very reliable.

The only reason we did not head to Panama on this occasion was that I still had a bad taste in my mouth from a previous occasion for a different client. About two years before, one of my clients had difficulty retrieving his deposit. I flew down to Panama City and had to become contentious and argumentative in order to retrieve his money. It worked out favorably, but there had been a tense moment and certainly no need for me to go there to retrieve the money.

Various countries claim to be the oldest tax haven: Switzerland, followed by Liechtenstein, make such claims. They perfected the system at the turn of the 20th Century as people fled upheaval in Russia and Germany. What makes a tax haven is nil or nominal taxes, lack of effective exchange of tax information with foreign authorities, lack of transparency in operation of legislative, legal, or administrative provisions, and, often, self-promotion as an offshore financial center.

All of this was changing now, but the Bahamas had a long history of illegal transit, rum, cash, and slaves. Many a wealthy Northeasterner had become wealthy in these trades, serving as the American elite filled with ethical piety. I did not know what the future held for the Bahamas, but the old saying of "the more things change the more they stay the same" was bound to apply.

I had never used a tax haven for tax avoidance for a client, but the same characteristics evidenced by tax havens also provided privacy, which does not exist in the United States. Clients came to me to hide assets that were potentially in danger from creditors, lawsuits, or others seeking to take away their assets. This was our purpose in making an offshore deposit for Ron's trust. In time, we would either divest the money to him personally, or reinvest it on behalf of his trust.

Cuatro and I had entertained ourselves on the flight by telling each other stories of our experiences in conducting international business for our clients. He had never recovered from how the Chinese watched him eat or how they came up and touched him like in the Pillsbury ads where a finger pokes the doughboy and he giggles. Cuatro's size intrigued the Chinese. He took it all in good humor, and we discussed how we had recently read that now, with the advent of Western diet, the Chinese were not so small as they once were.

The plane began to reduce altitude, and I could see the islands on the far horizon. I took the opportunity to tell Cuatro about the hot rod I'd built as a kid in West Texas. Cadillac had just come out with a new paint with metal flecks in it, the first time that had ever been done. They called it "Bahama Blue." I thought it was absolutely beautiful, so I painted my hot rod Bahama Blue. It made me want to see what the Bahamas were like. At the time, I had no idea I would ever see this island country. I could not have guessed that, one day, I would be a lawyer and conduct business here.

Dallas and his co-pilot brought us in for final approach to a private Nassau airfield where we could clear customs. The Lear doesn't land slowly, it comes in hot. But we could immediately see palm trees of all sizes, how green the island was, and different colors of tropical flowers popping out everywhere. The plane pulled up with military precision.

Dallas opened the door and dropped the stairs. I stepped out of the plane first with my aluminum metal briefcase, cash locked inside. I was met on the tarmac by a tall, black, well-built customs agent. I handed him an unsealed envelope with five one-hundred dollar bills in it, and, with my best smile and direct eye contact, said:

> "Thank you for the use of your services, and your
> beautiful island. We are here to see the P.M., and
> will be here for two days. We are most concerned
> about the safety of our plane, but I am confident you
> will provide whatever protection is necessary."

I learned long ago that every country except Nordic and North America countries operates on the basis of "tips." In Mexico, it is referred to as the mordido. In some countries, it is not referred to at all, you just hand it over. But it is always important to appear that you are the one in charge, that you are merely accommodating customs' procedure.

We were whisked through a cursory customs check of our passports. Dallas and the co-pilot stayed with the plane.

As Cuatro and I climbed into the taxi to head for the Atlantis Hotel, Cuatro grinned and said, "So we have an appointment with the Prime Minister." I laughed. "You didn't know that?" Years ago, I'd also learned that it helped at customs to drop the name of the person in power who might be expecting you. The agent would never take the chance of checking up on the statement. It would just be a question in his mind.

The taxi drove along the shoreline road. No matter how many times you have seen the green and blue colors of Caribbean waters, on each revisit you're nevertheless impressed by how they create new hypnosis.

Red bougainvilleas lined the highway, as if to greet us with loving warmth.

The windows were rolled down, and moist air blew into the taxi as it sped towards our destination. Cuatro broke into a sweat; I wasn't far behind. We had left arid West Texas, flown in rarefied air at forty-thousand feet, and were now adjusting to sea level island weather. It felt good. We would soon acclimate.

The Atlantis Hotel rises up at the end of the island with its own opulence and majesty. It's a bit overwhelming. You wonder how such a structure could be assembled on this tiny island, indeed, how the island could even hold the building's weight.

Cuatro and I were led to our rooms on a subterranean floor. A huge aquarium that transgresses the entire base of the hotel shares one wall of the room. I felt the irony of our trip seeking privacy; the room felt anything but private with all manner of sea life swimming by---sharks, grouper, and other species. They peered in, we peered out.

After settling in our room, Cuatro and I caught a taxi to the bank. As soon as we walked in, I could tell that things had changed. Even though this was a private bank owned by two Brits and a Turk, the last time I visited it had been full of activity handling international trades in currencies and fully staffed. Now, the atmosphere was cold and stiff; there was very little activity. I noticed some employees glancing at us suspiciously out of the corner of their eyes.

A nice lady with a bright smile, obviously the person assigned to greet walk-ins, approached us and asked if she could help. I asked to see Mr. Peabody, the man I knew to be the administrator of the bank, and whom I had dealt with before. She informed us that Mr. Peabody was not there, but she took us in to see a nice young man purported to have answers for any questions we might have.

The nice young man was young, British, obviously educated in England. He explained that Mr. Peabody was not in the country at the time, and that, basically, he could take care of our needs. I questioned him about the American crackdown on Bahamian banking. He tried to reassure me, but I could see doubt and concern in his eyes, not so easy to detect because of his broad, bright smile.

We spent some time talking generally about privacy issues and recent Bahamian legislation mandating certain disclosures by its banks. Finally, I explained that I could not make a deposit without a personal visit with Mr. Peabody. I left my card and wrote my Atlantis room number on the back.

With time and experience, you learn that it is almost standard practice that the bank officer with authority --- in this case, Mr. Peabody --- is not in at the time of your call. You're told that he is not on the island. The junior officer you speak with will also tell you that he or she can accommodate your needs. It's simply a delay tactic that gives them time to check you out, a whole process unto itself.

Three years earlier, I had done business with Mr. Peabody for a different client. I considered it was possible because of the U.S.'s recent crackdown on tax havens that Mr. Peabody may *not* be there, anymore. On occasion, offshore banks shift their people around but act as if they are still present, at least by name. I didn't know. I did know I would find out in time, but I couldn't be in an American rush. It didn't work that way. Previously, I had waited three days before Mr. Peabody had gotten down to brass tacks with me.

Cuatro and I returned to the Atlantis and wandered through the cavernous subterranean aquarium. It was huge and gave the feeling you were actually under the ocean, itself. Different sea creatures drifted by, maintaining their mesmerized pace. We two flatlanders knew the names of very few of them.

From there, we moved up to the main floor and into the casino, a full-blown casino of international style, and, throughout, exploding displays of Chihuly glass of greens, blues, pinks, purples, large leaves and upward-shooting spikes resembling stalagmites. Reflective lighting shot through the glass at various angles. At the far end of the casino, on this side of the high-end, glitzy shopping area, was a huge Chihuly glass fountain, again with glass spikes, some ten feet tall, some springing out from the others, all of varying, vibrant colors with reflective light shooting up through them in alternating fashion. Periodically, water sprung up through the spikes in a geyser spray. The only other Chihuly display I had seen, other than in pictures, was at the Spencer Theater. The Theater was beautiful; this was spectacular.

I went back to the room to rest for a while. Cuatro stayed at the casino to hit a few slots. No sooner had I walked into the room and stared down the shark on the other side of the glass wall (I was glad we were separated), the phone rang. A pleasant female voice asked:

"Mr. Aaron?"

"Yes."

"Mr. Peabody cordially invites you to dinner at his home this evening at half-past eight. He apologizes for the short notice. Would you be able to attend?"

"Of course. I look forward to seeing Mr. Peabody again," I said.

"Thank you, sir. The limo will pick you up shortly after eight p.m."

Shortly after eight, there came a knock on the door. I opened it to a beaming black lady, tall and beautiful:

"Mr. Aaron?"

"Yes. I am Glen Aaron," I said.

"My name is Tisha. I am here to accompany you to dinner. The limo is at the portico."

"Thank you. Let me grab my jacket. I hope I am not underdressed," I said.

"Oh, no. You look quite nice," Tisha said.

I had on a light blue, button-down, open-collar shirt, blue blazer and khaki slacks. Tisha, on the other hand, was dressed to the "nines." She was a little over six-feet tall in her very high heels. She had very long, slender legs covered with black hose of an intricate criss-cross design, and a skin-tight black dress that covered only her bottom. I knew this to be very much the European style for eveningwear. Her white silk blouse with wide collar was open deeply to reveal her smooth ebony skin, and she smelled subtlely of something delicious. Around her long, slender neck, she wore a fine string of small pearls.

Tisha was quite chatty, placing her arm under mine as we walked through the hotel foyer. She spoke with both a British and a Bahamian accent. There were times when I couldn't quite make out what she was saying, but it sounded pleasant to my ears. Jasmine! I was sure it was jasmine I smelled.

It is not uncommon for Caribbean or Latin American bankers or entrepreneurs to send a lady in a limo to fetch their clients. I had experienced it before, though, if I were honest with myself, I had never felt completely comfortable. I was probably a most boring client. My heart was with Jane, and I was never interested in "extracurricular" activity. Beyond that, I didn't care to party to the extent where I felt bad the next day. The business at hand was my priority.

As Tisha and I rode to Mr. Peabody's house, she feigned interest in Texas, where she had never been, and asked the usual, typical questions. I, on the other hand, asked about her life and education and found her quite interesting. She was Bahamian. Her father was a minister in the government, and she had a bachelor's in economics. She had worked in international banking for two years, and had been with Mr. Peabody for about six months.

The limo arrived at the villa, a sprawling one-story white stucco-and-glass modern structure. It was well lighted, and sat on a small point overlooking the ocean. Just as the chauffeur opened my door and I stepped out, Mr. Peabody came out of the front door of the villa to greet me. It was good to see him again.

He was a small man in his fifties, not quite portly at about five-foot-eight, with thin gray hair and very white skin. He was dressed in a silk, black wedding shirt, the island and Latin American shirt worn for all occasions, tan linen slacks, and Gucci loafers. Ours was an interesting mix of dress; my conservative khaki slacks and blue blazer, Mr. Peabody's island evening casual, and Tisha, dressed as if going out. It all seemed to work. It was clear that we each felt comfortable in our choice of attire.

At dinner, we sat at a smaller glass-and-chrome table covered with a white linen tablecloth, linen napkins, and full-place settings. The larger dinner table, which would comfortably seat a dozen or so people, was in the dining room behind us. While we looked out over the blue-lighted swimming pool, a tall, very courteous black man in a starched white uniform served Tisha, Mr. Peabody and me an appetizer of *saviche* in small ice-cold crystal dishes. Mr. Peabody asked me to taste the wine for approval. I noticed it was a Chateau LaFitte Rothschild of the late 1980s.

Mr. Peabody was British, quite intelligent, and not snobbish. He'd always been a great conversationalist, and this night was no different. Dinner, with its main course of grouper, took at least two hours. Our conversation ranged from American geopolitical empire-building with British support, to the rise of Asia in world economics.

After dinner, we retired to the patio where we were served a brandy and a selection of Cuban cigars. Our conversation turned to the American crackdown on Caribbean tax havens, and Mr. Peabody, who had always been a straight-shooter with me, verified that pressure had been tough on his bank. It was an 'inconvenience,' as he put it, but, because of the international complexion at the bank, they simply moved deposits to other countries.

By evening's end, the decision was made to accommodate our deposit through the private bank to a Swiss numbered deposit. I would bring the money the next morning, and they would provide me with documentation for the numbered account. We could retrieve the deposit through normal wire transfer, using the account number and certain passwords at such time as we may require.

Mr. Peabody and I said our goodbyes, the chauffeur brought the limo around, and Tisha accompanied me to the limo. She told me she would have the limo pick me up at the Atlantis the next morning and bring me to the bank so I could make the deposit. She would meet me there and make sure all went smoothly.

I asked the driver, as we rode along the coast highway, to turn off the air conditioner and roll down the windows. The feel of Caribbean night air after a good dinner and fine wine is its own poetic experience. I felt relieved that Tisha's retrieving me from the Atlantis for dinner was nothing more than professional courtesy. I have been in similar circumstances where the nuance was different, and I was uncomfortable.

This night had been enjoyable, efficient, and successful.

29

The days when the Rolls-Royce or the Bentley drove through the little mountain village of Ruidoso presented a most incongruous sight. (I later learned the Rolls had cost three-hundred-thousand and the Bentley four-hundred-thousand.) People stopped to watch as if a funeral procession were passing. Jackie and Ron periodically took in the races at Ruidoso Downs.

On a Sunday, I returned to Ruidoso to attend the races with them. The following day, I would meet with the utility company, expecting to be assured there would be no power line construction along the property line of the house across from the Theater. But Sunday at the races was the usual scene; dense traffic getting into the track and the Jockey Club section. Pickups, RVs and general transportation from all over the Texas-New Mexico border herded into two lines cueing up to the track. There we were, in the Bentley, stuck between a Texas "dually" Ford pickup truck and a New Mexico RV as large as a Greyhound bus.

Finally, we reached the valet station. I could see the young valet's eyes light up as we approached. I felt I knew what was going through his mind; you could see the glee wash over his face. No doubt he would go home that night with great excitement and exclaim to his parents, "I got to drive a Bentley today!" "Really, what's a Bentley?" would likely be the parents' response.

Race after race passed as the Jockey Club cowboy or faux cowboy gentry placed their bets, watching the short races, but mostly visiting with each other. I say 'short races' because, unlike Eastern thoroughbred races, which circle the entire track, Southwestern tracks are mainly quarter-horse races of only a few hundred yards. They pass in the blink of an eye.

Night came and we returned to Jackie's house. It always surprised me how tiring an afternoon at the races could be; it felt like I had been working in the sun all afternoon.

As we came into the garage and got out of the Bentley, we all agreed to retire for a quick shower, clean up, and then head to the club for dinner. I knew that Ron and I would be faster and we could visit in private while we waited for Jackie.

As we waited for Jackie in the downstairs den among all the racing trophies, I mentioned to Ron that he'd seemed tense all day. I asked him what was the matter. He evaded the question. After a few silent minutes, I decided to mention that I was going to ask Jackie if she would care to make a contribution to the battered women in Juarez. Over dinner, I could tell her their story and talk about the dilapidated facility the little lady, Esther Chavez, had established in Juarez to help these girls.

"Oh, no, you won't," was Ron's immediate response. "In fact, you have been talking to Jackie too much. I don't want you talking to her unless I'm present."

I was taken aback. I didn't realize there had been any problem with my talking to Jackie all these years. I realized Ron was protective of Jackie ---probably more for his own sake than hers --- but I had no secret agenda. I had felt I was one of the team. I meekly told Ron I would abide by his instruction. We went on to other business.

As it turned out, Ron was beside himself with frustration. The construction of their house across from the Theater was not moving quickly. This was no cookie-cutter McMansion.

From viewing the architectural renderings, one could see the house was massive, sprawling, yet it nestled nicely into the contours of its surrounding topography. It had its own privacy, shielded from the two-lane state road that separated it from the Theater. One would not sense the full impact of its richness until they had parked under the portico entrance and entered its various rooms, each with unique vistas of the Sacramento mountain range.

Working with exotic materials from other countries was not only a formula for delay; its weight on the subsoil caused problems. Harry Farah had contacted several experts about the matter, but there seemed to be no simple remedy. The last thing anyone wanted was to build a unique structure of this magnitude and immediately have settling cracks show up. Harry quipped that Jackie would have Ron's balls if she saw that happening.

Ron and Harry were having arguments. Though we didn't talk about them on this particular night, I knew I had to be peacemaker and try to work out their problems. As soon as one problem resolved, another arose. The money kept pouring out.

With each passing month, it seemed Ron became more tense and more paranoid. He and Harry were good friends, but, on one occasion, he accused Harry of stealing and delaying the project so he could steal more. I was dispatched from Midland to Harry's condo complex in El Paso to solve the problem. I called in advance to let Harry know I was coming. He said fine, he would put me up in a little guest apartment he had by the pool.

El Paso has a unique history regarding immigrants. It comes as a surprise to people who do not live there. One generally thinks of Mexican immigration and border problems when they think of El Paso, but the city has a solid Jewish community, merchant families who settled there before the turn of the 20th Century: a large German community came perhaps as a result of the air base there; and an Arab community of Mediterranean descent, like Harry's family. Some are clothing manufacturers, some are in the massive warehousing industry related to the *maquiladores* across the river.

Harry was a unique fellow. He was a small, gentle man in his 70s, very Mediterranean in his features, with a quick wit that easily threw someone who didn't know him, off-guard. Through the course of his career he had built some beautiful structures in El Paso. When he built something, it wasn't small or modest. Until Ron's project came along, he had been content with completing his unique condo complex, which was ornate, rich in stone, marble, glass, and had a view looking out across El Paso. His stone, marble-cutting business supplied special-request customers, and he used these materials in designs for his own complex. I had the feeling this house for Jackie and Ron at Ruidoso would be his "last hurrah."

When I arrived at his condo, his sister, who served as his secretary, directed me to the dining room where Harry was working. I would later get to know Harry's sister by solving a few legal issues for her. If Harry's personality was unique, it was nothing compared to his sister, herself very Lebanese-looking, as well, but, unlike Harry, forever caustic in initial greeting.

When I walked into the dining room, I didn't see Harry at first. I looked out through the tall glass windows over the pool and toward El Paso. I turned and saw a long, expensive-looking dining table that seated about twelve people.

Then I saw a scaffold and I looked up. The ceiling must have been twenty-five feet tall. There was Harry, lying on his back at the very top, placing 24-carat gold leaf on Italian-style beams arching the ceiling.

"Hi, there! Is that you, Harry?"

"Yep, it's me. Who's that?" he asked.

"Glen. Glen Aaron from Midland."

"Oh, hi, Glen. I'll be down in a minute. It's taking me forever to get this gold leaf on."

"You look like Michelangelo painting the Sistine Chapel up there," I said.

"Not hardly. I can barely get this gold leaf on, let alone paint Abraham or some angel," he said.

When Harry came down from the scaffold, he was a sight. His large Lebanese nose was almost completely gold. I couldn't help but laugh.

"You have a gold nose!" I said.

"Yeah. It's my most valuable asset," he said.

Harry showed me to the guest apartment by the pool and poured us a drink. He didn't waste any time discussing the matter.

"Glen, I am really hurt with this allegation Ron has made. I don't have to do this job, and I don't have to steal."

"I realize that. It's why I'm here. By tomorrow, I'll have this thing resolved, I'm sure."

"In the morning, I'll sit you down at a desk in my office, and you can go over the books," Harry said.

"Harry, it is really difficult talking to you with that gold nose," I said.

He laughed and said, "Well, I've got to get back up on the scaffold. I want to finish the job before dark. Tomorrow, you can ask me anything you want."

The next day, it didn't take me long to go through the invoices, inventory, and payments. I was finished before noon. There was no evidence of wrongdoing.

I called and gave Ron my report. Harry came in while I was talking with Ron and asked to speak with him.

"I'm cooking Mediterranean Cornish hen and quail tonight with champagne, and having a couple of fellows over. Come join us," I overheard Harry say.

Apparently, Ron agreed. Dinner was at seven, drinks at six. I had planned to return to Midland, but Harry insisted I stay another night and attend dinner. He said I had never tasted a real dinner until I tasted his cooking.

I was glad I stayed over. Ron came. He and Harry made up. Two other fellows came; one, a dentist, the other, a well-known entertainment promoter. They were all gay men. I was the only non-gay there. That didn't seem to bother anyone in the least. With the exception of Ron, any one of these guys could have made a living as a stand-up comic. It was truly an enjoyable dinner, and the food was fantastic.

Ron wanted to talk.

The next morning, he and I met at a Denny's diner for coffee before I left for Midland. It was the end of October. Ron told me that he and Jackie planned to leave in February for a five-month cruise on the Radisson Seven Seas. He wanted to push the house project as fast as possible before their departure. He also told me that, as he had done before, he would ship purchases from around the world to my law office in Midland. I was to store and protect the shipments, as usual, and he would have them hauled to El Paso when he got back.

Finally, Ron told me that Jackie seemed in good health at this age. She had had problems of various kinds in the past, including ovarian cancer which had been taken care of. She seemed healthy and certainly loved her daily golf, but Ron said he knew the day was coming. He was concerned about what would happen when she died. He had grown accustomed to his high standard of living and didn't want to lose it.

"You know her children are going to sue me and cut me out when she dies," he said.

"That's the way those things usually go, all right," I said.

"I'm trying to get her to change her will. I've given up a lot over these last few years. I've got a right to be compensated," Ron continued.

"If she changes her will --- and I don't have any idea what Jackie's will says --- but if she does change her will, they are going to come after you with the age-old arguments, Ron."

"What are the arguments?" Ron asked, looking surprised that there could be any.

"Undue influence and competency," I answered. "Those are the arguments that are always used, along with some vestige of fraud. They usually work pretty well," I explained.

"So, what should we do?" Ron asked.

"Well, you are looking at powerful people. People with a lot of money and a lot of influence. People who can buy judges, congressmen, or anybody they want. Jackie's children may not be the sharpest knives in the drawer, but they are powerful. Never doubt that."

"Well, I think I've got Jackie talked into talking to Mike Line about her will. That's the Ruidoso lawyer she likes. He's pretty good at brown-nosing her. I'll talk to him, too," Ron said.

"Well, let me know if there's any way I can help," I said as we got up from the table.

We said our goodbyes, and I pointed the car east towards Midland.

Windshield time soon set in. I recalled the night Ron had come into his house in El Paso with Lorenzo hiding in the kitchen, crying. The night he told me he was going to marry Jackie, stay married to her for a year, get all the money he could, then divorce her. My, how things had changed and become more complex since that night. Now Ron wanted to become a Bancroft heir. I really didn't see that happening.

As the miles burned on under the West Texas sun, I began to wonder about Jackie, still an enigma to me. I could understand Ron who was just there to get what he could get. He could be courteous, pleasing, charming, and accommodating, but he expected largesse in return. He was one up on Jackie's children on that one. At least her boys, Chris and Wink, cared only about the money, nothing else. However, there did seem to be affection between Kathryn and her mother, though I knew they had their own bouts about money. It did seem odd how Jackie had had so many money arguments with her children. I guess, in some ways, she felt abandoned by them, at least, by the two boys. But hadn't she now shifted that dynamic to Ron?

I wondered if any of Jackie's marriages had ever been more than associations of convenience. The original Bancroft, Jr. marriage hardly had time to flower, limited to five years, three children, and a husband out partying most of the time. Dr. Spencer, bless his soul, was married to Jackie for a long time. He was always there. Somewhat like Ron now, he was on hand when she wanted to play golf, take a trip, or play Rummikub. Clearly, Jackie respected A.N. She had named the Theater after him, in part.

Another thing seemed so strange to me. In her entire house, not one picture of husbands past, children, or grandchildren present.

The miles burned on.

30

If you are known to have money, you are constantly under attack for donations, or asked to invest in some venture. Jackie was never able to escape the requests, no relief nor safe haven from any quarter. No matter where she went or what she did, no one saw Jackie for who she was, ever. They couldn't see past the dollar sign. Oh, bridge partners, politicians, service providers such as lawyers and CPAs claimed to know personally this lady with an odd personality. But they didn't know *her*.

In spending time with her in the way I did, with an inquisitive but respectful eye, I could see Jackie in reflection, reviewing her life.

From her chair, Jackie gazes into the dusk at the mountain. As if in a dream, she thinks back.

There was a man; tall, structured, handsome. He came to her, riding his proud gelding. He was escaping family but not their fortune. He was escaping mountains he could not climb, running from loves he could not love. He told of searching for new life, and it could be found in the still frontier of New Mexico. There, freedom awaited. Freedom from the haunts of the East. In her blissful youth, she ran with him, but only for a short time. The man left. He left her alone. She was still young. She could return. But return to where? Why? It was not good to be alone. Something is missing when you are alone. What is it?

There is another man. He is not running. He is not looking to escape. He is fatherly, but not soft. He is reliable, but not pernicious. He is companionship, but not control. Why not? Why not be together? She drifts into peaceful sleep.

She jerks, suddenly awake, still in her chair. It is dark. The view through the window, the snowcapped mountain Sierra Blanca, is gone now. Jackie searches for the thought before drifting off.

What was it? Was it that the poor hate the rich, that the rich are never satisfied, that they always want more? No, that was not it. That was a dream from another time, a time when she had made a gift or a donation and it was not well accepted. All she could remember was that this recent dream was incomplete. Perhaps it would return to her on another occasion, but the thought of that ill-accepted donation brought to mind how this society of wealth is one of despicability yet conditional acceptance.

Even the family evolves from verbal commitment of donation to subliminal distrust. Every family has concerns about money. The rich are no different from those of middle income; the rich just have more to worry about. When the Bancroft children found their quarterly or semi-annual trust distributions insufficient to carry them through, they called their mother for more. Such calls, after so many years, can strain the ties that bind family relationships. Feelings of distrust and blame are seeded when one was questioned why he always needed more, or when answers to requests are "no."

Jackie wrestled with this dynamic through the years. Once Ron came into the family picture, the dysfunction intensified. As she reflected on this history, she knew the dream had visited her before. It always left her feeling depressed. She didn't know why, though. In an awakened state, she took on the world with an attitude of "so be it." She would not allow the defects of others, or society for that matter, to get in her way.

Jackie had built an invisible shield. How she felt, who she was deep inside, was insulated by what might be called "Jackie logic." In a personal encounter, she could be brutally blunt by pointing out a physical imperfection or character defect of the person she was talking to. "You're too fat. You should do something about it." "You're not my friend. You just want my money." She used innumerable clichés and platitudes for defensive purpose, designed to throw the other person off their game. Over the years, her repertoire grew with use. That "devil take the hindmost" attitude she had had since childhood gave her the confidence to not care what people thought of her. It was *they* who were after her, not she who was after *them*.

Wealth, extreme wealth, attracts a type of court, as in the days of Louie XIV, that some of these people want to be part of. It gives them meaning to be seen rubbing shoulders with others in coterie. Even if the queen, in this case Jackie, is not present, there is a sense of acceptance when the court is in session, each person wondering about the other's special relationship with Jackie. Is it more special, more personal than theirs? This is the social effect of it: The pushing and crowding for pecking-order position, to be that special one who knows the lady just a little better than the next. Or to casually say, "When I was having dinner with Jackie the other night..." or to drop some other offhand remark indicating one's special privilege with Jackie. None of this is so much about money as it is about being accepted and part of an honored, monied circle. To the social elite, real or imagined, you are known by the clubs to which you belong and those with whom you associate. If you can claim a special or private relationship with a very powerful, rich, or influential person, then you are one up on the rest of the group. You are who your friends are, whether they are really your friends or not.

This scene played out on many occasions, in many places in Ruidoso, Albuquerque, Santa Fe, and even Palm Springs, but perhaps none more than at the Spencer Theater's Founders Club when a by-invitation-only dinner would be held before a performance. The most honored location was always Jackie's table. If you were invited to sit there, you were at the top of the heap. But if not, you were still free to mingle among the court and to visit at leisure with Jackie, unless she told you to go away.

I saw a woman, blonde, small in stature, thin in weight, wearing a black lithe dress and large reflective diamonds, too large for the size of the woman. She moved quickly with energy and conversation through the crowd. Someone said her last husband, her sixth, was a Texas billionaire oilman. I was standing next to Ron as he socialized with the Ruidoso mayor and his wife. The woman worked her way to Ron.

"Ronnie! Where have you been? You stood me up in El Paso," she said as she approached our group. She bestowed the light, gentle, not-to-be-touched, hug and kiss on each of Ron's cheeks.

"I did not, Jehri," Ron defended. "I wouldn't stand you up, darling."

"We were to have coffee or a drink or something," she giggled.

Suddenly, the now-ignored mayor and his wife watched the exchange, fabricated as it had been on so many previous social occasions, practiced but never quite perfected, a ritual of affectation. The lady made a point of ignoring me and those around us. Her purpose was clear. She wanted to sit at Jackie's table, with Ron and Jackie. She wanted center stage.

I have seen many of Ron's female friends in the high society of West Texas and Ruidoso. I have marveled at how well the cosmetic surgical industry must be doing. Here again, a perfect example; pursed lips, drawn cheek bones, balanced melon-lobed breasts just peeking out above the dress line. Of the certain requirements to maintaining celebrity status, this little lady knew them all; which ones to play, the timing with which to play each taunt. Jackie was not impressed. She continued dinner as if the lithe vision had never materialized.

Jackie was neither a fool nor an egotist; she knew that this popularity, this magnetism, was not specifically about her. As wealthy people throughout history have experienced, it was the aura of wealth that brought the court. It was the idea that this person had special connections in high places and could buy or have anything she wanted, anything that gave rise to the energy filling the room when having drinks and dinner with Jackie at the Spencer Theater's Founders Club.

At home in Alto Village, Jackie looks at the walls of her house. Except for the periodic placement of art, there is nothing to remind her of family, of husbands past, or children present. It is better to be insulated. The years of first one child then another calling for more money has taken its toll. The tension, the arguments, the manipulative games now hurt and leave her "on guard."

It was not that way in Carrizozo, the little New Mexican village where she reared her children. There, they had escaped the Bancroft curse of wealth. The children grew up in the freedom of a small cattle town, and lived modestly, without knowledge of the vast wealth behind their mother. For a time, Jackie was able to protect them from the knowledge that they, too, would have an unending flow of money.

Once they left the little town for prep schools and colleges in the East, innocence and modesty and humility were destroyed. The curse flowed through the heritage of The *Wall Street Journal*. Though there would be mountains of money and trust distributions, none of the children would feel it was enough. They would always want more. There was always the phone call to mother asking for part of her trust distribution, "just this one time."

Jackie came into huge wealth in her late twenties. She didn't come to it from poverty but from a well-to-do Denver family. Until her dying day, she lived knowing people would ask her for money, try to get close to get her money, or try to cheat her out of her money.

Fifty years is a long time to live in that environment. The drive by others to get her money never let up. It was always intense. From presidents, to senators, to governors, every Republican politician of any repute lined up at her door at campaign time every year for fifty years, waiting for his contribution. She contributed, though she wasn't sure why. She could have cared less about their politics, but, somehow, if you were a

Wall Street Journal heiress, it's what you were supposed to do. So she did it. Amazingly, for her entire life, she never called in the political capital she had accumulated. She never called in a chip, a request for a favor from a president, or someone in power. She'd never had a need to.

She loved the performing arts since a child, so, when requests came in from theaters in trouble, she helped. Eventually, it was just easier and more satisfying to build her own theater. She never understood how philanthropic organizations worked, so she stayed away from them. She had some misgivings, some suspicions of ulterior motives resounding from an early experience that hadn't worked out. But when she saw someone in need, if she were of a mind, she would immediately help.

It was crucial for Jackie to develop a sixth sense about when someone was trying to get close to tap her for a business investment. The pros circle as they do in any wealthy society. The promoters circulate where the money is. If approached, Jackie threw up a fence. Her simple logic was complete and perfect. "If I have all the money I need to buy anything I want, why would I invest my money and lose it?"

Though she lived modestly in comparison to her wealth, she had consumption down to a tee. If the trainer said a well-bred colt was up for sale for two-hundred-thousand dollars and Jackie wanted it, it was done. Just that quick. But until the end of her life, when she met Ronnie Lee Morgan and went on her gala end-of-life spending spree and celebration, she lived a comfortable, semi-social, modest life.

All lives have stress, even those where we wonder, How could that be? Jackie's stress did not come from how to make ends meet. As the Carrizozo banker who knew her from the '50s and '60s said, "Jackie could never connect the dots on money. If she needed more, she just called Denver and told them to send it."

She could, however, connect the dots on those wanting her money, including her kids. If it were not for one of them calling needing money for yet another investment, horse, or other perceived need, it was some non-profit or politician wanting to tap her wealth.

Jackie sat in her living room now, looking into the dark. What had it all been about? To what gain? She knew she had lived modestly. She knew she had broken with the Eastern elite's view of wealth. She knew that her involution in the community in which she lived was both real and surreal. She didn't keep pictures of family in the house because pictures brought feelings of distrust as much as they brought feelings of family warmth. She did keep a picture of her granddaughter, Kathryn's daughter, who studied opera in Europe. Jackie adored the girl, who, in many ways, was a young replica of herself.

The source of the peace, the stability, had been A.N. Spencer. He had always been there for her, from delivering her babies to providing a stable home life while they grew up. The feelings weren't deep, perhaps, in the eyes of many, but they were stable, and the years provided equilibrium.

Now her social effete was giving way to this new thought. How many years did she have left? She had never participated in "positional" consumption -- feeling good because she possessed something others did not. That was not Jackie, and she knew it. When you have the complete confidence of immense wealth, you don't even think in those terms.

But, she wondered, how many years do I have left? How much longer shall I live? Five years? Ten? How should I spend that time? How, indeed?

Jackie decided to make an appointment with the psychic in California whom she and Kathryn had used on occasion. Twenty-five thousand dollars a session seemed extreme, but she had to know, and she had to know the meaning of these dreams. The psychic had proven herself before.

What was said in that psychic session we'll never know. What was clear was that Jackie returned from California energized and ready to get on with life.

31

Ron came to see me in Midland on a surprise visit. It would not be long before he and Jackie left for their cruise. He was worried.

"I don't know whether Jackie is going to change her will," Ron said.

"What do you mean?" I asked.

"Mike Line, the Ruidoso lawyer, and I have been talking to her. She understands that I have to be protected from her children in case of her death, but she's dragging her feet," he explained.

"Like I said before, Ron. If you get Jackie to change her will to make you an heir, at her death those Boston and Denver lawyers are going to be all over you."

"They are going to be all over me, anyway, even if she didn't change her will," Ron said.

"I hadn't thought of it that way. You're right, but that's why you've got your trust that we set up that Jackie has funded," I responded.

"Look, Glen, I need you to do something. I'm not sure what. She will get around to changing her will. I know she will. What can I do to protect myself?"

"Well, you need a game plan, Ron. You know that if Jackie changes her will to make you an heir, the Bancroft trust lawyers are going to argue that you pressured her, that she didn't do it of her own free will."

"So what should I do?"

"I would say, have Jackie examined by an expert, a competency expert, who could testify at a probate hearing as to her competency at the time of the will change."

"Do you know anyone like that?" Ron asked.

"No, but I could check around," I said.

Before Ron left, I pushed him on why the hubbub about Jackie's death, or, at least, her will. Was she feeling all right? He assured me she was. It was just that they had been married a long time, and he needed to be taken care of and protected when she was gone, he explained.

I didn't realize being married for four years was considered a long time, but I didn't quibble with Ron about it. He never appreciated being taken lightly.

So, I turned my attention to finding a psychologist-type who might be an expert on competency. I called John Judge, my trial lawyer friend in Austin, to make an inquiry. As a matter of fact, he did know of just such an expert who could both test and testify, and had done so in numerous trials on both sides of the fence.

I immediately contacted the man and, over the course of two one-hour conversations, explained the situation. Explaining the Ron/Jackie relationship to someone who has no idea who they are was always a taxing description. Fortunately, I wasn't required to do it often. Yes, Jackie Bancroft Spencer Morgan is a Bancroft heiress of *Wall Street Journal* wealth. Yes, this is her third husband, and yes, he is gay, and they have been married only four years and she is going to change her will to include him as a Bancroft heir. Yes, she is in her 70s, he, in his 50s. Time was of the essence because they were soon leaving on a six-month cruise.

The professional was actually a published psychiatrist, an expert in dementia, competency, and elements of undue pressure on the elderly. I felt that my Austin lawyer friend had sent me in the right direction, and, if Mike Line, the Ruidoso lawyer, and Ron were going to work with Jackie on redesigning her estate, this would be the man to back them up, depending upon what his tests of acumen and focus indicated.

I called Ron in Ruidoso and told him that I had found the man with proper credentials for testing Jackie. I asked how he wanted to proceed. He said he would talk with Jackie and Mike Line and let me know.

About a week later, Ron called and said to send the psychiatrist, Jackie was willing to go through with the testing. He wanted it done, without delay, the next morning.

"Ron, this guy is a professor, has a clientele. He's famous. He's not going to just drop everything, get on a plane in the morning and work his way to Ruidoso," I said.

"He has to. This has to be done now! Pay him more money," Ron demanded. "Send the Lear to pick him up and take him back."

He was frantic. I suspected the cause. He had Jackie in the frame of mind to change her will. He didn't want her to change her mind. Apparently, Mike Line had agreed that a competency test by a reputable professional was the thing to do, and they had raised Jackie's comfort level for the process.

As I suspected, the psychiatrist was not willing to drop his commitments for the Bancrofts, or otherwise. He gave me three dates on which he could interview and test Jackie in Ruidoso, if I sent the Lear and he returned to Austin immediately after the process. I called Ron and told him to get with Mike Line and Jackie and pick a date. They did, and I scheduled the round-trip flight and logistics for the doctor.

I never met the psychiatrist, though I later read a copy of his report. I chose not to be present at the interview or testing. I wasn't sure why. I did figure that, at some point, there would be one hell of a lawsuit over this will change. I saw myself as Ron's lawyer and trustee, and, although I, no doubt, would be called in to testify about the trust, I was not Jackie's lawyer. I had just spent a lot of time with her, but even that had dwindled since Ron's admonition that I had been talking to her too much. I figured that her estate matters would shake out, however it was to come about. I wouldn't be the lawyer involved in that battle.

The psychiatrist's report was a "hoot" to read; vintage Jackie. There were a few casual lapses of concentration, but nothing abnormal for Jackie. If she didn't care what happened on a certain day or major event that other people thought was important, she just didn't care. It wasn't of particular importance, at least, not to her. If most people were supposed to know how much money they had, she didn't. Did it really matter? If asked how much she paid for a particular item, she didn't recall. Did it matter? She could ask the accountant to look it up.

When it came to relationships, she was right on the mark. Yes, Ronnie was spending a lot of her money. "He's having fun, and I'm having the time of my life. No. I don't care if there is any money left when I die. My kids have their own money. I don't even speak to my son Chris. He is only interested in how much money he's going to get when I die. When Ronnie and I get back from this cruise, I will change my will so that, when I die, my kids won't cheat him. He will be taken care of."

The psychiatrist saw nothing incompetent about this woman who was approaching 80. Whether her decisions or attitudes would be rational for someone having a working class background may be up for dispute, but Jackie had never worked a day in her life and often reminded people of that fact. She was clear-cut and hard-headed about what she wanted and when she wanted it. She always had been. Nothing was different now.

As was so often the case, I didn't hear from Ron once he got what he wanted, until he wanted something else. Such was the case with his drive to have Jackie change her will to include him, and for me to find a competency expert who could testify, after interview and testing, as to Jackie's competency. I didn't have a relationship with Mike Line, so I hadn't expected any communication from him, but, at the very least, I thought Ron would let me know how the will thing came out with Jackie. He didn't. In fact, as it turned out from later revelations, he secreted from me and the world the nature of his meetings with attorney Mike Line in Ruidoso.

The relationship between Ron and me seemed to become tense before this last cruise, but I couldn't understand why. His original plan was to have me fund his blind trust in a manner that he could have sufficient income when Jackie passed away. That trust was now kicking off about twenty-five-thousand dollars a month, net. I knew he had become obsessed with the idea of perhaps becoming an heir to the *Wall Street Journal* fortune, at least to that portion of Jackie's inheritance, but there really was nothing I could do to assist in that effort. That was between him and Jackie.

To add to the growing strain between Ron and me, Jackie contacted me --- actually, sent word --- one day not long before that final, fatal cruise, that she wanted to talk to me. I was instructed to fly the Lear up to Ruidoso the next day for a golf game. She had something on her mind, and something she wanted me to do.

Of course, I did as instructed, and while we were playing, she told me about Claire Greenwood, her horse trainer. She liked Claire and felt she had worked hard for her, as well as having won some races for her. I knew about Claire. She was the trainer who had complained about how jockeys riding competing horses bumped Jackie's horse coming out of the gate at the races so the horse would be knocked off stride and could not win. I reminded Jackie that, at her request, I had sent my sons up to the track at Ruidoso Downs for a called meeting with the jockeys in the paddock to straighten them out. The message was simple and straightforward: If any bumping occurred coming out of the gate in that day's race, the boys would be doing some bumping of their own. Not surprisingly, Jackie's horse won.

Jackie laughed at the remembrance and told me I should have been there in the winner's circle after the race with Claire and my sons. She would have given me the Waterford crystal vase trophy.

But what Jackie wanted to talk to me about on this day was that she wanted to give the race barn at the Ruidoso Downs track to Claire --- just give it to her. Now, this was no farm barn. It was an elegant structure for stabling, training, and exercising pampered racehorses. It also had a very nice living quarters in which Claire lived. I estimated its current value was probably around a million dollars, and I could have been off by a million.

I asked for a second time, "Jackie, are you sure you want to just give the race barn away?"

In true Jackie style, she indicated that I should not ask that question again. She wanted the papers drawn, signed, and filed before she and Ron left on their next six-month cruise, which was to be within the next few weeks.

After the golf game, the Lear brought me back to Midland. The next morning at my office, I began working on the papers to assign the race barn to Claire. About mid-morning the intercom interrupted me. Ron was on the phone, calling me from his home in El Paso. The phone call began friendly enough. Ron greeted me on a beautiful morning, asked about Jane, my wife, and how we were doing, and then asked what I had been doing relative to work.

I explained that Jackie had called me up to Ruidoso the day before and instructed me to convey the race barn to Claire. I was working on the necessary instruments to do so. Ron went into a tirade. He told me that under no circumstance was that going to happen. He detested Claire. He called her a cheat and a fraud and told me to drop the whole thing immediately, so that's what I did. I called my secretary in, gave her my work to that point, and told her to just make a file.

About a week later, I was in Ruidoso for a Spencer Theater dinner and show performance with Ron and Jackie. We had driven the Bentley, and there was a lot of oohing and aahing as we drove up under the portico. At some point in the evening, Jackie asked me if I had given Claire the race barn, as if I could have just done that on my own. I told her that, "No, Ron instructed me not to." She said it was her barn and Claire was going to have it. Jackie told me to get the papers to her immediately so she could sign them.

I wasn't sure how to handle this, but, when I returned to my office the next day, I finished the conveyance instruments and just mailed them to Jackie's house in Ruidoso. I would later learn that, after Jackie's death, she had, indeed, given the trainer, Claire Greenwood, a tremendous gift -- the race barn at Ruidoso Downs.

That event occurred just before Jackie and Ron's last cruise, a few months before her death. Jackie could be hugely generous when she wanted to be and for whatever reason, which she usually kept to herself.

As she chose to make this generous gift to her horse trainer, perhaps she had observed just how difficult it was for a woman to succeed in that environment but admired Claire's fighting spirit. I would also wonder, as I do now, why make that gift then, why at that time? Did Jackie have some foreboding, some premonition about this last cruise?

32

The spring of 2003 came to Texas as it had for centuries. The Hill Country popped with blue bonnets, Indian paintbrush, and a myriad of unnamed colorful flowers. The Llano River, a clear spring-fed river, rushes through pink granite boulders where bass spawn and life begins anew.

My son Cuatro and I made our annual spring trek to the Llano to get away and rejuvenate from the daily strain of law practice and business administration.

Ron's trust had stabilized over the few years of its existence with its Internet casino out of Belize and a developing trade out of China. It was all so unorthodox because we never completely knew what Ron was putting into or taking out of the trust. Everything was supposed to flow through the law office so we could keep up with additions, but that's not what happened. There was no disciplining Ron in a business sense. There never had been. But, as far as I could tell, the trust was in good shape.

Ron was in the process of buying yet another villa on the beach at Puerto Vallarta. This one was about six-thousand square feet and cost over two-million dollars. As far as properties purchased, it was number four: two condos, two villas.

The first villa, located on the mountainside overlooking the bay and Puerto Vallarta's red tile rooftops, opened onto the quiet, private sandy beach of the bay, itself. The view of the sails and boat activity was at bay level. The villa's catacomb of rooms was separated by fountains that offered pleasing sounds of rushing water. Of traditional Spanish style, with tile floors and stucco walls, the villa was of new construction.

Much of the art and high-end furnishings warehoused in El Paso represented just a mass of inventory to us at the law office. We really had no idea what it was or how much it was worth. I had been at a loss to value the Bentley or the new property and house being built across from the Spencer Theater. I had yet to file a trust tax return with the government because, about the time we felt we had a handle on things, here came something else we hadn't known about. Representing Ron was not an easy task, perhaps more so because we had to guess at things rather than have full knowledge. But my little law firm was well paid for its services; a nice change from the earlier years of representing Ron.

As for the rest of our practice, it had been a busy winter and spring with new clients coming in and new problems to solve. It was nice spending a few days and nights in the Hill Country wilderness.

Clairvoyance was never my forte. There was absolutely nothing in my mind in the spring of 2003, on the Llano, that would portend the events to come. In fact, Cuatro and I talked very little business. We fished, we joked, we told stories we'd told many times before, and enjoyed them as much as ever. We did what you do in spring: renew.

I had not been home long when I received the Mayday call from the Radisson Seven Seas. Ron was panicked, but I could not pick up on the underlying source of his panic. That ship had been in Cape Town only a few days before. In fact, we had received a large, expensive shipment of varied art objects and sculptures that Ron had purchased at Cape Town.

If Jackie was this ill and desperate at this point, she had to have been quite ill while docked at Cape Town, which certainly had adequate medical facilities to address her health problems, or, at the very least, temper her medical condition.

Now, we were out in the middle of the Atlantic without even a diagnosis. Ron was suddenly afraid. I not only heard the fear in his voice, I could tell by what he said and how he said it. He was inconsistent, as if he wanted to design a story but hadn't thought how.

At first, he told me Jackie had just gotten sick, as in last night. Later, he told me, well, she had been sick for about a week, hadn't left the ship at Cape Town while he shopped for several days and met a young guy he had had a fling with. When he got back to the ship, Jackie was very sick, but he hadn't told the captain.

Just before he left on the cruise in February, Ron said he couldn't stand being married anymore. He had had it. He went through these fits periodically but got over them. This time, however, he seemed particularly irate. Apparently, Jackie had not yet changed her will, and they were leaving on the cruise. It seemed to be of huge importance to Ron that, before the ship left the dock, she had to have changed her will to make him a beneficiary. I could never make out why, and Ron was never forthcoming with a reason, other than Jackie owed it to him.

Discussions about her will had wavered back and forth for about a year-and-a-half, yet Ron never wanted me involved. He would, seemingly, confide in me at times, but he was never fact-specific.

I could tell that he periodically talked to family members. He seemed to have a rapport with Jackie's daughter-in-law, Wink's wife, the one we called the "trophy wife." I thought he was trying to drum up support for becoming an heir, but his rendition of what he tried to do, or how he tried to do it, was always vague. I doubt it was even clear in his mind, other than just wanting to be a Bancroft heir and richer than he already was.

The three days and nights my team spent getting Jackie off the Radisson Seven Seas and into the hospital in Albuquerque where she wanted to be were exhausting. After that intense period, all communication ceased. It was as if Ron and Jackie and this persistent saga of the last five years had suddenly dropped off the map, as if the earth had opened up in some surreal fashion and swallowed the whole thing up.

Teresa, my legal assistant, called the hospital daily to get a status report on Jackie's condition. Like most hospital calls of that nature, the report she was given was pretty sanitized, and we didn't really know how Jackie was doing.

On the evening of May 10th, Jackie passed away after surgery for an abdominal obstruction.

I sat at home thinking about Jackie, about her history, her life. I thought about playing golf with her, and how she loved the game, of how she laughed at me at how poorly I played card games and Rummikub. I wondered if she really did receive the satisfaction she sought on her gala, end-of-life spree. She had been like the Merry Widow after A.N. Spencer's death. She had made it clear that she wanted to travel, play, spend money, and have the "time of my life." As she had indicated to the examining psychiatrist about her competency, she didn't really care whether or not there would be any money left.

At the end, there was about sixty million in *Wall Street Journal* stock, and roughly another sixty million in Jackie's personal assets. This did not include the approximately forty million in Ron's trust. As personal American wealth compares in the new millennia, that is not large.

What *was* large was The *Wall Street Journal* stock, itself. It was not known at the time, but three years later, Rupert Murdoch would pay five billion for The *Wall Street Journal*. This block of stock represented a significant position of ownership in the most important, the most influential financial reporting system in the world. Until its founding by Charles Dow and Edward Jones and the development of Dow's formula for averaging equities traded on the New York Stock Exchange in the 1890s, there had been nothing like it. Worldwide, the publishing company grew to mammoth proportions. Its prestige and power had not diminished, and its future worth seemed incalculable. But, as far as I could tell, this was the end of the Ron/Jackie Bancroft Spencer Morgan saga.

I had never seen anything like it. I sat in my chair at home, wine glass in hand. I reminisced about this lady and her life as I had come to know it. I thought about Ron Morgan and how my representation of him had brought me into bizarre circumstances. I couldn't help but be glad I had been part of it. The experience had stimulated my curiosity and observations of what people think and why they do what they do. Originally, I just wanted to observe and see where events led, but I had become too involved. I sat in judgment when it was not my place to judge but rather to observe and to represent.

Soon after Jackie's death, Ron called and said he had arranged a memorial at the Spencer Theater. He wanted Jane and me to attend, sit in the row behind the family and directly behind him. Seating was assigned and preferential, as it had been in the Founders Club where it was always important to be close to Jackie because your seated position lent credence to your own importance.

Jane and I left Midland before daylight and headed for the Spencer Theater.

As one crosses the Texas/New Mexico state line, the vast prairie, historically known as the Llano Estacado, reaches out for a hundred miles as the steppes of the Rockies and then up the foothills to the mountain village of Ruidoso. The land is flat and covered with knee-high golden grass waving in undulating gentle winds. The morning sun reflects back a golden aura to a crisp blue sky, a vista often painted by landscape artists as they attempt to capture the beauty and the feel of freedom. Soon, the snowcap of the great mountain, Sierra Blanca, came into view. Jane and I were silent as we absorbed this sunrise.

We arrived at the Theater mid-morning but a few minutes late. Due to road construction in the foothills, the drive had taken a little longer than expected. The valet immediately took our car, and we hustled into the auditorium.

As we entered the Spencer Theater, Jane and I had wondered what picture, what scene, we would encounter. From his seated position in the front row, Ron saw us coming down the aisle. He quickly rose, intercepted us as we tried to slip quietly into a back seat, and brought us to our assigned position in the third row.

We had not seen Jackie's son Wink nor her daughter Kathryn since the wedding almost five years earlier. We had never met Chris, since Jackie preferred not to be around him.

There, in the rows ahead of ours, sat the disconnected family seamed by one value, the value of money, and always wanting more, the Bancroft legacy.

I noticed that Jackie's brother, who had been institutionalized with schizophrenia since childhood, was there with his caretaker. I thought it a touch of class to include him, and wondered who had caused that to happen.

Chihuly may have been there, but I didn't see him.

I caught a glimpse of the Governor and several other politicians whose names I couldn't remember.

Sitting in the third row at a memorial, one can hardly crane one's neck for too long to view attendees without becoming obvious and crass, so I stopped looking. But I did wonder what was going through the mind of each relative.

I wondered at the people who filled the Theater, at what had brought them here. Was there a deep-seeded feeling for Jackie, or were they just part of the entourage, the court?

Ron had orchestrated his usual perfection for show and presentation. We sat below the stage, looking up with a clear view. In the center was a tall glass pedestal encasing the urn holding Jackie's ashes, and at least five thousand red roses splayed, tossed and surrounding the pedestal. It was simple yet elegant.

The non-denominational preacher from Palm Springs eulogized the glories of Jackie. I could not recall if he was the one who had married Ron and Jackie. To his credit, he did not proselytize a particular faith or browbeat the necessity for a hereafter, so often encountered in funerals and memorials in the Bible Belt. I have observed that such gatherings are more for perpetuating a religion than the celebration of a life, well lived or not.

Chris took the podium and spoke of his mother as if there had never been a moment of estrangement or dysfunction but only closeness and love. I assumed he was appointed for the eulogy since he was the eldest of the children. His words fell on ears that could care less.

From years of observing this family dynamic, I was sure those interested in control of the *Journal*, those with Machiavellian thoughts, were already at work trying to anticipate Chris's next move. It would be Chris, the self-proclaimed venture capitalist, who would try to capture *Journal* stock. Wink and Kathryn would have to be careful not to let that happen to their detriment. Ron sat in respectful silence in the first row as part of the family. Surely, his mind was at work countering the litigious charge that was soon to come, now that he had made himself a Bancroft heir.

Jackie's granddaughter, who Jackie idolized and who had been in operatic training in Europe, followed Chris on stage, and tried to sing one of Jackie's favorite arias. But her emotion was too great and she couldn't complete it. She was young and not yet insulated with the cynical shell that wealth and family in-fighting bring.

The preacher came back onto the stage. As he talked, my mind wandered.

This auditorium, in this magnificent structure that Jackie built, was, this day, but a cave. We saw the stage and Jackie's glass pedestal as light, but it was the reflection of light, not the light itself. There were no forms, not in this cave. There were shadows on the wall, and they danced --- the shadow of materialism, the shadow of social acceptance, the twin shadows of power and control. Puppets --- deceit, envy, and delusion --- played their parts. There was a way out of this cave, there was a way to reach the light where the shadows did not dance. But no one would reach it. Not these people, not here.

The memorial which honored Jackie but did not do her justice came to a close. It had failed to capture the spirit of a young, preppy girl from Denver running away with an older Eastern elite to live a wealthy private life in the mountains of New Mexico with three different husbands; a spirited life that ended with a fling of travel, consumption, and entertainment.

The front three rows, with the first row family and the third row friends of the last husband, were led out. The gallery followed.

Politicians and family members rushed to the small commercial airport down the road from the Theater to their waiting private jets. For the politicos, a money source had dried up. Yet, it was important to be seen at memorials, funerals and weddings of the wealthy, not just for future contributions but for continued backing of the powerful.

For family members, it was time to leave. There was nothing to stay here for, not in Ruidoso. It was time to meet with lawyers to prepare a strategy that would capture a larger share of Jackie's estate, most importantly, her share ownership of The *Wall Street Journal*. Ron, who remained, had to decide what law firm to hire to defend his trust. No doubt that would be the first target.

Ron said his goodbyes to various attendees as we stood in the Theater foyer next to the reflections of the red Chihuly art glass tree. The noon sun streamed through the segregated glass and stainless steel room, with the gathering of people wearing their finest.

I pulled Ron aside and said that we needed a short meeting before Jane and I headed back to Midland.

He and I stepped into one of the Theater's private meeting rooms. I intended to discuss or ask how we were going to defend his trust, and if he had a specific law firm he wanted me to contact. The conversation didn't start out that way.

Past experience in representing Ron had planted a seed of paranoia in me. There had been a rush, or so it seemed, to cremation after Jackie died in the hospital. Not only that; it had been strangely quiet from Ron's quarters since the night of his hysterical call from the Radisson ship. I didn't believe for a moment that he was sitting quietly by Jackie's side in her final days at the hospital, but I had no idea what was going on. Nor did I know if Jackie's children would demand an inquest or a private investigation involving the ship's personnel. God only knew they had the power to follow that line of thinking.

As we stepped into the quiet privacy of the room, I said:

"Ron, I haven't heard from you since you got home. I'm a bit uneasy."

"What do you mean?" Ron asked.

"Some things don't add up about the final days on that ship. Did you do something you shouldn't, or not do something you should?" I asked.

"What are you saying? What are you accusing me of?" Ron went into reaction.

"I'm not, but, Ron, if there are facts I need to know, you need to let me know if I'm to defend you. Don't get us blindsided as you've done in the past."

"I can't believe you are accusing me, after all I've done for you. I'll tell you what. I think you've stolen one-hundred-thousand dollars from my trust, and I'm going to get a lawyer and come see you," Ron said.

"What the hell is this --- stick and switch? I haven't stolen anything from your trust, Ron. We'll have that conversation any time you want it. All I'm saying is that, if there is an inquest and you want me representing you, I need to know what went on, on that ship."

Ron was livid. I was upset.

I gathered Jane up in the foyer and we headed out of the mountains of Ruidoso for Midland. Jane could tell I was upset and tried to get me to talk, but my head was spinning. Ron's attitude had suddenly changed. Suddenly, after five years of near-total dependency, it was as if I was no longer the advisor and protector. It almost seemed as if I were the enemy. But why?

33

The glow of Jackie's memorial at the Spencer Theater nestled in the Sacramento Mountain foothills and the shadow of the great Sierra Blanca had hardly faded before the battle for inheritance had begun. Ron chose to keep me uninformed as to how that battle might be shaping up. He had always anticipated that the Bancroft children would sue him upon Jackie's death. That was why he had acquired all the jewels, art, vehicles, real estate, and cash he could, placing most of them in the trust I designed for him. It had been his original intent that the trust would be his war chest for defense, as well as his survival kit, during the course of the ultimate legal battle.

In the first few years of representing and advising Ron, I made it clear that, in addition to properties in the U.S., like the Century Club house at Palm Springs and the Alto Village house at Ruidoso, he needed properties and income beyond the jurisdictional reach of a U.S. court. Thus, the international aspect of the trust, with its cyber casino out of Belize and its international import/export trade out of the Hong Kong corporation. I felt that the trust, along with the foreign corporations it owned, was reasonably designed to withstand the onslaught of litigation once Jackie had passed from this world.

Jackie knew about the trust. She understood that it had to be utilized for whatever she decided to give Ron, or whatever Ron talked her into giving him.

On one occasion, the occasion when Jackie decided to deed the Palm Springs house to Ron, she suggested to me that using Ron's trust was too complicated. It seemed to me a complaint of cosmetics.

When she looked at the deed, Ron's name was not on it. The three-million-dollar home was going into Ron's trust. She wanted the deed to somehow show Ron's name. We sat at the Century Club where the notary patiently waited to notarize Jackie's signature on the deed. I went back over the reasons for the trust, that Ron owed over two-million dollars to unpaid creditors, and he was in bankruptcy. Those were the reasons why his trust had to be utilized. I did not mention that the trust's alternative purpose was as a vehicle of defense against the Bancroft children upon Jackie's death. With simple clarity, Jackie suggested that we just pay off these creditors. Then Ron could take whatever she gave him in his own name. I didn't doubt for a minute that Jackie could call Denver for enough money to do that very thing.

At that point, Ron stepped into the conversation and told Jackie he was dead set against such an action. For one thing, the Verlander trial had been a bitter struggle. Even though Ron may have been wrong in his double-billing, the verdict with its million-dollar punitive damage award was overkill. He would have no part in paying off the creditors and coming out of bankruptcy. In fact, he drove to El Paso for the last creditors' meeting of the bankruptcy court in the Rolls Royce and wore his diamond Cartier watch, appraised at one-hundred-thousand dollars. Ron loved pushing the debt of his creditors in their faces.

He told Jackie that transferring the house to his trust was just like giving the Century Club house to him, individually. Jackie signed the deed.

But all of that was in the past. Now, Jackie had died and I didn't know what was going on. I figured I had really pissed Ron off, questioning his care of Jackie, or lack thereof, on their last cruise. It seemed as though he was shutting me out, while the day-to-day work of running his trust continued.

At the same time, I was embroiled in a difficult and unrelated trial in Midland that usurped all of my attention. In fact, the night I finished that trial, a constable met me coming out of the courtroom and served me with papers.

I didn't look at the papers right away. Being served with papers as a registered agent for some corporation I represented was not an unusual occurrence for me. I didn't even look at the lawsuit until the next day.

When I did read the lawsuit, it took me a while to understand. Even then, I didn't completely comprehend what was going on.

Mike Line, the Ruidoso lawyer, along with Jackie's CPA and her son, Chris, all as co-trustees of a twenty-year-old trust of Jackie's, was suing me as the villain who had had undue influence on Jackie and pressured her into making transfers of property and cash into Ron's trust. I was being sued, personally, and as trustee of Ron's trust. The premise seemed to be that, by Jackie funding Ron's trust, this older trust of which Chris was a beneficiary was deprived of distributions from Jackie.

One never knows the machinations contrived by lawyers as they design litigation. Trial lawyers pride themselves, indeed spend both waking moments and dream sleep, on creating slippery traps for their opponents. I had not expected to be sued personally when Jackie died. I hadn't doubted

I would be the lawyer defending Ron's trust, or, if conflicted out, as a witness required to testify on behalf of the trust.

This first volley was an interesting one. I hadn't known that Jackie had some sort of trust in which one of the co-trustees was her son Chris, the son she detested and wouldn't even speak to.

About the time I digested Mike Line's strategy with this lawsuit, along came the constable, again. This time, he served my legal assistant, Teresa, my office manager, Cuatro, and he had papers for my wife, Jane. All of us had been sued, as acting in concert to defraud Jackie and cause her to make transfers and gifts to Ron's trust.

I tried to call Mike Line in Ruidoso to discuss these allegations. I wanted to make it clear that suing my office staff and my wife was outrageous. My office staff had worked their butts off for Jackie, separate and apart from Ron. Most of the time it was done as a favor, such as the time Cuatro and his brother straightened out the jockeys at Ruidoso Downs. Jane hardly knew Jackie, except for being at her wedding to Ron, and she was present at a few social occasions. I understood the litigation strategy: divide and conquer, separate and polarize, bring extreme defense cost to the opponent. It was a cheap stunt, but litigators are known for their cheap stunts. It's all part of the game.

Mike Line would not accept or return my calls.

That night, I sat down in my easy chair with a glass of wine. Perhaps if I could relax, I could clear my mind.

Mike Line was making me the villain, but why? I knew that, just a few months before that final cruise, he and Ron had been working on Jackie to change her will to make Ron a Bancroft heir. This former trust of Jackie's, where Line was a co-trustee with her son, was suing *me*, not Ron. How interesting; if a culprit there be in this court of manipulation, wouldn't that culprit be Ron? That was my thinking, anyway. I could just envision how the various parties were aligning and realigning to perfect their respective vantage points to acquire Jackie's inheritance. No doubt there was a lot of confusion and switching of who was to be loyal to whom.

I always knew this event, Jackie's death, as it occurred in May '03, at 77 years of age, would be like the kickoff to a Super Bowl game. I had never thought much about how that game might shape out. I realized, as I sat in this room on this evening, sipping my glass of wine, that lapse had been very unlawyer-like of me. Lawyers are supposed to "anticipate and manipulate," but never admit it and never show it. That's what I had done in defending Ron against his creditors, and in protecting his income and largesse outside the bankruptcy with the trust.

What I had not done was to anticipate my personal exposure upon Jackie's death. I ended the evening feeling a very strong disappointment in myself.

The next morning, before I could think further about this lawsuit, I was met once again by the constable as I came into the office, and served with papers. This time, I did not delay in reading them.

This latest lawsuit was filed in a different court. The first lawsuit had been filed in Carrizozo, New Mexico, the county seat where Jackie resided at the time of her death. This suit's allegations were the same, but the plaintiffs were the Bancroft children. Oddly, it was filed in Lubbock, Texas. I say "oddly" because the law states that a defendant has a right to be sued where he lives, or where the transaction(s) occurred. Neither applied to Lubbock.

I sat down at my desk and began reading the allegations that I had forced Jackie to transfer property and deposit money into Ron's trust. I noticed the lawsuit had been filed dually by a large Lubbock law firm and a sole practitioner whom I knew to be Mike Line's best friend and Texas Tech college roommate. I had met the friend once when I attended a Theater function. I particularly remembered him because he repeatedly addressed Line as "Judge Line." I thought he was acting as courtier, but I had no idea why. It just seemed odd. True, Line was the municipal judge for the little mountain village of Ruidoso, but, in my mind, I could never associate the purveyor of traffic tickets as being properly addressed "judge" or "your honor" in a social setting.

While I had underestimated Mike Line, I hadn't projected how he might act, or what he might do. It hadn't seemed relevant. Sometimes he represented Jackie, and he had worked with Ron while Ron was trying to get Jackie to change her will. I ran Ron's trust. Until now, I did not know the twain would meet.

But to file this lawsuit in Lubbock when I lived in Midland? What shoe would fall next? It would be two months before it became clear why this suit had been filed in Lubbock and what the connection was between the plaintiffs' lawyers and the presiding judge.

I spent the rest of the week locating lawyers I could hire for defense.

This was going to be expensive. One lawyer could not represent all of us; that would be a conflict. Each person in my office, and my wife, would have to have a separate lawyer, a separate law firm, from the other.

Not only that; we didn't have just one lawsuit. We had two each, one in each state. That is, we had two separate lawsuits --- until Monday of the following week.

Here came the constable again. This time, it was Ron suing me. He had hired the largest law firm in town, substantially alleging the same things the other two lawsuits alleged. At least, in this one, I had been sued in my hometown and, at least, there was consistency in the three suits. The consensus was that I was the culprit, the villain, the one who had spent the last five years making Jackie do the things she did, which, each suit alleged, she wouldn't have done otherwise.

You have twenty days in which to answer a lawsuit. In an uncomplicated world, that would have been adequate time to find a lawyer and get at least a cursory answer filed.

However, I needed not only separate law firms for myself but my staff and my wife needed separate law firms, as well. There had to be separation to avoid conflict in respective representations.

The process was expensive, time-consuming, and grueling. Each lawyer was hearing this complicated tale for the first time. It took patience to bring each one up to speed while the clock was ticking for all of us. Then, each lawyer had to take the whole thing to the firm's weekly committee meeting to see if their firm would accept representation, check their conflict-of-interest file, and establish an adequate retainer fee, taking into account any risk of nonpayment.

Fortunately, no law firm rejected representation. Teresa, Cuatro, Jane, and I all had lawyers before default time. Unfortunately, the average retainer deposit was twenty-five-thousand dollars for each. I knew those retainers would be expensed out quickly and more money would be needed.

In trial practice, there are numerous strategies for winning. One typical approach is to break your opponent, financially. If the adversary can't pay for defense, you win. Not only was this multi-lawsuit strategy costing a good deal of money, there was precious little time left to practice law and earn more money. When I defended against allegations affecting Ron's trust, I was placed in the position of bankrolling that defense.

Because of a pending court order prohibiting me from touching the trust, I could not tap the trust for its expenses. I wasn't sure how long I could last with this financial drain, but I was sure that Jane and the staff had to be taken care of first.

Although there were litigators from firms in Las Cruces, Albuquerque, Santa Fe, Lubbock, and Midland with myriad lawsuits and unending allegations between the parties, I was surprised that neither the trust firm in Denver nor the trust firm in Boston had intervened.

The Boston Bancroft trust, originally created in the early 20th Century, was the mother of them all. The '41 Trust was the one Hugh Bancroft, Jr. created in 1941, when he had just moved to Denver from Cohasset, to hold his Dow Publishing and *Wall Street Journal* shares.

As I thought about it, these were old, established estate firms. They probably sent trial lawyers from other firms to do battle, and the trust firms likely stayed behind the scenes. Some of the firms already in the fray, suing me, were probably their warriors.

Mike Line sat in the preferred position, or so it seemed. I knew that Jackie liked Mike, even though she viewed him as she viewed most lawyers. On a number of occasions, she later talked with me after she received advice from Mike to see what I thought. I didn't doubt that she had double-checked with Mike on things I had advised, also. I was aware she used us alternately to call the Denver trustees for more money.

I would later learn that Mike had gone with Ron to change Jackie's will, make Ron an heir, and name himself the personal representative of Jackie's estate. I could not tell whether this had occurred in Jackie's hospital room, or just as Jackie and Ron were leaving on their last, fatal cruise. He had used his wife as the notary who acknowledged Jackie's signature.

However, in these lawsuits, there were no allegations against Mike, nor any contest of his position as personal representative of the estate, a powerful position in probate matters.

Clearly, Mike Line was playing his cards well with the Boston and Denver trustees, and with the Bancroft children. On the other hand, who but Jackie could contest his position as personal representative of her estate? As long as Mike had all parties together and was the vanguard against me and Ron's trust in the attempt to return the trust's assets to Jackie's estate, Mike was serving as he should. It might get a little touchy for Mike once that was accomplished and he turned on Ron to excommunicate him as a Bancroft heir.

Nevertheless, there was no evidence of impropriety on Mike's part, other than how he had acquired the lucrative position of personal representative. He was doing exactly what each of the parties wanted --- to attack Ron's trust and remove me from defending the trust as trustee by alleging mismanagement and theft on the one hand, and my undue influence of Jackie on the other. I had to admit it was a brilliant strategy, one that he could only have posed with Ron's cooperation.

The coterie of the very wealthy, like the court of aristocracy, is filled with intrigue and Machiavellian maneuvering. Mike Line had worked his way into a powerful position as the personal representative of Jackie's estate under probate law. In the process, he had taken care of the Lubbock lawyer, his friend from college, so that his friend could represent him in that position and charge the estate lucrative legal fees.

Ron, through social grace and friendship, had gone from interior decorator to husband to heir of a vast fortune. He had played his game well up to this point.

However, he was too dense to realize that he was the odd-man-out. By trying to ally himself with Mike Line and Jackie's children in hopes of an easy compromise, he had taken the bait they designed, the idea that if he brought everything back to the estate, everyone would get along and be happy. By joining in the initial attack upon his own trust, and me as its trustee, he destroyed his war chest for his own defense when the tables turned, as they soon would.

In time, Ron would be led to the largest law firm in Midland by his Midland jewelry connection, whose daughter happened to have been recently hired by the firm. Ron's strategy was to appease the Bancroft children and Mike Line by suing me as trustee of his trust, alleging that I had mismanaged and misappropriated funds from the trust.

His was a poorly thought-out strategy. It completely nullified any ability I had in defending his trust and its assets against Mike Line's lawsuit on behalf of Jackie's estate. Ron didn't realize it but he was playing into Mike's hands. It would only be a matter of time before Mike Line and the Bancroft children would turn on him with a vengeance, which they did.

To eliminate me from defending Ron's trust was poor strategy, indeed. Ron, or his lawyers, clearly thought his position as a Bancroft heir under Jackie's last will, as drawn by Mike Line, was strong enough that he couldn't be extricated as an heir. Therefore, it would be better to join in the destruction of his trust, revert all monies and properties back to Jackie's estate, and share in a friendly distribution with the Bancroft children. It didn't work.

Death attracts lawyers like vultures to a fresh kill when that death involves millions of dollars. Large law firms, filled with well-compensated professionals bound by oath to abide by a rigorous code of ethics, operate in a rarefied strata of money and power.

What most people don't know is that law practice among the well established revolves around the circumvention of two aspects of law, ethics and procedure. Just as every procedural law in jurisprudence is enacted for a given protection, it is utilized to destroy protection somewhere else. Just as every canon is set forth to maintain veracity, it becomes a tool of attack for ulterior purpose. Such is the art of the practice of law. Those who are most creative at the art, succeed. Those who are not, lose. Lawsuits are seldom, if ever, a search for the truth. They are a game of position.

I could not get over the insanity of Mike Line's lawsuits alleging that I was the perpetrator of undue influence upon Jackie, that I caused her to transfer all that money and property to Ron's trust. In the years I had known her, Jackie was too strong-willed for anyone, including me, to exert undue influence. Mike, who had known her well, knew this.

However, in trial strategy, sometimes the most outrageous allegation sings the best in peoples' minds. In the culture of degeneration in which we live, pernicious allegations take on the cloak of veracity, regardless of truth.

I had often wondered what went through Kathryn's, Wink's, or, for that matter, Chris's minds at seeing their mother, in her 70s, off on a fling with a 50-ish gay man spending her money with abandon. It was not as if they didn't have *Journal* wealth distributions of their own, but I wondered how they must have felt.

I had observed that Kathryn didn't seem to mind. She had had her own disastrous fling with a Greek lover and temporary husband. Now living in Boston and somewhat reclusive, she was close to her mother. She and Jackie spoke by phone frequently.

Wink was always in need of money in order to maintain pretensions in California. He may not have cared about his mother's late-life fling, but I was sure, at some point, he would be concerned about Ron's maneuvers on Jackie's money, and certainly about his design to become a Bancroft heir.

Chris, whom I didn't know, would be the resentful one. I observed from talking with people in Carrizozo that, growing up, he was the wildest, most aggressive one of the three children. At Jackie's late stage of life, she often complained that he cared nothing for her but rather for her money. I had always thought he would be the one with the greatest resentment. Now, in these lawsuits, it was proving out. He seemed to be in the lead and directing Mike Line.

It was a foregone conclusion that there would be an avalanche of litigation upon Jackie's death. Wink and Chris must have viewed Ron as stealing from them.

I felt sure that even less materialistic families would feel this way. Theirs was not a close family. Its closeness, if it could be called that, was money --- who had what, and how could they get more. It did not seem that way with Kathryn. She was gentle and simply wanted her mother to be happy, no matter how bizarre or expensive a late-life fling might be. In the final analysis, however, it would make no sense for her not to be a party in the lawsuits. She was an equal heir with her brothers.

Ron always knew the children would sue him after Jackie died but, in the end, he had fooled himself into believing they would accept him equally, as a wish of their mother. In the early stages of litigation, the children and Mike Line supported him in that belief, or fantasy, as it were, but only long enough for him to assist in destroying his own trust.

Once the Puerto Vallarta condos and villas, the Palm Springs Century Club home, the Spencer Theater construction site for the new home, and cash assets were returned to Jackie's estate, the comradeship was over. Ron then became the defendant, the villain, who all along had created undue pressure and influence on the children's mother and should, therefore, be extricated from her will. Bancroft heritage is well steeped in the ways of trust fights and heirship litigation.

As they say out West, this was not their first rodeo.

I once discussed with Ron that, if he were moderate in his desire for wealth, in what he received in his trust, it may be that, upon Jackie's death, though the children may not like what had occurred, they would not sue him. If he had just one villa in Puerto Vallarta and perhaps a few hundred thousand dollars conservatively invested, he could live well. I asked, "How much wealth does one need?" Ron acted as if I were betraying him at the suggestion, and pointed out that what he acquired was no one's business but his own and was not up for second-guessing. My job was to manage and protect it.

34

It was late at night when the phone rang. I had been asleep for only a short time. The male voice on the other end of the line was ominous.

"Mr. Aaron, I'm not going to give you my name. You helped me once. I'm just returning the favor."

"Okay."

"I believe that Ron Morgan caused Mrs. Spencer's death on that ship," the voice said. "He told me things."

"Why would he do that? He wasn't an heir. He would have no motivation," I said.

"He was her heir. She changed her will. He went into her room on her deathbed and made her sign the paper."

I wondered who the caller was and why the person felt the urgency to call me. *He told me things*. It must have been someone who knew Ron pretty well to have been able to say this.

I didn't recognize the voice. I thought I caught a hint of Hispanic accent, but I wasn't sure.

Aside from reinforcing my thought, that I had hit a nerve with Ron when I inferred he had not acted as perhaps he should have on the ship when Jackie fell ill, the caller raised another issue I hadn't thought of. What will was being probated in Carrizozo, New Mexico? How many wills had Jackie drafted over the years? Since my pending litigation was not in probate court, I hadn't even thought about Jackie's will. It seemed that each party was too busy attacking the others --- and particularly me --- for me to consider what was actually stated in Jackie's will.

It was the middle of the night. Nevertheless, I decided to get in my car and head for the district clerk's office in Carrizozo, New Mexico. If I left now, I would be there about the time it opened.

Besides, some windshield time would be good for me. I had spent weeks chasing my tail, trying to defend myself, my staff, and my family. I counted the number of law firms already involved in those cases, which was really one but spread among three different courts in two states. Ten firms were already involved; I was sure there would be more. Lawyers lined up, everyone wanting a piece of the pie.

Dawn broke as I crossed the Texas/New Mexico line, and a new realization hit me.

There are certain practices commonly used among the civil trial bar because they are consistently successful. One is to attack opposing counsel on ethical issues, so as to weaken his/her resolve for fear of being called up before a state bar ethics committee. Statistics show that less than one percent of all lawyers are ever called up on ethical violations, and very few of those ever lose their license. Nevertheless, the trial tactic, *in flagrante delicto*, usually has a mollifying effect.

Ethics among lawyers. I laughed to myself. It's an oxymoron. Law is the womb of hypocrisy, and lawyers in large law firms serve it well. I recalled Dean Schlitz, at Vanderbilt, writing: "Let me tell you how you will start acting unethically. One day, not too long after you start practicing law, you will sit down at the end of a long, tiring day, and you just won't have much to show for your efforts in terms of billable hours. It will be near the end of the month. You will know that all of the partners will be looking at your monthly time report in a few days, so what you'll do is pad your timesheet just a bit. Maybe you will bill a client for ninety minutes for a task that really took you only sixty minutes to perform. However, you will promise yourself that you will repay the client at the first opportunity by doing thirty minutes for the client for 'free.' In this way, you will be 'borrowing,' not stealing.

"And then what will happen is, it will become easier and easier to take these little loans against future work. And then, after a while, you will stop paying back these little loans...You will continue to rationalize your dishonesty to yourself in various ways until one day you stop doing even that. And before long --- it won't take you much more than three or four years --- you will be stealing from your clients almost every day, and you won't even notice it."

Yep, that's the law biz, I thought to myself as I drove to the clerk's office. And those same lawyers then become the judges who decide the cases and the fate of the people before them. Ethics become a tool, not a standard.

I pulled the court's probate litigation file on Jackie Bancroft Spencer Morgan. There it was, Jackie's last will and testament. I had to look at it several times to make sure I wasn't fooling myself.

The will was dated just a few months before she and Ron left on that final cruise. Jackie's signature was witnessed by Mike Line and notarized by his wife. It gave her house in Alto Village to Ron, and all the racehorses, but then it did something I had never seen before. It said: "I give my tangible personal property in accordance with a written statement signed by me or in my handwriting which I leave at my death."

Then, the will appointed Mike Line as the personal representative of her estate, giving him full authority over the estate.

For the first time, I realized that Ron and Mike Line had succeeded in having Jackie write a new will within nine months of her death. Ron had never told me, perhaps because the will didn't say much. From a legal and practical viewpoint, it was unique in that it said, This is my will, but how I distribute my wealth or to whom I leave it will not occur or be known until I write a handwritten note at the time of my death. In all of my years of practice, I had not seen this technique used.

What the will did immediately accomplish was to make Mike Line Jackie's personal representative of her estate upon her death. What a powerful position that is. I didn't doubt that Mike Line danced all the way to the bank. For a guy who had never been anything more than a traffic ticket and DWI judge, that was quite a jump up the ladder.

The "handwritten statement," as the will referred to it, was a mystery. It was not public record, but, of course, that was its purpose.

I have observed that wealth is never enough. The insidious drive for wealth never has a stop-gap. It perpetuates until it self-destructs. Ron's trust had approached forty million, but, clearly, that was not enough. The battle for more revolved around the handwritten note. If Mike Line was the man to control Jackie's estate and follow her last direction via the handwritten note, then Ron had been under Mike Line's thumb for the last nine months of Jackie's life.

The crown jewel was The *Wall Street Journal* stock, protected by the '41 Trust of which the Denver lawyers were trustee. The stock could not be willed but the distributions from the trust by way of dividends or sale could be, and that involved millions upon millions.

Ron seemed to distance himself from me in those last nine months, and perhaps this was the reason: his new relationship with Mike Line, his posturing to become a Bancroft heir by way of a note written upon Jackie's death.

But, then, why did he call me when frantic in the middle of the ocean?

It seemed as though the required handwritten statement had not been written, or, at least, not signed, when Jackie fell so desperately ill on the ship. I could almost visualize Ron trying to get Jackie to sign it in her weakened state. When she refused, he panicked. He had to get Jackie to the States, in cogent enough condition to talk to Mike Line and sign the handwritten statement mandated by her will. She wasn't going to sign it until she talked to Mike Line, the designated personal representative of her estate. I had heard Ron's panic on the ship-to-shore calls that night. For a decade, whenever he was in a tight spot, he called me, just as he had done that night.

I got in my car to drive back to Midland. I knew more than I'd known before.

I knew, for instance, that Jackie had signed a new will before she left on her final cruise. This gave me some idea of why Ron had begun to distance himself from me. His new game plan was to become a Bancroft heir and not rely solely on his trust.

I assumed Ron could not have been happy about how Jackie's new will was drafted. "I give my tangible personal property in accordance with a written statement signed by me, or in my handwriting, which I may leave at my death." Jackie would have to be at least cogent enough on her deathbed, either to have Mike Line draft her written statement pursuant to her instructions and then sign it, or to draft the statement herself, in her own handwriting, and sign it. She was capable of neither from what the nurse, the Captain of the ship, and Ron told me on that fateful night in the Atlantic.

That must have been the source of Ron's panic. He had to get her back to New Mexico and bring her around well enough to prepare and sign that final statement.

The will had pointedly left the Alto Village house and horses to Ron. He wasn't interested in that house, nice as it was, and he sure didn't care about a bunch of racehorses. His goal was to become a full-fledged Bancroft heir under the umbrella of The *Wall Street Journal* stock and Dow Jones Publishing empire. That could only be done through this final "written statement at the time of my death."

A picture of Ron and Jackie arguing while on the cruise kept surfacing in my mind, Ron forcing the issue, Jackie gradually becoming more ill and frail. I had witnessed their arguments on various occasions. Jackie could be stubborn and Ron beside himself with frustration. I returned to the conclusion that Ron realized he had to get Jackie to New Mexico for proper medical care, and to Mike Line, the personal representative of her estate.

The caller to my home the night before had said something about Ron going into Jackie's room to have papers signed. The call was such a surprise and I wasn't awake enough to question the caller as I should. He said Ron went into Jackie's room on her deathbed and had her sign the paper. Was he referring to the "written statement?" Had Ron succeeded at the very last in becoming a Bancroft heir? Then, the caller alleged that Ron caused "Mrs. Spencer's death on that ship." Why did the caller refer to Jackie as "Mrs. Spencer," instead of "Mrs. Morgan" or "Jackie?"

And who was the caller? I would never know.

While I did know more now, I was still looking through a glass darkly.

Upon returning to my office, I pulled the copy of the will contest filed by the Bancroft children in probate court. I had not seen it before because I had not been a party to that lawsuit, but, while I was in the clerk's office that morning anyway, I made a copy of it.

One particular allegation stood out. I laughed so hard at it Teresa and Cuatro came into my office to see what I was laughing about.

Jackie's children alleged that Jackie and Ron were never legally married because the marriage was never "consummated," which meant they had never had sex. As evidence of this fact, aside from Ron being gay, Jackie and Ron never shared a stateroom on their voyages but were, instead, berthed in two separate rooms. I'm not sure how one retrospectively proves they had sex. I'm not sure how one retrospectively proves they didn't.

Nevertheless, I guess the separate-but-equal staterooms on the ship, not to mention separate household bedrooms, had some evidentiary value. The lawyers seemed to think so.

Many Southern states have laws that "protect the husband's needs" by stating that, after a marriage license is obtained and civil ceremony is performed blessing the vows of marriage, the union must be "consummated" by a completed act of sexual intercourse.

Somehow, these laws came from Biblical foundations of Southern legislatures years ago. The attempted logic, or illogic, here was that if Ron was not legally married to Jackie for failure of consummation, he was not her "husband." When her will or "written statement" referred to her husband, that person, then, could not be Ron.

The South has always had ridiculous sex laws. After all, it is the Bible Belt. But, somehow, I would have expected New Mexico to be a little more advanced. Besides, how did the Bancrofts know that Jackie and Ron never had sex? Granted. It was a pretty good bet, but how do you prove such a thing? Or, if the proponent of the argument makes the allegation, does the burden of proof shift to Ron to prove he had sex with Jackie?

There is no end to the arguments that lawyers will contrive. At least, we all had a good laugh about the very thought.

35

The weeks following my trip to the clerk's office in Carrizozo were intense with lawyers filing discovery motions, wanting to know every aspect of Ron's trust, most particularly, what was in it and where its assets were located. It was difficult for me from a legal standpoint. While the beneficiary, Ron, was suing me in the Midland lawsuit, alleging mismanagement, theft, and seeking damages, he had joined the Bancroft children in the Lubbock lawsuit, claiming the trust was illegal and should be abolished.

Beyond that, I had been served with a court order to take no action regarding the trust or its assets. The practical effect was that Ron's trust was standing there naked, and I could do nothing to defend it.

My lawyer and I had entered the courtroom first and were seated at counsel's table. From the time I first walked into the Lubbock courtroom, I could see that the judge detested my very existence. Our eyes met briefly and he literally glared at me, staring me down. When Mike Line and the Bancroft lawyers entered, the judge literally stood up from behind the judge's bench and greeted them with great energy. I knew then it was going to be a long day.

By the end of the hearing, the judge had ordered me to deliver every file relating to Ron's trust to the Lubbock lawyers within the following week. He made it plain that if I didn't or if anything was missing, I would be held in contempt of court and placed in jail until I either delivered the files or cured the incompleteness.

This provided an impossible situation, an age-old trap which litigators love. It usually occurs when dealing with a "hip-pocket" judge. It was obvious that, no matter what I delivered, the lawyers on the other side would claim it was incomplete and file a motion to hold me in contempt of court.

In trial practice parlance, a "hip-pocket" judge is one who is either on the take or, for some reason, is under the influence of the other side. In Texas, it happens all too often because judges are elected. A judgeship is nice to have, even for those not into power. Judges receive an upper-middle income salary, great healthcare, and good benefits. The higher up they are in a court's pecking order, the higher their salary. When they retire, they receive anywhere from half to eighty-percent of their salary for the rest of their lives. Judges are respected and looked up to as leaders in their communities. Their campaign coffers are wide open and unlimited. The general electorate seldom knows who is running for a judge position, and, furthermore, doesn't care. However, law firms do care, and contribute heavily to the judge's campaign fund. In important judgeships, corporate America follows this practice, as well. There is no limit to the amount that can be contributed, even if the judge has no opponent.

Neither my lawyer in the Lubbock suit nor I had any idea why we were not being heard by this judge. Every time my lawyer opened his mouth, the judge jumped down his throat. The Bancroft lawyers hardly had to say anything. They sat at their table and smirked. We didn't know whether we had a hip-pocket judge for sure, but one thing was clear. "There was a bear in the courtroom," another trial lawyer euphemism meaning this judge was clearly prejudiced.

It had seemed odd to be in court in Lubbock. A person has a right to be sued in his or her home county. That apparently didn't matter to this judge. He was there to "home-town" me and was doing a very good job of it. Every time I requested a hearing on why he had jurisdiction, he set a hearing requiring me to show why I should not be held in contempt of court for not fully responding to the opposing Lubbock lawyer's discovery requests. My argument was, if you don't have jurisdiction over me by law, then these discovery requests are invalid. The logistical tail kept chasing the dog. I was the dog.

Instead of answering my argument, the judge kept demanding that I produce everything that existed about Ron's trust. The judge threatened me with jail for contempt. He said I could just sit there until I decided to answer every question and produce every scrap of paper the Lubbock lawyer demanded.

It was clear the judge was frothing at the mouth to render that contempt order. He no doubt surmised the Bancrofts would be impressed.

Ultimately, the judge declared Ron's trust invalid from its inception in order to then rule that every property transfer from Jackie to Ron's trust was invalid, therefore, the deeds supporting those transfers conveyed nothing.

It would be several weeks before he made that ruling, but, when he did, that action would drive me to the Department of Justice to explain that, by this judge's ruling, I was now guilty of federal bankruptcy fraud.

It would immediately remove jurisdiction from this Lubbock state judge to federal jurisdiction where he couldn't get me. His parting shot was to fine me twenty-five-thousand dollars for contempt. By appeal, I was able to have his contempt ruling reversed, but the legal fees for the appeal were about twenty-five-thousand dollars. There's nothing quite like being "home-towned" in Texas.

Upon returning to Midland, I called a friend of mine in Lubbock. I knew he would know about this court and how it advocated for the Mike Line/Bancroft children/Ron Morgan coalition.

It turned out that the judge, a lawyer in private practice, was temporarily serving as the judge of this court while the regular judge served a tour in Iraq. That didn't explain his attitude, but I suspected he had designs on being elected to one of the other courts. What better way to gain support than to pander to the Bancrofts and their large law firms. There was nothing I could do about it. Clearly, this was a court trap, one that every lawyer fears and tries to avoid.

In the weeks to come, we had several hearings in Lubbock, and the tenor of the court never changed. If anything, it got worse. In the last hearing, the judge ruled that Ron's trust was invalid from its inception, and, therefore, everything in it must be returned to Jackie's estate.

He set me for depositions at the opposing counsel's office in Lubbock for the following week. Just as I had anticipated, the Bancroft lawyers had filed a motion alleging I was not disclosing everything regarding the trust and that I should be held in contempt. The judge made it clear that if I did not bring every last file I had to the Lubbock lawyer's office at deposition, I was going to jail. Going to jail for contempt is not a good thing. It is not like committing a crime. You can't bond out. You stay there until the judge decides you can leave.

This judge had struck the death blow, his intent all along. That ruling, a state court ruling that effectively said Ron's trust never existed, placed me in immediate violation of federal bankruptcy law. I doubted that the judge knew the full effect of his ruling, or that he even cared as it applied to me. I had placed Ron in federal bankruptcy to keep him from paying creditors such as the Verlanders, on the one hand, and created a trust where he could legally receive properties and money without disclosure to the bankruptcy court, on the other. Some forty million dollars in jewels, art, real estate and corporate ownerships had passed through that trust. None of it had been reported to the bankruptcy court. If there had never been a trust, as the Lubbock judge ruled, I was guilty of bankruptcy fraud and laundering money for an illegal purpose, the purpose of keeping money away from the creditors in Ron's bankruptcy proceedings.

Driving back from Lubbock to Midland after that last hearing, I thought of appealing the judge's ruling. The impediments to doing so seemed endless. I was sure the judge was wrong in both law and fact. Early on, he had overruled my objection to his jurisdiction that, since Jackie and her estate had no connection to Lubbock, neither did I. From a procedural standpoint, I felt that was a strong argument. Declaring Ron's trust invalid from inception used a very weak legal argument for its basis. I felt now, as I had felt at the ruling, that it was patently incorrect. I wasn't sure, however, that I even had standing to appeal. The one beneficiary, Ron, was suing me at the same time I was under a court order from a different court to take no action in regard to the trust or its assets.

I was becoming paranoid in my thinking and fearful in my emotions. If Bancroft influence could totally dictate to a Lubbock judge, what could they do at the appellate level? Those judges were elected, too. They had campaign coffers just like lower level judges did.

Texas history was replete with appellate courts being owned by the rich and powerful. Beyond that, the cost of defending Ron's trust would be substantial, and I was prohibited from using any trust funds. Up till now, I had been pulling the money out of my own pocket, not only for my staff, my wife, myself, but for Ron's trust defense, as well. There was no way I could continue to do that. It's one thing to stand on principle and fight to the death, but principle dies broke, as often as not.

It was a long drive back from Lubbock.

For two days, I stayed away from the office. I tried to think through every aspect of what was occurring, but depression set in and made it increasingly difficult. I knew the penalty for what I was now retrospectively guilty of --- twenty years in the federal pen.

I also knew there was no safe harbor I could turn to. My client, Ronnie Lee Morgan, had, for whatever reason, turned on me. Jackie's children saw me as a villain in concert with the gay man who contrived and married their mother and stole their inheritance.

Just as there is no honor among thieves, there is no honor among lawyers. They would keep coming at me in these lawsuits until my practice was destroyed and Jane's and my savings were depleted. I knew this from experience and observation in a lifetime in law. Not only that; each of my staff had been noticed for deposition in the Lubbock case. It would only be a matter of time before that occurred in each of the other cases.

The trial tactic would be to call Teresa and Cuatro for cross-examination in deposition, over and over, from one case to the next, then move the court to hold them in contempt based on any slight inconsistency between their testimonies or statements when they did not know the answer to some question posed.

When they were through with Teresa and Cuatro, the lawyers would start on Jane. The fact that there was no wrongdoing was irrelevant. This was the accepted tactic of trial strategy.

Had Jackie been alive, I felt in my heart, she would have intervened. But then, if she were alive, all of this wouldn't be happening.

I have observed that, just as nations do, people tend to invent their own morality to justify their desires. Lawyers are hired to perfect that justification and to argue it in courts of law. The Bancroft children, Chris, Wink, Kathryn, believed their mother's wealth was their own, and that Ron had no right to it. Ron believed he had a contract with a wealthy woman to assist as her companion in her last years, but underlying that, to participate in her wealth. Each had their own character defect, their own dysfunction, as they focused blame on the other. They made their own rules, bent them into new interpretations, or altogether disregarded the rules they made.

While in-fighting continued between the separate Bancroft families over the wealth that existed and their desire for more, Ron would move from one to another, seeking an ally, playing a game that seemed sensitive to social norms, trying not to appear as a pariah, all the while preparing for what would ultimately occur --- the battle for heirship.

Now, the worms would turn, and Ron, who seldom perceived matters as they truly were, would be struck like a drone attack from the sky. Mike Line, as representative of the estate, and the Bancroft children, through their New Mexico lawyers, would attack Jackie's last written statement making Ron an heir, and take him to task on every event over the last half-dozen years, from how he came to marry Jackie, to how he acquired each distribution to his trust. I knew he had good lawyers in Midland, but I doubted they realized how much they would have to defend.

It would be a long, expensive battle to keep Ron in the legal fold as a Bancroft heir.

It had been over a decade that I represented Ron. I reflected over the numerous cases, I questioned the ethics.

What were the rules, or had they been bent so many times there was no moral fiber left? A person comes into a lawyer's office with a problem, part legal, part social. Mixed within are matters of morals and ethics separate from the law, itself. Does the lawyer apply the facts to the law, only?

At what point does the lawyer go beyond counseling on legal effects and structural planning, and become a co-conspirator in manipulation and moral breakdown? Had I done that? I questioned myself, and I didn't like the feeling. I didn't like the feeling because of the facts dealt me by Ron, the double-billing on invoices, claiming personal injury to his arm in order to sue a paramour, making statements like, "I'll stay married for one year, get all the money I can, then divorce her."

At what point should I have pulled away and said, No more? I thought back over the years I represented Ron. What were the rules? Had they changed? Or was there just a total lack of morality?

I tried to determine in my mind: had I failed Jackie in any way? She knew what she wanted, and told me what to do. I could not recall one time that I told Jackie what to do.

I came to realize I was at the end of my rope. Too long had I witnessed the selfishness and pain people bring upon themselves and impose upon others. Too long had I witnessed the manipulation of justice in trial law. Too much had I seen the power of the wealthy over the poor. These allegations against me, my staff, and my family were false and contrived. I knew in time they would fade away, but the ruling by the Lubbock state judge dissolving Ron's trust from its beginning placed me in a federal box of illegality from which I could not extricate myself.

One of my choices was to spend the next ten years fearing indictment, and, sooner or later, have to defend myself on federal criminal charges of bankruptcy fraud.

Or I could bite the bullet, now.

On the third day of seclusion, I returned to my law office. If you have walked the halls of a law school for three years preparing yourself for a life's work; if you have worked long hours and many weekends with people you admire and trust as you prepare for yet another trial; if you have a legal assistant, and combination office manager-investigator who take to heart the problems of each client just as you do; if you have been in the line of fire together with your blood up and a pace that left no time for fear, you have known the vicissitudes of professional life and the deep friendships that come with it.

But now, the end had come. I had no alternative but to close the office.

I brought the staff together. The mood was somber and all could tell that whatever was about to be said, whatever was about to happen, it could not be good. Most would not feel so deeply. It would be an inconvenience, but they were qualified and finding other employment would not be that difficult.

But I looked into my legal assistant Teresa's eyes, and then into my son Cuatro's. He had worked in this office since he was fifteen, he'd been trained as an investigator, and was now the office manager. They knew my quirks, but they also knew how to succeed for our clients. They were one hell of a team. At this moment, they knew what I was going to say before I could say it. The hurt ran deep. The eyes talk.

I'd researched the matter and determined that the Federal Sentencing Guidelines would, indeed, incarcerate me for a required twenty years. The guidelines are based on the amount of money involved, and, at forty million dollars, the maximum would be required. I would be dead before I got out.

Jane returned home that evening from teaching at the college. She had never become overly involved in my law practice, though she knew things hadn't been going well of late. We each had our professional lives and were good about leaving them at the office.

This night was different. It was time for me to explain just how difficult the situation was, how it was my belief that my breaking the law should be addressed now rather than living in fear of when it would surface. She knew I had been spending a lot of our money on lawyers to defend us.

But that was civil. She did not know the criminal ramifications I was now faced with.

We talked well into the night, affirming our faith and dedication to each other. I explained how I could go to prison, that if I reported my crime and how it came about, perhaps I could get probation. I explained how the Federal Sentencing Guidelines worked, and how the gauge to punishment was always quantity. Its purpose was to quantify punishment throughout the nation. If the crime was dope, punishment depended on how much dope. If the crime involved money, punishment depended on how much money.

However, there is a process of plea negotiation between the prosecutor and the defendant. That negotiation is dependent upon agreeing to the quantity. If the quantity, in this case money and asset value of the trust, can be agreed upon without a trial, then the agreed amount becomes the sentencing guideline basis for punishment.

My goal was to get the prosecutor to agree that the amount unreported to the bankruptcy court in Ron's bankruptcy proceedings was equivalent to ten million dollars. An audit would show around forty million, but that would be a contested amount and would require a trial.

In the federal system, the prosecutor, not the judge, controls punishment. If I succeeded in negotiation and the federal prosecutor agreed to cap the amount at ten million, and then, because of my cooperation give the judge a letter recommending probation, I would avoid prison.

As I explained these things, the night wore on. Jane and I sat for many hours, sometimes just holding each other, sometimes talking, sometimes crying. I have been told that looking into the future, trying to anticipate outcomes, only creates fear. Jane and I had a wonderful life together, and now the future didn't look too bright. We were fearful.

The time had come to release clients, find them new representation, and wrap up business. Many had been clients for years. Some were close friends. Many asked questions. There was no simple, clear way to explain what was going on.

At the same time, each of my employees worried about their own future, where they would find a new job. They were loyal to me, they were there to support and complete the job of closing the office, but they also had families to support. I knew what was going through their minds. I felt their feeling of insecurity.

The task was further complicated because of the international structure of Ron's trust. The cyber casino in Belize had to be dissolved, and that staff terminated. The import-export company I had established in

Hong Kong had to be disbanded, and that staff, one of whom was a lawyer from our Midland office, had to be notified. However, he would have no difficulty going to work for our other contacts in China.

The closing days were long, the tasks intricate. The air in the office was thick with depression.

My mind kept returning to how I would negotiate --- plea bargain --- with the Assistant U.S. District Attorney (AUSA).

I knew him. He was an aggressive prosecutor. I had tried cases against him; he had always seemed fair-minded, at least as fair-minded as one could expect from the Department of Justice. Federal laws are heavily-weighted toward the prosecution. The power is very much in the hands of the government.

Convincing the AUSA to give the judge that letter recommending probation would be the most I could hope for. Surely, he could see there was no original criminal intent, that the whole invention of diverting Jackie's contributions to Ron's trust was legal until that Lubbock state judge destroyed the trust from its inception. Of course, even getting to that point in negotiation would come after an agreement to use a figure of ten million dollars as the amount contributed to the trust.

I could see this was not going to be an easy presentation. The more I practiced it in my mind, the more nervous I got. I had spent a lifetime being nervous as hell on the inside but never showing it on the outside, and I was well practiced at it. This was going to be one of those times when professionalism was the characteristic required of me, regardless of what I was feeling on the inside.

I had researched these nuances of federal criminal law, and I was certain this was the approach I should take. I told Jane I would go to the Department of Justice in downtown Midland the next morning and begin the process.

For each of us, life takes unexpected twists. If you are a lawyer and representing humanity and its layered relationships, the view can be surrealistic. I never again saw Ron Morgan. I had had no inkling we would never again meet after all those years of closeness, his relying on my advice, even at the last, calling me in the middle of the night in a panic from the middle of the Atlantic Ocean. By posturing himself as an adversarial litigant, he and I could no longer just sit down and talk. It may well be he didn't understand that. Ron didn't understand most things about law, nor did he spend much time worrying about the legal consequences of his actions.

I had surmised that Ron's strategy was to sue me regarding his trust, to have its assets returned to Jackie's estate on the assumption he was now an heir. No doubt the Bancroft children and Mike Line had supported the idea.

That strategy had backfired, and now, the suit against me was nothing more than a sideshow. Ron and his new Midland lawyers were scrambling for all they were worth defending Ron against lawsuits filed by the Bancrofts and Mike Line. Ron fought frantically to survive as an heir. I could just imagine how the legal bills were mounting. In the wash, his trust was abolished.

For me, the die was cast with the Feds. It would make little difference who inherited what of Jackie's estate, or if lawyers ended up usurping it all.

Once Ron's trust was abolished, and realizing that all of these related cases were high profile not only from the public's view but from the government's, as well, I was sure that, one day, the IRS and the Department of Justice would show up with indictments. Whenever they did, and it could be years because there is never a need for the government to be in a hurry, I would spend the next ten years defending myself, paying attorney fees, and bankrupting my own family, not to mention the prolonged emotional stress it would bring upon them.

That is the way things work. This period was trying enough. Had I waited for those events to take their course in their own good time, the emotional trauma would have been fatal. No. Now was the time to cut bait, as they say, and make the best deal I could with the Feds.

In my introspection, I came to realize the line of demarcation for me was being faced with defending myself. I could have stayed and fought and defended the trust as trustee until the end of time. But there is no perfect way to express the particular pain so deeply felt when personally attacked.

I had spent a lifetime defending people, protecting their property and standing as an advocate for their rights. The time had come for me to be an advocate for myself, a position that, by its very nature, felt empty and self-serving.

I came to realize more closely what all those clients through all the years must have felt in their time of need, the sudden fear of self-deprecating advocacy, the realization that the cost of defense would cost more than they had, and the picture of the emotional stress on their families. Now, I could see so clearly what I had always suspected --- that it is easier to present a client's case than to defend oneself. A lone voice may howl from soul's depth, "I am not guilty," but there are no ears to hear, no belief in veracity. One cannot prove they are not guilty. A negative allegation is proof enough. Thus it has been throughout all of history.

Even now as I contemplated my own fate, I thought of the insanity of what was going on.

In all this litigation, there had not been one question, one concern, over how Jackie died, of what her last days, her last hours, were like, not in the hospital but on the ship, of whether she could have been saved if attended to sooner.

I had thought ultimate litigation would center around Ron's actions or lack of actions on the ship, which I saw as the center of attack to show ulterior motive on Ron's part. It could be argued that his actions later in her hospital room, the plan to make himself a Bancroft heir, affirmed that ulterior motive.

Jackie had left port at San Diego a happy, vibrant, 77-year-old, with the energy of a person in her fifties.

Clearly, she took ill on the voyage, but why hadn't she been given medical attention at Cape Town and flown home, if necessary?

Why didn't a luxury cruise ship with a stateroom cruise costing a hundred-thousand dollars a month have a medical doctor?

Why had Ron waited until the last moment to call for help?

Had he been serious when, just before leaving San Diego, he confided he couldn't stand it anymore, that he couldn't stand to be married to Jackie any longer?

Had he seen delay in attending Jackie's illness while cruising in the middle of nowhere as his way out?

Was his plan to force her to write her last written statement, as her will required, while helpless in the middle of the Atlantic, but she refused until she could get medical attention in Albuquerque?

Was that the inception of his panic?

Was none of this of interest or concern to the litigants?

There *were* no allegations regarding how Jackie had died. No one cared. They cared only about her money and who would get it. Where were these people when I was trying to get Jackie off that ship in the middle of the Atlantic? I knew where Ron was. I concluded that, if Jackie could see what was going on now, she would not be surprised; not in the least.

After the memorial at the Spencer Theater, I was distracted from thinking about how Bancroft lawsuits would take shape because I was knee-deep in an unrelated jury trial.

In the pit of my stomach, from time to time, I felt a deep unease. Like a Pavlov dog coming to food at the sound of a bell, whenever a legal entanglement arose involving Ron, I knew there was something he was not telling me. In the office, we had come to call them "oh-by-the-way" moments. "Oh-by-the-way, I double-charged Mrs. Verlander," or "Oh-by-the-way, I was arrested last night for lewdness," or "Oh-by-the-way, there was a marriage contract with Sam Vest."

The thought would come to mind, then leave, then reappear at another time: "Will there be a lawsuit against Ron? Will his actions or failure to act regarding Jackie's health be suspect? What will be the 'oh-by-the-way' moment this time?"

I had always felt nervous about the whirlwind speed at which Jackie funded Ron's trust over the course of their five-year marriage. Perhaps my premonition was because I anticipated the day when I would have to defend the trust. Perhaps it was just because I had never seen personal wealth tossed about with such abandon.

I had prepared the trust for defense. Defending myself had not entered my consciousness, and the destruction of the trust was simply not in any picture I could see. Nor could I envision such a move as Ron suing to abolish his own trust.

Lawyers spend long hours planning actions and anticipating reactions. This time, in this case, I had failed the test of anticipation.

36

It's true for anyone: There is cause for trepidation when dealing with the federal government. You never quite know what you will get. Every aspect of government is a huge bureaucracy, and one governmental employee's decision might be pre-empted by another employee in a different agency. Often, policy overrides good sense. Over my professional career, I have seen lives literally ruined by such agencies as the IRS, U.S. Attorney Civil Enforcement, as well as other agencies within the Department of Justice.

I was about to enter one of those agencies and lay out for them a forty-million dollar crime I had designed and committed for a client. I kept reminding myself I could either do this now or wait in fear every day until the FBI or the IRS, or both, showed up at my door. The government is never in a hurry. It doesn't have to be. It may wait years before it decides to act, but, when it does, it arrives with great power and intensity.

In the Midland office of the Department of Justice, four AUSAs, all of them young, aggressive prosecutors, are looking to put another notch in their guns. I knew each one. The bulk of their caseloads was narcotics since Midland is just three hundred miles from the Mexican border and sits on Interstate 20. Just outside of El Paso and to the east, Interstates 20 and 10 converge, thus allowing for convenient transportation of drugs and boxes of drug money awaiting deposits to either the Eastern or Western United States.

As I approached the tall office building housing the governmental prosecutorial agency, my heart sank, my palms broke out in sweat. I could hardly make myself get out of the car. I knew this was the termination point, the end for a lot of things on this earth for me.

I had already closed my office and done what I could to help my staff readjust in new employment.

Rumors circulated in every corner of the town about Ron Morgan, Jackie, the wealthy lady up at Ruidoso, and allegations against me of fraud and deceit. People would never look at me the same; this taint would always remain. Somehow --- I didn't know how --- Jane and I would get through this.

I was convinced this was the only way to go at it.

Denial is a common character defect but so is confession. I had observed through years of law practice that a defendant's first reaction is denial. Many times I observed that my clients never broke out of their denial, regardless of fault clearly being theirs. They just wouldn't own it.

But I have also observed those who readily confess when accused of anything. This is true of those raised in strong religious environs. I thought of my wife, Jane, raised Catholic. It was always easy for her to feel guilty, even when she had nothing to do with the issue at hand.

In the federal system, it is not uncommon for people to self-deny their guilt, only to be snapped up by the Department of Justice years later.

I didn't want to be in that position. I didn't want that to happen to Jane and me, certainly not at an age later in life.

I had already depleted half our savings defending myself in the various lawsuits and hiring lawyers for my staff. These cases were nowhere close to ending. Even when they did come to an end, I didn't doubt for a moment that the Feds would be there next, and that would call for a whole new round of expense and defense. At my age, close to retirement, the combined litigation could last through most of the rest of my life.

Jane and I had talked it through. I had to make the best deal I could with the government, and the only way to do that was to go in and take responsibility. The day had come. It's why I was here.

The AUSA received me courteously. I think I caught him off-guard. Once he began to hear my story, he asked me to stop. He called the FBI's bureau chief and asked him to come over.

I debriefed for at least a couple of hours and, by the time I left, was given a long list of documentation to supply at our next meeting.

I returned home where Jane anxiously awaited. Of course, she wanted to know if the government had agreed to probation. She didn't want to lose her husband. I had to explain that the government never solidly agrees to anything. They "indicate," and the indication was they would agree to the ten-million dollar cap for sentencing guideline purposes.

Since I had disclosed the commission of a crime of which they were unaware, and had taken responsibility for that crime, I should get the required letter from the AUSA to the judge, recommending probation.

From the time of my FBI debriefing forward, the Bancroft lawyers, Mike Line, and Ronnie Lee Morgan all turned on each other as if in a shark-infested feeding frenzy. I never heard from them again. I was out of the picture.

37

It had been several months since that fateful day I drove to the Department of Justice and confessed my guilt to bankruptcy fraud on behalf of my client, Ronnie Lee Morgan. I learned from a friend who worked in the Justice Department that, when the Bancroft attorneys found out what I had done, they sent an envoy to meet with the U.S. Attorney in San Antonio, the head of our federal judicial district, to make sure a criminal investigation would not ensue or follow through into the civil litigations surrounding Jackie's estate. The Bancrofts and The *Wall Street Journal*, like most wealthy families and corporate entities, shy away from adverse publicity and place pressure where pressure is needed to insure that it doesn't occur.

I didn't really care about that, and I didn't care how the lawsuits between the litigants turned out. Alan Dershowitz is said to have once told his Harvard Law School students that they must never trust their client, and to always protect themselves. I don't know that I ever trusted Ron. I just considered the source, and tried to represent the client. What I had not done was protect myself.

The date for my sentencing in federal court was coming up in about two weeks. All the work had been done with a pre-sentencing report to the judge.

I had prepared my statement at the time he asked to hear from me at my sentencing. My statement would set forth that I did not agree with a system in which a state judge could declare a trust, created in good faith within the rules of bankruptcy law, void *ab initio*, from the beginning, and thereby activate a federal criminal statute that would cause me to become a convicted felon. To me, this was the nuance of power and money, not the veracity of law, and it was not fair that I should pay the price.

In the federal system, I knew it was a requirement of federal procedural law that the judge gives the defendant, indeed requires the defendant, to make a statement before he/she is sentenced. It mimics the French Revolution habit of allowing the defendant to utter last words, usually a prayer, before chopping his head off at the guillotine.

The statement changes nothing. The punishment has already been predetermined by the probation department who applies Federal Sentencing Guidelines to the crime and advises the judge of the required punishment.

It does, however, give the defendant an opportunity to accept responsibility for his/her actions. For me, it was an opportunity to speak my mind, which I intended to do. Jane was fearful of what I might say and how I might say it at sentencing.

We now felt confident that I would receive a probated sentence, we would not be separated, and we could reorganize and continue with our lives.

However, a surprise occurred less than two weeks before my sentencing. My office personnel was down to Teresa, Cuatro, and me. Cuatro came into my office and advised that three dark blue Suburbans with dark-tinted windows were quickly, as if in military fashion, pulling into my parking lot. They were probably Feds.

Indeed they were. They presented me with a search warrant and began hauling off boxes of files. These files primarily related to Ron's trust, but I noticed that, occasionally, a different client's file got mixed in.

I didn't like the surprise or the action, though the agents were courteous. I felt I had been straightforward with the AUSA and the FBI. I had laid all the chips on the table, and the indication was that we had worked something out, including the AUSA recommending probation.

I felt an acidic tightening in my gut.

Many times throughout my career, I had seen law enforcement and the prosecution lead a defendant on to get what they wanted, only to turn on him at the very last. Is this what was happening here? Because I was upset, I chose not to call the AUSA to find out what was going on. I would wait until I calmed down. I didn't have to wait long.

Two days later, the Bureau chief called and asked that I come down to the FBI office and meet with him and the AUSA. He was quite polite and acted as if nothing were the matter. I responded by saying that I appreciated his call and that I expected an explanation for the unannounced search of my office and seizure of my files.

I arrived at the FBI offices, which took up two floors of an office tower. I signed in and announced myself to the receptionist. The chief agent quickly came out to the reception room and escorted me back to a conference room.

The AUSA was sitting at the conference table. He didn't look up, but looked as if studying some papers before him.

The mood was cold. The air felt tense. I suspected this room was wired, perhaps it even had a video camera.

FBI: "Glen, I'll begin. We've been going through the organizational design of how you protected the trust's money."

I nodded. I wasn't sure where this was going, but both men wore a deadpan, serious look.

AUSA: "No one could have developed such a complex offshore structure without having done this before. A first-timer couldn't have figured all of this out."

I nodded, again. I had an idea of where this was heading, but why now, just two weeks before my sentencing?

FBI: "Glen, we want to know every person you have ever done this for, and how."

"Fellas, I can't do that. I've protected assets of families here in Midland who ran into one problem or another, but nothing criminal. I've never done anything for a criminal intent," I said.

AUSA: "That won't work, Glen. You'll have to disclose your client list."

"And if I don't?" I asked.

"You will probably do time," the AUSA said.

"Does that mean you won't give the letter to the judge for probation?" I asked.

"No letter," the AUSA responded.

"Then I'll have to do time. These families don't deserve to be on your Big Brother list," I said as I got up and stormed from the room.

By the time I got home, I was shaking. I needed Jane. I needed to talk to her so bad, but she was at the college, teaching.

All of this time, as bad as the situation had been with closing the law office, facing the questioning eyes of friends and even some family members, there had been the modicum of relief that we wouldn't be separated from each other, that I wouldn't actually go to prison.

In the two weeks leading up to the sentencing, there were long periods in which Jane and I sat in total silence, just holding hands. My son Cuatro and I had worked in the law office together for so many years; my legal assistant Teresa had been with me a long time. We were like family.

At other times, we all sat for long periods, trying to bolster each other's spirits. There was not only the sense of loss, but of helplessness. After all the battles we had fought for so many clients, never giving in, it seemed so odd there was nothing we could do, that this era had come to an end.

Jane, Cuatro, Teresa, and I arrived at the federal courthouse promptly on time the day of my sentencing. The courtroom was packed with friends and supporters, and the sentencing ritual proceeded as it had millions of times for countless others throughout this nation.

When the gavel came down, I had been sentenced to federal prison for two years, followed by three years supervised release. I was given the liberty to turn myself in on a specified date to the federal prison at Butner, North Carolina.

It was as the FBI and AUSA had said. No disclosure, no probation. I would do the time.

38

No longer did I think of the Bancroft history. No longer did I think of Jackie or her gay man whom I had represented for many years, or her bizarre last fling at life on this earth.

In time, and after numerous lawyers had siphoned millions of dollars in fees, Jackie's children and Ron Morgan ceased fighting and settled. I read that the Bancroft estate would buy off Ron for twelve million and remain intact as the Bancroft estate and heirs to The *Wall Street Journal*.

By 2006, Ron would be hurting for money again. He sold off an alleged three million dollars in assets on eBay. Listed were Warhol, Cezanne, Peter Hurd, Matisse, and Picasso art; European and Asian antiques, and Buddhist Temple artifacts, including a rare ten-foot Buddha statue and temple bell. There were fine furnishings and accessories by Kreiss, Swaim, Design Directions, J. Robert Scott, Lalique, and estate jewelry, watches and accessories by Henry Dunay, Yurman, Cartier, Gucci, Philip Stein, Corum, and H. Stern.

Ron's grand design to marry this rich woman and set himself up for life had succeeded, but at what price, I wondered, does great wealth bring happiness? The great lesson of history reveals that it does not.

By 2007, media mogul Rupert Murdoch paid five billion dollars for ownership of The *Wall Street Journal*, enough money to extend trust baby heirship for at least another century.

It is difficult for the mind to grasp the difference between millions and billions when it comes to numbers or dollars. The huge estate battle between the Bancroft children and Ron could not have been more than a hundred million dollars, including all that was in Ron's trust.

The crown jewel, however, was The *Wall Street Journal* stock still in Jackie's trust in Denver, set up by Hugh Bancroft, Jr. in 1941. It was that stock ownership that parlayed into the billions paid by Rupert Murdoch only three years after the court battles surrounding Jackie's estate had ended.

Had Ron succeeded in having Jackie sign a written statement at her death, leaving that stock to him? If he had, and if the court upheld that provision of her will, Ronnie Lee Morgan would be the billionaire, not Jackie's children, the Bancroft children. No doubt none of the parties could have foreseen Murdoch's purchase just a few years later. The stakes of the litigation had become even higher than they had realized, and Ron's settlement of twelve million dollars ultimately looked like small change. All things are relative, I suppose.

The decision was made in my family that Jane and my son Cuatro would accompany me to North Carolina, to the federal prison which would be my home for the next two years. My other two sons and daughter wanted to be with me, as well, but because of all the expenses involved in litigation of the lawsuits, travel costs were a consideration.

It was appropriate that Jane was with me, for we had always been soulmates, friends and lovers. The separation for the next two years would be hard. We knew we were strong people, but we had never been apart. I could see the fear of the unknown separation as my eyes reflected in hers. Cuatro had been locked at my hip since a toddler. He was not only my son but my friend, and for ten years had been my most faithful and intelligent employee.

As the commercial air flight lifted from Midland, Texas, and eventually brought us to the East Coast prison where I was allowed to self-surrender, Jane sat on one side of me, Cuatro on the other.

The air was heavy, the mood so dark it oppressed the heart. There was no feeling of failure, no thought that we had not served well in practice of a legal profession. There was no sense of guilt, no acknowledgment that a crime had been committed. Law is what statutes say it is, and mere mortals write the statutes, while enforcement is layered with egocentrism.

We had no feeling of any of this, nor had we felt embarrassed or ostracized by society. We felt sad because we would not be together for the next two years, and I knew that Jane and Cuatro, though they didn't say it, feared for my safety. I have observed that people commonly think that, when a lawyer, banker, or businessperson goes to prison, they go to a locked-up country club. The place I was going to was a hard prison, with hard people, and high security.

As the plane banked out of Midland airport, I watched out the window at the community below.

The city sat in its piety, its broad, simplified view of the world, its belief that it could consume forever and have a God-given right to do so. I viewed the flat landscape once flowing with buffalo grass for hundreds of miles now pockmarked with hundreds of thousands of pump-jack locations, some pumping dribbles of oil, some dry as a bone. I observed the massive cotton fields north to Lubbock as they pumped and irrigated what was left of the Ogallala subterranean water formation, and wondered when the sandstorms would return.

I turned and, with tears in my eyes, looked at Jane. She squeezed my hand and cried back.

There was no epiphany here. No sudden realization of insight or truth. It is a story partly told, but a mystery never solved. There were more answers about Ron than questions. There were more questions about Jackie than answers. The Bancroft street at Sierra Blanca, New Mexico, told the story for those who cared to read it. It was a road to nowhere. No destination required.

In August 2004, I entered the iron door of federal prison at Butner, North Carolina, to the tears of my wife and son. It was a lockdown prison and many long hours would pass in my cell as I watched the seasons pass: fall, winter, spring, and then again, summer.

As Christmas approached that year, the mood of the prison population changed. It was not a happy mood, though the staff and administration put up a lot of decorations and attempted to improve the mood. We come to realize that prison is our home. Some people had been there twenty or more years. Some were there for life. Some die there. We learn that we are not getting out, that we may never get out.

Thoughts turn to family and loved ones back home. For me, it was knowing they were suffering as a result of my absence, as well as the social stigma of my being in this prison. For others, the thought of home brought a picture of the dysfunction of family dynamics, or who is kissing her now. Then, there were those who had no one back home, not anymore. Christmastime only intensified the feelings.

My most peaceful time was the two hours we were allowed outside to walk around the track in the recreation yard where I covered many miles every day. The small asphalt track was about a quarter mile in diameter with grass in the middle; soccer, softball, or flag football were often played there. I began to observe things of beauty during my walks. Even though the electric fence and razor wire were distractions, I could see the beautiful pine tree forest beyond, with its rich shadowy green color. There was a whole troop --- perhaps it's called a gaggle --- of not-so-wild geese that marched by the outside of the prison fence at a certain time each day, as if all were well. I never knew where they were going, but they knew, and they proceeded with purpose. The sky often held a certain spectra of blue between puffy clouds. It was a different blue than what I was used to in my West Texas home. I came to call it "freedom blue," and often peered into its vastness. There was a certain peace in these walks, a certain presence, not the rapid motor of the mental computer that plagues one even in prison, but indeed a presence.

Christmas passed. New Year's Eve came. On this final day of the year, I saw the last act of human kindness I would witness that year, and it touched and moved me deeply.

As I took my daily walk around the recreation yard, I observed that a beautiful Canada goose had landed in the middle of the yard. This had never happened. No prisoner approached or bothered her. We kept walking, silently, each to his own.

In time, it became evident that this majestic bird who eyed us curiously was ill. No doubt she had stumbled upon some of the pigeon poison the prison dispenses around the prison compound. Pigeons pose a health concern. Geese do not.

From the corner of my eye, I saw movement. It came from the far end of the yard, where the mentally ill were celled. One of them came out of his confines carrying a large white bowl, arms outstretched so as not to spill the water contained within it. He gently set it down in the middle of the yard within reach of the goose. Then he backed away, quietly.

In the days to come, as the goose grew weaker, it often came to the water to drink. The poison caused it great thirst. After each drink, she stood, proud, head high, chest out, as Canada geese are wont to do.

At last, she was too weak to drink, too weak to stand. She roosted down upon the grass, and tucked her beak back under her wing one last time.

I never doubted she was grateful for the water that eased her pain. But I wonder what she thought of the strange human who was kind enough to bring it. I wondered even more what made her seek a group of prisoners living behind an electric fence and razor wire as her hospice in her final hours.

Could it be that she saw in us something that others could not?

EPILOGUE

On August 6, 2004, I entered the Butner, North Carolina federal penal institution as punishment for my actions in shielding Jackie Bancroft Spencer Morgan's monetary and asset distributions to Ronnie Lee Morgan. As a lawyer, I had visited prisons before, representing an inmate, but I had never spent the night in one, much less been an inmate.

A guard led me through iron-locked and secure doors. I was first taken into a medical triage and clothing room for incoming inmates.

The initial process is quick and efficient. First, the strip search with "spread the cheeks" inspection. Vitals, height, weight, identifying scars, tattoos or marks are taken and listed, and mandatory tuberculosis inoculation is administered, as well as a test to check for the presence of tuberculosis. My street clothes were replaced with a thin, cotton pullover top and drawstring pants. Soft cotton non-support slippers are provided for the feet. After exhausting initial, rapid efficiency, it begins: the process that time is nothing and there is nothing for you but time.

I was placed in a large concrete and metal holding cell. It would probably hold a dozen men, although, in the year to come, I would learn that my estimate of space sufficiency and that of the Bureau of Prisons' (BOP) differed significantly.

After an hour in the holding tank, I became chilled. It was cold. The air conditioner blew full blast with a large vent directed right into the cell. The prison-issue clothes were so thin they could provide no warmth. I tried walking the length of the cell, faster and faster. It helped for a little while, but the depression of the day, leaving Jane and Cuatro, eating nothing --- soon, I became weak.

After the second hour, my head began hurting with sharp, throbbing pain. Over and over, I banged on the iron door.

After about fifteen minutes of hitting the door with my fists and hollering for help, a voice came over a hidden speaker inside the cell. "Is there a problem in there?" I asked for aspirin and a blanket. The response was simply that I would be assigned to a cell soon. I was, but it was four hours more before I was led to a cell on the third floor of the prison.

I felt pain and loss that first night.

The time was "lockdown." All inmates are removed from TV rooms and halls and returned to their respective closed cells. Every solid iron cell door shuts and locks with a resounding, almost echoing, clank at lockdown time.

My guard took me up in the elevator to the third floor, then past a row of closed gray cell doors. We stopped and he opened one of the doors, which looked identical to all the others. "Your bunk is on the left," he said.

I peered into pitch-black darkness. I could see nothing. The door was slammed shut behind me, metal to metal. I tried to feel along the wall, but almost immediately I rammed my knee on something. It was the metal toilet. Fortunately, four inches beyond was a metal bunk, empty. I laid down on it. The cold metal base agitated my already cold and hurting bones but I felt a folded blanket at the foot and pulled it up over me.

My head was exploding. If only I could lie there on my back, I thought, wrapping myself tightly in the blanket, the pain would, hopefully, subside.

It was quiet, prison quiet. I wasn't sure if there was another person in the cell or if I was the only one.

Later that night, when my eyes had adjusted to the darkness, though it was still densely black I saw a body. The dark shadow moved towards either the door or the toilet, I couldn't tell which. I said "Hello." There was no answer, only silence.

When daylight came, the reverberation of the synchronous unlocking of the iron cell doors woke me.

The other person in the cell was already up. He was an Indian, Native American, with a long black ponytail. Again I said "Hello." Again there was no return greeting. Instead, he immediately went out the open door and into the hall where inmates flowed in one direction. I later learned this was one of three times a day when inmates rushed to the main excitement of the day, chow.

Gradually, I adjusted to the system and its procedures. I would come to realize that my cellmate ("cellie") was a Lakota Sioux from the Montana reservation. He didn't talk. He moved quietly with uncommon stealth but meant no harm, nor did he want to be harmed. Early on, I realized that, if I followed his every move, I would learn my way around. He didn't seem to mind. Instead of being taught verbally how to adjust to prison life, I mirrored my cellie's every move. Monkey see---monkey do.

As the weeks moved into months, I learned what to do and not do, how to survive. In prison, all Native Americans are called "chief," regardless of their true name. I shall never forget my "chief," my first cellie. He wasn't much on talking, but he was a good teacher. I learned a lot from him about the fundamentals of prison life.

Before closing my law office, I had made sure that each employee had another job or a new profession. So it was with Teresa.

Though she had been an outstanding legal assistant to me for many years, we felt there may be a taint in her seeking new employment in view of what happened with me. Not only that; as a paralegal passes the age of forty or forty-five, law firms are wary in hiring, for fear the individual has burned out. It is an unwritten "law" and an applicant would have the devil trying to prove such a thing, but it does exist.

I had insisted that Teresa take the private investigator's licensing exam and hang out her shingle as a P.I.

She was reluctant, but I insisted. She passed the exam, missing but one question. At first, business was slow, as it is initially in building any client base. It's a pull-yourself-up-by-your-own-bootstraps type of thing. Ultimately, she became the most sought-after P.I. in West Texas. Law firms loved her. She could find out things that seemingly no one else could uncover.

It was clear that another law firm was not going to hire Cuatro. The allegations by Ron's law firm in his suit against me --- that I had stolen from the trust --- placed an ethical cloud over us all. Cuatro had been my "go-to" man in problem-solving, and ironically, one of his duties as office manager was to make sure no thefts occurred. I was encouraged that he was not deterred regarding his own future. His concern was more about me than himself.

Cuatro had always been an outstanding cook and harbored a dream of owning his own barbecue place. I suggested he make it a Texas honky-tonk and that he should get on with building it.

He did. He built it out in the county, in the middle of the "oil patch" between Midland and Odessa, and named it "The Hog Pit."

By the time I returned from prison, I was amazed to find that it was well known across Texas for its ribs and cowboy ambiance. On Tuesdays and Thursdays, over a hundred people sit playing Texas hold-um poker. On weekend nights, the dance floor fills with people dancing to country music. In prison, I had no idea things were going so well. I just worried for Cuatro and his family, as any dad would, and hoped for the best. On my return, I was so happy to see that I need not have worried.

Over the course of my incarceration, Teresa kept me abreast of Ron's activities and what was going on in his life.

Why, I'm not sure. I know that what happened to Ron continued to be of burning interest to Teresa, in part, because it was good practice as she developed her investigation skills, in part, because she felt we had all been wronged and damaged. She felt both resentment and a desire for retribution. I think Teresa was looking for justice, for a time when federal law enforcement would come in and make the same accusations against Ron that I had gone to the pen for, bankruptcy fraud.

I had never told Teresa because I had been sworn to secrecy by a reliable source: That wasn't going to happen. When lawyers for the Bancrofts and Jackie's estate got wind that I had gone to the Department of Justice and exposed my game of shielding distributions from Jackie to Ron, a legal entourage took a private jet to San Antonio, the seat of the head of the Department of Justice for the Western District of Texas, and acquired an agreement that there would be no federal criminal intervention other than what already related to me. All else would be left to civil courts.

Aside from personal power, the wealthy also have influence when they contribute heavily to the party in power, as Jackie and the Bancrofts had faithfully done. I observed the irony that Jackie, in her life, had never called in a favor from a politician in return for years of contributions.

In her death, the time had come. The blanket of protection had been broad enough to cover Ron; of course, the meeting of that legal entourage with the DOJ came at a time when Ron played nice with the Bancroft children and vice versa, and before they brought suit against each other. Nevertheless, the Feds never entertained criminal prosecution against Ron. He had dodged the bullet, as they say in West Texas.

I did learn from Teresa that the first year without a monthly distribution and credit card paid by Jackie was difficult for Ron. Apparently, the Midland law firm that took his case to enforce his position as a Bancroft heir saw potential. They even provided him with an office at their law firm. I never quite understood what that was about; Ron was not the office type. It would, of course, provide an *entre* to wealthy clients should he desire or need to continue working in interior decorating or special jewelry sales. The newly-hired lawyer in the firm was the daughter of Ron's jewelry connection, the source of several hundred thousand dollars in sales to Jackie. I assumed some influence was used for Ron's accommodation at the firm.

By the end of my second year in prison, all lawsuits had been settled. The allegations against me had been dismissed in return for my conveying, as putative trustee, all trust assets back to Jackie's estate, which I was more than happy to be rid of.

The Bancroft children settled with Ron for around twelve million, which included one of the seashore villas in Puerto Vallarta. Regardless of the apparent wealth, the net liquidity was substantially reduced by legal expenses and an IRS investigation and settlement.

As before, Ron had numerous paramours; in time, he gave Lorenzo his walking papers.

Though Ron maintained the trappings of wealth --- an expensive car and even more expensive jewelry he had acquired from Jackie and secreted from the lawsuits --- money became tight and the same cycles that existed before Jackie, creditor problems of major magnitude and client disagreements, returned.

However, Ron never lost his knack with wealthy women who became excited with the idea of going to Market with him, nor did he lose his knowledge of how to work the high-end jewelry market that served him well for so many years with his Midland and Lubbock contacts.

As for me, I had encountered a completely new experience.

After my cellie, the Lakota Sioux, was transferred out of Butner prison, my new cellie was Colonel George Trofimoff, the highest ranking U.S. Army officer ever convicted of spying. We would be cellmates for a year and become good friends. I would write his appeal, and he would serve as my paralegal, and a good one, at that. It was time I left the Bancrofts and Ron Morgan for what they were, each to their own. Instead of dwelling on a past saga, I became totally enthralled with the case of George Trofimoff.

NOTES ON SOURCES

In writing creative nonfiction about one's own experience, it is evident that memory must be relied on. I had ample time and solitude to remember and take notes on my memories. My former legal staff also had remembrances, notes, and files, which helped. To the largest extent possible, what I have written is my observations of the relationships between Jackie and Ron and Jackie's family, as well as how I observed each, individually. Although my first reference of Ron and my early encounter with him was in the late '80s, the Jackie-Ron references are from the late 1990s through 2003.

All quotations of dialogue and descriptions of states of mind are as I recall them and as I can most honestly relate them. But readers should bear in mind that remembered conversations are rarely an exact reproduction of the words actually spoken. This is my story. This is how I remember it. I would suggest that anyone having a different remembrance write their own story.

When it comes to historical facts such as those that relate to the Barrons, Bancrofts, and The *Wall Street Journal*, most of what is written is based upon historical research. That history is fascinating and there is much more to it than what is related here. I did take the liberty of characterizing Hugh Bancroft in a way that I felt was likely from my research of his life. Often, Jackie would give me some historical snippet relating to either Hugh or The *Wall Street Journal*, and off I would go on a research binge.

The following is a bibliography of the principal written source material that I relied upon, but a great deal of help was acquired from different genealogical researchers in Denver, Colorado, and Massachusetts. Several books are included that were used as general background on The *Wall Street Journal*, itself, the Panic of 1907, the Panic of 1929, and changing social conditions during that period.

Finally, I wish to thank the people of the little town of Carrizozo, New Mexico, where Jackie spent much of her life. Their hospitality and frankness were greatly appreciated. All interviews were used as background information, and none were quoted directly.

BIBLIOGRAPHY

BOOKS

Chernow, Ron. *The House of Morgan: An American Banking Dynasty and the Rise of Modern Finance.* New York: Grove Press, 1990.

Dealy, Jr., Francis X. *The Power and the Money.* New York: Carol Publishing Group, 1993.

Weisman, Steven R. *The Great Tax Wars.* New York: Simon & Schuster, 2002.

Rosenberg, Jerry M. *Inside The Wall Street Journal.* New York: Macmillan Publishing Co., Inc., 1982.

Brown, Dorothy M. *Setting a Course: American Women in the 1920.* Boston: Twayne Publishers, 1987.

Wolock, Nancy. *Women and the American Experience: A Concise History.* New York: McGraw-Hill, 2002.

Murray, R.K. *The Politics of Normalcy: Governmental Theory and Practice in the Harding-Coolidge Era.* New York: W.W. Norton & Company, 1973.

ARTICLES

On Hugh Bancroft:

Crowe, Earle E. "Previous Crises Compared: Hugh Bancroft, Financial Publisher, Finds No Evidence of Panic or Depression in Current Situation," *Los Angeles Times* (California), Nov. 22, 1929.

"Hugh Bancroft, 53, Publisher, Is Dead," *New York Times* (New York), October 18, 1933.

Larson, Dominic. "A Tale of Wealth and Intrigue: The First Family of Wall Street," *The Independent* (UK), June 9, 2007.

On Hugh Bancroft, Jr.:

"Marjorie Dow Engaged; uuuu Newton Highlands Girl to be Bride of Hugh Bancroft, Jr. of Boston," *New York Times* (New York), December 25, 1932.

"Cinderella Wins Devon Show Blue," *New York Times* (New York), May 28, 1921.

"Hugh Bancroft, Jr. Hurt; Son of Late Boston Trolley Head Hits Bridge Stanchion With Auto," *New York Times* (New York), December 25, 1936.

On Jackie Everts Bancroft Spencer Morgan:

Denver Post (Colorado), Society page, Jan. 13, 1948.
www.denverpost.com

Rouse, Karen. "WSJ Sale Points to Bancroft Local Ties," The *Denver Post* (Colorado), Aug. 6, 2007.

Romo, Rene and Logan, Paul. "Arts Benefactor Jackie Spencer Morgan Was 'Always Giving,'" *Albuquerque Journal* (New Mexico), May 14, 2003.

DATABASES

Hugh Bancroft:

NNDB "Tracking the entire world," www.nndb.com

New England Historic Genealogical Society, 2001-2009 (Orig. pub. New England Historic Genealogical Society, Boston, MA.) The New England Historical and Genealogical Society Online database: New England Ancestors.org.

"The Register – 162 vols., 1847-2009," database.
"Thomas Bancroft and Some of His Descendants," Vol. 97, Page 68, January 1943.

Hugh Bancroft and Hugh Bancroft, Jr.:

Paul Pratt Memorial Library, Cohasset, Massachusetts.
www.cohassetlibrary.org/research_database

Cohasset Historical Society, Cohasset, Massachusetts
www.cohassethistoricalsociety.org

Boston Public Library database, Boston, Massachusetts
www.bpl.org; www.bpl.org/research/socsci/genealogy

Hugh Bancroft, Jr. and Jackie Orthwein Everts:

The *Denver Post* (Colorado)
www.denverpost.com/archives

U.S. Death Records Search
www.govdeathrecords.com

The Colorado Genealogical Society
www.cogensoc.US

Colorado Genealogy on the Internet
www.genealogybranches.com/colorado

Forbes Magazine Archives
www.forbes.com

Newspaper Archive
www.newspaperarchive.com

The *Wall Street Journal* Archive
www.wallstreetjournal.com

Kent Denver School, Denver, Colorado

www.kentdenver.org

Connecticut College, New London, CT
www.conncoll.edu

"About Spencer Theater Founder Jackie Spencer," Spencer Theater Home Page, May 2003.

Barrett, William P. "It's My Money," *Forbes*, Oct. 11, 2004.

Arango, Tim. "Shaking the Bancroft Family Tree," CNN Money.com, May 14, 2007.

On Ronnie Lee Morgan:

Monte, Gabriel. "Late heiress's property up for auction," *Lubbock Avalanche Journal* (Texas), July 22, 2006.

LITIGATION FILES REVIEWED and REFERENCED:

In the Matter of The Separate Trust for the Benefit of Bettina Bancroft Klink under the 1941 Hugh Bancroft, Jr. Trust, Case No. 96PR1979, Probate Court, City and County of Denver, Colorado.

Application For Informal Probate of Will and Appointment of Personal Representative In the Matter of the Estate of Jacqueline Spencer Morgan, deceased, Cause No. PB-03-14 Division III, In the District Court of Lincoln County Twelfth Judicial District Court, State of New Mexico.

Ronnie Lee Morgan v. Glen D. Aaron, II, individually, Glen D. Aaron, II, as Putative Trustee of the 657 Trust and Putative Officer and Director of the 756 Corp., Michael Sylvester, individually, Aaron, Sylvester & Associate, P.C., Robert Sean Aaron, individually, Robert Sean Aaron dba Aaron Insurance Agency, and Glen D. Aaron, IV a.k.a. Quattro, Cause #MO-03-CV-144, In The United States District Court For the Western District of Texas Midland – Odessa Division.

Michael S. Line, as the Personal Representative of Jacqueline Spencer

Morgan, Deceased and 756 Corporation v. Ronnie Lee Morgan, Glen D. Aaron, II, Individually, d/b/a Law Office of Glen D. Aaron, II as Trustee of the Aaron Grandchildren Trust, as Trustee of all Iotta Trust Accounts associated with the law practice of Glen D. Aaron, II, and as Trustee of purported 657 Trust; Jane Hellinghausen Aaron; Glen D. Aaron, IV (a/k/a "Quatro"), Individually and as Trustee of the Aaron Grandchildren Trust; Robert Sean Aaron, Individually, d/b/a Aaron Insurance Agency, and as Trustee for the Aaron Grandchildren Trust, Ashley Aaron, as Trustee for the Aaron Grandchildren Trust, Teresa Cornelius and Lorenzo Sevilla, Cause No. CV44984, In the 238th District Court of Midland County, Texas.

Ronnie Lee Morgan vs. Michael S. Line, Ronnie Hemphill and Hugh Bancroft, III, as Trustees of The Jacqueline Spencer Morgan Trust, Civ. No. 03-259, Twelfth Judicial District, County of Lincoln, State of New Mexico.

In Re: 657 Trust, In the 99th District Court of Lubbock County, Texas; Appellate Case No. 07-03-0461-CV, In Re: 657 Trust, Court of Appeals, Seventh District of Texas.

Glen D. Aaron II v. U.S. Bankruptcy Court for the Western District of Texas, El Paso County, Texas, No. 00-32072-LEK, In Re: Ronnie Lee Morgan, Debtor, et al.

United States of America vs. Glen D. Aaron, II; Cause No. MO-04-CR-027, United States District Court, Western District of Texas, Midland-Odessa Division.

CPSIA information can be obtained
at www.ICGtesting.com
Printed in the USA
LVHW02s0240120918
589880LV00010B/347/P